THE MACHIAVELLIAN COSMOS

THE MACHIAVELLIAN COSMOS

Anthony J. Parel

YALE UNIVERSITY PRESS

NEW HAVEN AND LONDON • 1992

Set in Bembo by Textflow Services Ltd.

Printed and bound in Great Britain by The Bath Press, Avon

Library of Congress Cataloging-in-Publication Data

Parel, Anthony.
    The Machiavellian cosmos / by Anthony J. Parel.
        p.   cm.
    Includes bibliographical references and index.
    ISBN 0–300–05169–7
    1. Machiavelli, Niccolò, 1469–1527—Contributions in political
science. I. Title.
JC143.M4P35 1992
320'.01.'1092—dc20
                                                                                    91–26722
                                                                                         CIP

To the memory of my mother and to my father

Never was Machiavelli more wrong than when he wrote *gli uomini sdimenticano più presto la morte del padre che la perdita del patrimonio.*

CONTENTS

ACKNOWLEDGEMENTS

The argument developed in this book first took shape in the Fellows Seminar given at Lonergan College, Concordia University, Montréal, for the academic year 1982–83. I thank the then Principal Sean McEvenue for inviting me to be the Lonergan Visiting Fellow, and James Moore and the other members of the Fellows Seminar for their stimulating comments and criticisms. The late Professor Felix Gilbert and Professor Harvey C. Mansfield, Jr. read specific sections of an earlier draft of this book; Professors Sergio Bertelli, John G. A. Pocock and Nicolai Rubinstein read the entire text and made many valuable suggestions for improvement. My intellectual debt to all of them is gratefully acknowledged. Many thanks to Professors Kenneth Minogue, Barry Cooper, Edmund Jacobitti, and Victor Santi for their interest and encouragement. Judi Powell prepared the various drafts of this text with her customary speed, cheerfulness, and efficiency. Robert Baldock and Rosemary Amos, both of Yale University Press, have been extremely generous with their expert advice and guidance.

My deepest debt, however, is to the members of my family – Rolande, Tara, and Kamala – who cheerfully tolerated my decade-long association with Machiavelli and his very interesting cosmos.

Calgary, October 3rd, 1991

ABBREVIATIONS

P.	*The Prince.*
D.	*The Discourses on the First Decade of Titus Livy.*
I. F.	*Florentine Histories.*
A. G.	*Art of War.*
'Discursus'	A Discourse on Remodeling the Government of Florence.
'Ghiribizzi'	Ghiribizzi Scripti in Perugia al Soderino.

NOTES ON THE USE OF
MACHIAVELLI'S TEXTS

Considering the importance attached in this study to specific terms such as *il cielo/i cieli, umore/umori, licenzia, virtù, fortuna*, etc., I have given my own translation of Machiavelli's texts. But in doing so I have consulted other English translations, especially Allan Gilbert's *Machiavelli, The Chief Works and Others*, Durham, NC, 1965, and Harvey C. Mansfield, Jr.'s *The Prince*, Chicago, 1985.

Unless otherwise noted, all references in footnotes to Machiavelli's works are to *Niccolò Machiavelli: Tutte le opere*, ed. Mario Martelli, Florence, 1971.

I have given the Italian texts in footnotes wherever I felt that they were important for the reader to verify my claims. However, in doing so, I have been rather selective: not every citation from Machiavelli in English is followed by its corresponding Italian text.

In footnotes I have used the author-date system, except in the case of notes referring to Machiavelli's works. Here I have followed the short-title system.

INTRODUCTION

In this study I explore two themes generally neglected in Machiavelli scholarship. The first is the theme of heaven/s (*il cielo, i cieli*), used by Machiavelli not in a theological sense, but in the natural science sense of pre-modern, Renaissance physics and cosmology. The second is the theme of humour/s (*umore, umori*), taken from the pre-modern science of medicine and applied to the analysis of particular human nature as well as to the analysis of the body politic. According to pre-modern medical thought, changes in one's bodily humours are linked to changes in the motions of the heavens. As such, there is a theoretical connection between the ancient science of medicine and ancient physics and cosmology.

But this study is more than a study of these two Machiavellian themes. For what I have found from the study of these themes is that they throw new light on Machiavelli's political thought taken as a whole, as well as on specific Machiavellian themes such as *virtù, gloria, ambizione, fortuna, ordini*, and *stato*.[1] As every student of Machiavelli knows, he is concerned with how 'things of the world' (*cose del mondo*) and 'human things' (*cose umane*) are governed. Our investigation of his notion of heaven/s will give us at least a partial explanation of how he considers things to be governed. Indeed, it will become apparent that Machiavelli did study politics both in terms of human motions – humours, motives, desires, appetites – and in terms of the natural and occult motions that operate in nature and in the cosmos. Accordingly, the purpose of this study is to test the hypothesis that these themes do in fact throw new light on Machiavelli's political thought taken as a whole.

Now the hypothesis that Machiavelli entertained an astrological world-view might come as a shock to many of us, and especially to these who think of him as the founder of modern political philosophy. For here we are very much under the influence of the Enlightenment interpretation of the Italian Renaissance in general, and of Machiavelli's political thought in particular. The Renaissance has often been interpreted as a time when rationality overcame superstition, when human autonomy asserted itself against all 'alien' forces and entities, and human beings took their destiny in their own hands. At the same time, we notice that these very same interpreters have made passing judgements on the prevalence of many astrological ideas and practices. Jacob Burckhardt, for example, has declared astrology to be 'a miserable feature in the life of that time', something to be excused, perhaps as the result of being carried away by the passion for knowledge and scientific prediction. He does not see anything positive in astrology.[2] The initial shock could be considerably reduced, however, if it were remembered that in the Renaissance, astrology was considered the natural philosophy of the day. As Lynn Thorndike writes, 'during the long period of the scientific development before Sir Isaac Newton promulgated the universal law of gravitation, there had been generally recognized and accepted another and different universal natural law, which his supplanted. And that universal natural law was astrological.'[3] The heavenly bodies were thought to be composed of incorruptible matter, and their eternal motions were thought to have qualities which, in turn, were supposed to affect the motions of elemental, sublunar bodies, including the 'mixed bodies' of states, churches and religions. The heavens and the earth constituted a hierarchical, superior-inferior continuum. This rule of earth by the heavens should be kept constantly in mind, Thorndike counsels, by every student of the history of ideas of the pre-modern period.[4]

Eugenio Garin has lent the prestige of his name to the enterprise of rescuing Renaissance astrology from neglect and disrepute. He reminds us that astrology was an important part of the Renaissance intellectual land-scape, that as a science and as an art it affected every aspect of Renaissance life: religion, politics, medicine, philosophy, philosophy of history, and the conception of reality itself.[5] The recent *Cambridge History of Renaissance Philosophy* has also done much to balance the scales of historical knowledge on Renaissance astrology. As Quentin Skinner and Charles Schmitt state in their Introduction, 'magic and astrology not only occupied an accredited position in the heartland of philosophy during the Renaissance, but also entered from time to time into "purely philosophical" contexts . . .'[6] According to Paul Oscar Kristeller, although astrology was not a part of humanist philosophy as such, Renaissance Platonism did take an interest in it, as it provided the intellectual context for such debates as those on fate, fortune and free will. 'The great role played during the Renaissance by astrology, alchemy, magic and other occult sciences has few links with humanism or for that matter with Aristotelianism, but came to be associated with Platonism. But this area of thought was cultivated by at least some humanists and was influenced by some ancient sources made available by the humanists.'[7] James Tester's *History of Western Astrology* also speaks of the 'ascendency' of astrology in the Middle Ages and the Renaissance, and of how its cultivation was considered a perfectly respectable intellectual activity. And a recent collection of historical essays entitled *Astrology, Science and*

Society has underscored the point that in the Renaissance, astrologers were performing important social and political functions as advisers and consultants to rulers, both lay and ecclesiastical.[8]

Given the widespread influence of astrology, considered as a science and as an art, in the Renaissance, it is not unreasonable to hypothesize that Machiavelli also might have been affected by it. We have no accurate way of knowing the extent of Machiavelli's knowledge of subjects other than politics. But we do know that in writing on politics he did encroach upon fields other than politics – history, moral philosophy, natural philosophy, and theology. Thus, one is not surprised to see him saying in one of his letters to Francesco Vettori that he could illustrate the point he was making in the letter with examples taken from Greek, Latin, Hebrew, Chaldean, Persian, and other sources.[9] What is striking from the point of view of our present concern is the mention of 'things Chaldean'. For it should be recalled that in contemporary literature astrology was sometimes called the Chaldean science because of its connection with both ancient Babylon and its present successor, Baghdad. Abu Ma'shar, the famous Baghdadi astrologer/natural philosopher, was well known in Renaissance astrological literature.[10] Furthermore, we learn from Machiavelli's father's diary, the *Libro di Ricordi*, that Nicolo Tedesco, a family friend from whom the Machiavelli family obtained a copy of Livy's *Deche*, and for whom Machiavelli's father made an index of place names appearing in Livy, was a priest and an astrologer.[11]

We are not without some concrete evidence which suggests that Machiavelli had an interest in the political uses made of astrologers and astrology. In the *Discourses*, for example, he recounts how Emperor Antoninus Caracalla made use of his astrologers to find out if any of his rivals were aspiring to the emperorship. As a matter of fact, Machiavelli points out that Caracalla met his death because of the interception of the letter containing the advice from his astrologer. Unfortunately for Caracalla, the letter of his astrologer warning him of the threat from his prefect, Macrinus, fell into hands of Macrinus himself, who, of course, successfully contrived to have the emperor assassinated.[12] Elsewhere he notes how Emperor Domitian kept a close watch on the horoscopes and the birthdays of his senators. He was in the habit of assassinating those senators whose horoscopes indicated that they were a threat to the throne. For this astrological reason he was thinking of killing Nerva until his astrologer-friend advised him against the killing. No danger from Nerva was forthcoming, the astrologer said; and besides, Domitian himself, being very old, was soon to die a natural death. The advice was heeded, Nerva was spared, and he eventually succeeded Domitian.[13] Certainly, one ought not to make too much of these accounts recorded by Machiavelli. Yet they cannot be ignored either, for they indicate that he was not ignorant of the political uses being made of the 'Chaldean art'.

In any case, many highly respected authorities in Machiavelli studies have made remarks *en passant* which do link Machiavelli's name to astrology. Nearly a century ago, L. Arthur Burd noted that contemporary Renaissance speculations on Fortune were usually combined with a discussion of astrology and that Machiavelli had mentally connected the relationship of astrology to Fortune. For he saw plainly, says Burd, that certain questions of politics could not be discussed without encroaching upon fields other than politics, and that astrology was one such field. And when he did so, adds Burd in typical Burckhardtian fashion, his 'natural acumen' seemed to desert him and he seemed to share 'the superstition of the age'.[14]

Ernst Cassirer has also noted the existence of a connection between astrology and Machiavelli's thought. But he seems unable to give a coherent assessment of its significance. On the one hand, Cassirer credits Machiavelli with having been a revolutionary thinker, yet on the other he thinks that he did not overcome the pressure from astrology. 'What Galileo gave in his *Dialogues* and what Machiavelli gave in his *Prince* were really new sciences,' writes Cassirer. 'Just as Galileo's *Dynamics* became the foundation of modern science of nature, so Machiavelli paved a new way to political science.'[15] They were founders of two new sciences both based on 'a common principle'. Both started from 'the axiom of the uniformity and homogeneity of nature'. In physics and cosmology, this axiom led to the destruction of the distinction between 'the higher' and 'the lower' worlds. In politics, it led to the recognition, under Machiavelli's guidance, that all ages were of 'the same fundamental structure'.[16] The parallel that Cassirer draws between Machiavelli and Galileo, however, soon breaks down: for, says Cassirer, Machiavelli always remained under pressure from astrology. No one, with the exception of Pico della Mirandola, tried to overcome this pressure. 'Even Machiavelli could not entirely free himself from astrological conceptions. He thought and spoke in the manner of his age and contemporaries.'[17]

Hans Baron also had difficulty attempting to assess Machiavelli's position on astrology and modernity. On the one hand, Baron believes that the changes introduced by Machiavelli in political science contributed indirectly to the cosmological changes introduced in the natural sciences. The same vision, he says, inspired changes in both the human and the natural sciences. According to Baron, by the end of the Quattrocento a dynamic, decentralized view had emerged in history and political science, finding its first great expression in the works of Machiavelli and Guicciardini. 'In the sixteenth century the same vision began to transform cosmology and, indeed, all notions of nature. Machiavelli's *Discorsi sopra la prima deca di Tito Livio* (finished, in substance, in 1513) and Galileo's *Dialogo sopra i due massimi sistemi del mondo* (finished in 1632) were contemporary phases of one historical process.'[18] At the same time, Baron recognizes that by the beginning of the fifteenth century 'a new era of astrological ascendency' had begun in Italy – an ascendency which was to last until the middle of the seventeenth century.[19] The popularity of astrological medicine in the Renaissance was owed to this ascendency. And Machiavelli's naturalistic analysis of politics, as Baron correctly notes, is an outcome of the influence of astrological natural science. 'Had scientific pursuits as yet not played a part, side by side with classical and political interests, in the Florentine groups which influenced the growth of Machiavelli's thought, he would hardly have possessed the intellectual tools he needed for his naturalistic analysis of political disintegration and growth.'[20]

Leo Strauss also finds himself in a quandary. On the one hand, he is persistent in his claim that 'The founder of modern political philosophy is Machiavelli.'[21] While in the 1936 edition of his work on Hobbes, he had declared that Hobbes was the founder of the new science of politics, in the 1951 edition he changed his mind: 'not Hobbes, but Machiavelli, deserves this honor . . . The immediate and perhaps sufficient cause of my error was inadequate reflection on the opening of Machiavelli's *Discorsi*.'[22] On the other hand, Strauss also recognizes that Machiavelli's claim to modernity was open to serious theoretical difficulties since 'The theoretical or cosmological basis of his political teaching was a kind of decayed Aristotelianism.'[23] Elsewhere he wonders whether Machiavelli's cosmology might have been Averroist, or 'Democritean-Epicurean', or 'some other'.[24] He is fully aware that Machiavelli followed the 'astrologers' or 'scientists' of his age.[25] Even though Strauss hesitates on the question of the specific school to which Machiavelli's cosmology belongs, he has no hesitation on three issues: first, that there is a cosmology underlying Machiavelli's political philosophy; secondly, that 'there is no place in his cosmology for a ruling Mind'; and thirdly, that he 'favored a cosmology which is in accordance with his analysis of morality. His analysis of morality will prove to be incompatible with a teleological cosmology.'[26] A question arises, however: if Machiavelli adhered to an antiquated cosmology, and if there is a connection between his cosmology and his ethics, how could he at the same time be the founder of modern political philosophy?

Perhaps it is Eugenio Garin who has gone farther than any other critic in pointing out that an astrological pattern of thought is present in Machiavelli's works. According to Garin, Machiavelli's general view of nature, of history and of the theory of change in political regimes and religions was strongly influenced by contemporary astrological speculations.[27]

Finally, Gennaro Sasso, in the course of a lengthy commentary on *Discourses* II.5, recognizes that there is a cosmology underlying at least this particular text. And, according to Sasso, the cosmology in question is neither Democritean-Epicurean, nor Stoic, nor Biblical, but quasi-Aristotelian. The problems raised in *Discourses* II.5, Sasso believes, accord better with Aristotle's lost work, *Peri Philosophias*, than with any other work of antiquity. Just as in that work Aristotle is said to defend simultaneously the eternity of the world, so, in *Discourses* II.5, Machiavelli takes a similar position. 'Absolutely speaking, the Machiavellian cosmos does not perish; it is eternal, though some parts of it may perish.'[28]

Whatever the differences of opinion among scholars may be, there is no denying the fact that they have noticed the certain existence of astrological themes in Machiavelli's writings. The question which our hypothesis addresses concerns, then, not their existence, which is incontestable, but their extent and significance.

Turning now to the theme of humours, here too scholars have made observations *en passant* on the place it occupies in Machiavelli's writings. Federico Chabod, for example, sees *umori* as a 'basic concept' (*concetto base*) of the naturalism of Machiavelli's political philosophy. The notion of *umori* clarifies his idea of the parallelism between the natural organism of the human body and the political organism of the state. Each follows the cycle of birth, growth, decline and death. Each has its pathology, which ideally must be foreseen in good time, and strong medicines should be applied when necessary. Malignant humours must be purged, and good ones constantly satisfied.[29] Gennaro Sasso speaks of 'the doctrine of humours' (*la dottrina degli 'umori'*) in *The Prince* and the *Discourses*, which he believes is fundamental to Machiavelli's political philosophy.[30] Elsewhere, he puts the case even more strongly and says that Machiavelli speaks of a 'quasi-natural law of humours': the conflict of the two humours exists in every society, 'as if by the law of nature' (*quasi per legge di natura*).[31] Quentin Skinner, in his assessment of Machiavelli's use of the theme of humours, speaks of it as an 'axiom' of his political theory. The argument in the *Discourses* starts out from the 'axiom' that 'in every republic there are two opposed factions (*umori*), that of the people and the rich.'[32]

'*Concetto base*', '*dottrina*', 'quasi-law of nature', 'axiom' – these are serious claims made by serious scholars. And what I have attempted in part in this study is to articulate the implications of these claims. The fact remains, however, that there is no sustained analysis of the theme of *umori* in the existing literature on Machiavelli. Also, *umori* has disappeared from our contemporary political vocabulary; seeing the term in an early writer does not produce any immediate reaction in us. Even the reading of Machiavelli's texts, by itself, is not of much help, since a full understanding of the texts on *umori* is virtually impossible unless one goes outside the texts and understands their intellectual context. Such an approach of going to the context in order to understand the text need not result in making Machiavelli's thought appear 'derivative' and unoriginal.[33] On the contrary, such an approach, if properly applied, would give us a better appreciation of Machiavelli's originality. Indeed, without such an approach the precise extent of his originality may never be known. And for the readers of Machiavelli in English translation there is an added difficulty: the significance of the concept is further obscured by the difficulties of translation. Allan Gilbert, for example, translates *umori* as 'factions', 'parties', 'divisions', 'traits', 'disagreements', 'partisan hatred', 'partisan views', 'partisanship', 'party quarrels', 'strife', 'party feelings', 'disputes', 'factional differences', 'tendencies'. This list is not exhaustive; the plethora of words used to translate the same word indicates the problem faced by both the translator and the reader of the translation. A reader relying only upon an English translation would hardly guess that these words refer to *umori* in the original Italian.

My exploration of Machiavelli's use of the two themes led me to read some of the vast amount of Florentine literature on astrology, medicine, and politics. The literature on the astrological debates, in particular, is truly formidable, and I have done little more here than to scratch the surface of this area. But Machiavelli's meanings of the notion of heaven/s become better understood as we understand the tenor of these debates, the most significant of which was taking place before his very eyes. Pico della Mirandola's *magnum opus*, *Disputations Against Astrology* (*Disputationum in Astrologiam*) appeared in 12 books in 1496, and Savonarola's popular tract, *Treatise Against Divinatory Astrology* (*Contra Astrologiam Divinatricem*), in 1497. Machiavelli was appointed Secretary in 1498. He had opportunity to observe the stir which the debate caused especially among such contemporaries as Pontano, Ficino, Bellanti, and Pomponazzi. An attempt to situate Machiavelli in the context of this particular debate on astrology is made in chapter 1.

Regarding the theme of the heaven/s, Machiavelli appears to accept the contemporary position of astrological natural philosophy that the heavens are the general cause of all the particular motions – human, elemental and natural – occurring in the sublunar world. That is to say, the motions of history as well as of states are subject to the motions of the heavens. The significance of this idea for Machiavelli's conception of history and politics is explored in chapter 2. Religion for Machiavelli is also the product of the motions of the heavens. His position on the origin and the function of the pagan Roman religion is certainly guided by this idea. It is my hypothesis that his position on Christianity is also influenced by it. These and related questions will be discussed in chapter 3.

The relationship of the heavens to Fortune, and that of the operations of the unchanging laws of the heavenly bodies to the ever-changing phenomenon of chance, remains a vexed question in any treatment of Machiavelli's thought. Sometimes he speaks of the heavens and Fortune as if they were the same entities, but more often he speaks of them as if they were distinct. Indeed, there is some basis for this manner of speaking in the thought of his day. Certainly, in the contemporary popular thought, the heavens and Fortune were often equated, and Fortune often given the status of a divinity, symbolizing the powers of the heavens. In the contemporary natural philosophy, however, the heavens were thought to be the source of the unchanging determinism, fate, or necessity operating in the universe, while Fortune referred to the chance events which occur in a universe so determined. It is fair to say that Machiavelli often swings back and forth from the popular to the more philosophical understandings of Fortune and the heavens, making life difficult for his readers and critics. His conception of Fortune and its relationship to the heavens will be examined in chapter 4.

If, as Machiavelli often states, 'things of the world' are always in motion, and if all earthly motions have their general cause in the eternal motions of the heavens, what, then, is the meaning of human freedom? If the world is subject to astral necessity, and if chance events may also occur in such an astrally determined world, what place is there in this scheme for human initiative? Indeed, Machiavelli's thoughts on the heavens and Fortune force us to reconsider his thoughts on human freedom, human causality, and human virtue. This will be undertaken in chapter 5.

Turning now to the specific uses Machiavelli makes of the notion of *umore/i*, I was led to recognize that unless I was familiar with at least some of the available literature on humours, medicine and related subjects, I could not correctly ascertain Machiavelli's meanings. Accordingly, a brief sketch of the use of this notion in classical and medieval political philosophy is attempted in chapter 6. Surprisingly, in Machiavelli's hands *umore/i* becomes a means of classifying political regimes – in my view, this is surely one of the most original achievements of Machiavelli's political thought. That he uses this concept to distinguish princedoms, republics and *licenzie* permits us to wonder whether *The Prince*, the *Discourses*, the *Florentine Histories*, and the 'Discourse on Remodeling the Government of Florence' (hereafter the 'Discursus') could be read from a new perspective. Seen from the perspective of *umore/i, The Prince* appears to present us with the picture of a body politic whose humours are not in proper proportion, and whose cure would require the intervention of an able 'doctor' prepared to administer purges, strong medicines, or whatever else it might take to improve the health of the organism. Machiavelli's 'new prince' is such a 'doctor', and political ethics appears to acquire the features of a natural science, admittedly a pre-modern natural science. The *Discourses*, on the other hand, presents us with the picture of a healthy body politic. Rome is able to develop itself into a free, virtuous, and expanding republic precisely because here the humours were operating in an ordered manner. The *Florentine Histories*, in its turn, presents us with the picture of a body politic whose humours are malignant, and which is unlucky enough to be without an innovator – until, that is, Machiavelli himself was asked by Leo X to write a constitution for it. And while Machiavelli could not be a new prince for Florence, he could certainly be its legislator. And although he did not think highly of those philosophers who wrote only of imagined republics, he himself, when given the chance to submit a *discorso* for a real republic, could not do much better than to produce a draft on paper. Yet the insights from which Machiavelli starts his legislative enterprise are insights derived from the theory of humours, and the recommendations which he makes for what he variously calls 'the perfect republic', or 'this republic of mine', are also based on the same theory. Chapters 6-9 consider the varied aspects of his use of the theory of humours.

The hypothesis of this study, as mentioned already, is that a certain type of naturalism, derived from the two themes under discussion, pervades Machiavelli's political thought. I am encouraged to find a partial confirmation of this thesis in the judgement of someone who knew him better than do any of his critics, viz. Giuliano Ricci, his grandson and the transcriber of his works. Ricci believed that what, more than anything else, caused the opprobrium against his grandfather was the latter's penchant for explaining everything in terms of 'natural and fortuitous causes'. 'In all his compositions,' Ricci wrote, 'Niccolò indulged in much license, as well in blaming great personages, lay and ecclesiastic, as in reducing all things to natural or fortuitous causes.'[34]

'Natural cause' I interpret here to mean the causality exercised by the heavens on both the 'things of the world' and on 'human things'. 'Fortuitous cause' I interpret here to mean the causality ascribed to a personified figure of Fortune. According to Machiavelli's naturalism, individual human beings are thought to be subject both to the qualitative changes allegedly attached to astral motions, and to the limitations imposed on them by their own individual humour. Accordingly, their freedom of choice is limited both by the 'quality' of the times in which they engage in their actions and by the fixity of their temperament. Their chances of success in what they do, then, depend not only on their mastery of their own human capabilities, but also on the 'cooperation' of the non-human factors involved. Human causation and astral causation must work in tandem if human action is to be successful. As can be seen, divine Providence is replaced by the naturalistic providence of the stars. Thus, history, politics, and religion are to be explained partly in terms of natural causality and partly in terms of human causality. Machiavelli was led to adopt this position because of the particular world-view he adopted; one which, I believe, was more akin to an astrological world-view than to any other.

Now, reducing all things to natural and fortuitous causes was precisely what the astrological natural philosophers of the Renaissance were doing in Florence. Savonarola, for example, criticized astrology for promoting this type of naturalism. 'These philosophers and astrologers,' he pointed out, 'wanted to resolve everything they see into its natural cause or attribute everything to heaven rather than to God.'[35] His criticism led him to see a connection between tyrannical rule and the reliance on the alleged predictive power of astrology. Tyrants are without God's grace and special providence; generally speaking, they are without faith and understanding. They rule and govern according to astrology, and astrology goes against not only the teachings of Sacred Scriptures, but also those of natural philosophy, since it claims to have knowledge of future contingent events and the many accidents that occur in life.[36]

Modern critics have also noted the naturalistic flavour of Machiavelli's political philosophy, though they may not always have seen its connection to astrological natural science. The case of Chabod has already been mentioned.[37] Eugenio Garin believes that Machiavelli 'imported a rigidly naturalistic and causal conception into his vision of purely concrete, mundane and human affairs.'[38] The 'naturalism and lack of piety of Machiavelli, Pomponazzi and Bruno, even where they seemed most bold and most new, turned out to be quite old. In fact these men were the heirs, more or less consciously so, of medieval Alexanderism (condemned as early as 1210) and of Averroism and, through Arabic science, of other Hellenic currents.'[39] Gennaro Sasso devotes many penetrating pages to a discussion of the naturalistic themes in Machiavelli.[40] Vittorio de Caprariis also attests to the existence of a *filosofia naturalistica* in Machiavelli's thought.[41]

At the root of Machiavelli's naturalism lies his conception of the relationship of the heavens to earth and to humans. And, as Garin points out, 'The heavens of the astrologers did not behave like the mechanical heavens of the post-Galilean age.'[42] If Machiavelli's world-view is astrological and pre-Galilean (and it appears that it is), and if his theory of humours has something to do with his ethical theory, we are faced with interesting questions regarding both his modernity and his ethics. Certainly, this study underlines Machiavelli's naturalism, and in doing so it also provides an opportunity to take a fresh look at the question of his modernity, and at the nature of Machiavellism itself.

CHAPTER 1

The Astrological Debate

The Background

The rapid diffusion of works on astrology in Western Europe began to take place by about the middle of the twelfth century. Astrology appeared then both as a science of the stars and as an art of prognosticating and predicting their alleged effects and influences on human affairs. While the first kind of astrology was called natural or theoretical astrology, the second was called judicial, divinatory, or practical astrology. But, as Thomas Kuhn has observed, from the second century BC until about the eighteenth century AD 'astrology was inseparably linked to astronomy, and the two constituted a single professional pursuit.' Those who gained fame in the one also gained fame in the other. Ptolemy's *Almagest* is an astronomical work, and his *Tetrabiblos* is its astrological counterpart. Brahe and Kepler, both great modern astronomers, were also the best horoscope casters of their times.[1] This professional interdependence between astronomy and astrology, which lasted until about the eighteenth century, is crucial to our understanding of why it is that such famous thinkers of the Renaissance as Ficino and Pomponazzi accepted astrology as the basis of natural philosophy.

The two major figures most influential in setting the background for astrological thought in the Renaissance were Claudius Ptolemy and Abu Ma'shar (Albumasar of contemporary literature). Ptolemy's classic work on astrology, the *Tetrabiblos*, was translated into Latin in 1136 by Plato of Tivoli, and his equally classic work on astronomy, the *Almagest*, was translated twice in 1150, by Herman of Carinthia and Gerard of Cremona. The *Centiloquium*, a collection of a hundred aphorisms attributed to Ptolemy, was enormously influential and was translated in 1136. The most celebrated astrological formula of the times, 'the wise man will overcome the stars' (*vir sapiens dominabitur astris*) (referred to in both *The Prince* and the 'Ghiribizzi'), is thought to have had its origin in the *Centiloquium*. And two of Machiavelli's contemporaries, Giovanni Pontano and Agostino Nifo, published commentaries on the *Tetrabiblos*.

Two works of Abu Ma'shar also wielded great influence in circles which cultivated an interest in astrology. His *Introductorium Maius in Astronomiam*, an amalgam of Aristotle's *De Caelo, De Generatione et Corruptione, Metereologica*, parts of *Physics* and *Metaphysics*, the medical theories of Hippocrates and Galen, and the basic ideas of the *Tetrabiblos*, was translated twice into Latin in the middle of the twelfth century. His *De Magnis Conjunctionibus* also was made available in Latin around the same time. In this work Abu Ma'shar outlines the theory of the causal effects of planetary conjunctions on history, politics, and religion. Indeed, we know for certain that the work was available in Renaissance Florence; Cosimo Medici owned a manuscript copy.[2] The impact of Abu Ma'shar's conjunctionist theory on Renaissance astrological thought was enormous; what it attempted to do was 'nothing less than the reduction of history into natural philosophy'.[3]

Some of Ptolemy's ideas are particularly relevant for our purpose at hand. The first of these is his division of astrology into two major parts: the general, or catholic, and the particular, or genethliacal. The first concerns the fortunes and ethos of nations and states, while the second concerns the temperaments and fortunes of individuals.[4] The influence of this fundamental division between general and particular astrology can, I think, be detected in Machiavelli's most famous treatment of Fortune in chapter 25 of *The Prince*. (But more about this later.)

Secondly, Ptolemy divides the planets into the beneficent and the maleficent, according to the effects they have on the four humours. Thus Jupiter, Venus and the Moon are thought to be beneficent because of their tempered nature and because they abound in the hot and moist humours, while Saturn and Mars are thought to be maleficent because of their excessive coldness and dryness; the Sun and Mercury are thought to be either beneficent or maleficent, depending on how they are aligned with the other planets at any given time.[5] This is the basis of the belief that there is the same amount of good and evil in the sublunar world. Prognosticating and predicting the effects of these good and bad qualities of the planets on human affairs is the great object of the science and art of astrology.[6]

Thirdly, the motions of the planets are thought to determine the 'quality of the times', both for individuals and countries. The humour, temperament, or 'personality' of each individual is believed to be determined by the influence of the planets at the time of conception, or birth. Time, according to this mode of thought, has an effect on both character and human action. To this extent, the planets are thought to control the chances of success or failure in human actions. For this reason, the planets are called chronocrators, 'time lords', and 'lords of action'.[7] Next, Ptolemy raises the question of the relationship between astral motion, necessity, or fate (they are essentially the same), and individual freedom. He tries to reconcile them to each other by claiming that astral motion is only a general cause which permits particular individuals to act according to their temperament and according to the 'fortuitous antipathies' of the heavens.[8] In other words, the universe is only imperfectly determined, and humans can, with proper 'scientific', astrological knowledge, escape the worst effects of universal determinism. Hence the emergence of a widespread interest in prying into the secrets of an allegedly occult order operating in the universe, as well as an enormous trust in prognostications and predictions. This also accounts for the great prestige of the astrologer: the natural scientist of the day. 'In the case of events that may be modified,' reads Ptolemy's injunction, 'we must give heed to the astrologer, when, for example, he says that to such and such a temperament, with such and such a character of the ambient, if the fundamental proportions increase or decrease, such and such an affection will result.'[9] The astrologer enjoyed the status of the wise man: the wise man of the famous astrological adage, 'the wise man will overcome the stars', was none other than the astrologer, the expert who 'knew' how everything worked.

Among the early proponents of astrological natural science in Italy were Guido Bonatti (d. *c.* 1300), Peter Abano (d. *c.* 1315), and Biagio Pelacani da Parma (1347–1416), who taught at Florence for a time. Called 'the restorer of astrology in the thirteenth century',[10] Bonatti's major work was *Liber astronomicus*, 'the most important astrological work' produced in that century.[11] An amalgam of ideas taken from Ptolemy, Abu Ma'shar and other Arab writers, it enjoyed wide circulation in the courts and chanceries of Western Europe: Henry VII of England possessed one of five manuscripts of that work available in England alone.[12] Bonatti is of special interest to students of Machiavelli because his involvement as an astrologer and consultant to the Duke of Montefeltro is duly noted in *Florentine Histories*: 'When they were besieging Forlì, Guido Bonatto, an astrologer, directed that the people should attack the French at a time (*un punto*) he set; thus all the besiegers were captured or killed.'[13] Peter Abano, 'a second Aristotle' and the founder of Paduan Averroism,[14] was enormously influential in bringing Ptolemaic astrology into the philosophical heartland of Averroism. His *Conciliator* (1303) and *Lucidator* (1310) attempt to harmonize ideas taken from Aristotle, Ptolemy, Abu Ma'shar and Averroes. He firmly defends the theory of the alleged correspondence between changes in the celestial spheres and historical changes. 'It is then important to know whether historical events began when the terrestrial sphere was moving in the same direction as all other spheres, or was it during the first precession, or was it before the first precession, and so on ad infinitum.'[15] He contends that the correspondence between planetary conjunctions and their corresponding effects on earth accounted for the successes of such great conquerors as Alexander the Great, Darius, and Julius Caesar.[16] And, as Garin remarks, his *Conciliator* remained a favourite reading in many chancellaries and royal households.[17] Abano is one of the early Italian pioneers who attempt to make astrology the predictive arm of political science. Abano's 'confidence' in astrology's predictive power reminds one, notes Thorndike, of 'the confidence of the political or social scientist of the present in his methods compared to those of the mere politician or indiscriminate philanthrophist'.[18]

As Vescovini has pointed out, by the end of the fourteenth century adherence to astrological naturalism in physics and medicine had come to mean taking an implicitly anti-Christian stand against such doctrines as providence, the immortality of the soul, and the supernatural character of Christianity itself. Religion was to be treated as a product of nature, valuable for its utility, not its truth. As such, God, or the first cause, was thought to be completely separate from religion. Thus it was a common contention of astrological natural science to say that the rise and fall of religions (or 'sects', as religions were sometimes called) are the result of the great conjunctions of the planets: Judaism, the product of the conjunction of Jupiter and Saturn; Zoroastrianism, of Jupiter and Mars; the Egyptian religion, of Jupiter and the Sun; Christianity, of Jupiter and Mercury; Islam, of Jupiter and Venus; and the 'religion' of the anti-Christ, of Jupiter and the Moon.[19] This 'scientific' theory of religion commanded such respect that even such figures as Roger Bacon and Cardinal Pierre D'Ailly tried to work within it. Indeed, they were willing to accept it, provided an exception was made in the cases of Judaism and Christianity. Bacon accepts the theory of the horoscope of religions.[20] And D'Ailly goes still further, believing that the heavenly bodies played a role even in the case of the Incarnation.[21] This idea is reiterated in *De legibus et sectis* (On Laws and Sects) and *Apologetica defensio astronomice veritatis* (Apologetic Defence of Astronomical Truth). 'And, therefore, I conclude that not only the blessed conception and nativity of Christ or of the blessed Virgin, His Mother, but their entire mortal life, like the natural condition of other men, insofar as it was subject to natural laws, was subject not only to the stars or heavenly bodies, but also to the celestial elements.'[22] The point of our interest in all this is that astrological natural science predisposed even a number of orthodox thinkers to look upon many aspects of religion, including Christianity, from a naturalistic point of view.

The so-called Abu Ma'sharian theory of conjunction came to be accepted as an explanatory theory of the birth, rise and fall not only of religions but also of states. This was a doctrine frequently referred to by contemporary authors. We hear an echo of it in *Discourses* I.56. In D'Ailly's version, the doctrine reads: 'all astronomers are agreed in this that there never was one of those conjunctions without some great and notable changes in this world.'[23] On the basis of this theory, he maintains that the flood of Noah, the rise of the Israelite Kingdom, the appearance of Moses and Charlemagne, and the origin of the Franciscan and Dominican orders find their explanation in astral causes. He even predicts that a 'great mutation' will occur in France in 1789![24] Pomponazzi also supports the theory of conjunction:

I cannot ever remember having read in history books that any notable political change, or the life of any man worth mentioning, be it because of his virtue or his wickedness, did not take place without having those great celestial portents present at birth or at death, at the beginning or the end. And since such portents are given always or frequently, then they must have a natural cause. Furthermore, it can also be argued that they draw from the power of the celestial bodies from the fact that, as histories tell, the astrologers forecast them or interpret them on the basis of observation of the stars.[25]

Savonarola too takes note of this theory for special attention: 'They [the astrologers] say that no great event happens in this world which is not preceded by a great conjunction and all the great things of the past are attributed to certain conjunctions, which, they say, had occurred in those times.'[26]

It was not only in physics and cosmology that astrology left its mark; on medicine also its impact was quite considerable. Nothing illustrates this fact better than Ficino's *De vita triplici* (1489). Ficino considers it a general principle that 'medicine without the favour of the heavens (as Hippocrates and Galen confessed, and as we have discovered, too) is often worthless, in fact very harmful.'[27] The very title of the Third Book is itself quite revealing: 'On making our lives agree with the heavens' (*'vita caelitus comparanda'*). The key idea here is that the humours are the basic constituents of the human body, and bodily health is subject to changes occurring both in the quality of the times and in the positions of the planets. A good doctor must also be an expert astrologer. Machiavelli appears to have been quite familiar with these fine points of astrological medicine. Callimaco, in *Mandragola*, it may be remembered, is presented as being a medical doctor, recently returned from Paris after medical training. He could not only rattle off medical formulas in Latin but also could 'administer' the mandrake to Lucrezia at the astrologically propitious time: 'This evening after supper, because the moon is right and the time can't be more suitable.'[28]

Knowledge of the patient's horoscope was an important part of the medical knowledge required of a doctor. This, in part, accounts for the widespread practice of horoscope-casting in Medicean Florence. Ficino cast the horoscope of no less a personage than Giovanni Medici (Leo X), predicting that one day he would be pope. Cristoforo Landino predicted the reform of Christendom from the conjunction of Saturn and Jupiter, which took place on 25 November, 1484.[29] According to Roberto Ridolfi, Francesco Guicciardini always carried with him for constant consultation his horoscope file, 'a quarto volume of hundreds of pages . . . bound in brown morocco, with chiselled and gilded edges', in which his favourite astrologer had analysed his entire life for him – past, present and future – on the basis of his birth-hour, humours and inclinations.[30] By the standards of the day, there was nothing unscientific in this: knowledge of one's horoscope was part of self-knowledge necessary for keeping good health as well as for enjoying good fortune and avoiding bad fortune.

Court astrologers were even busier than were medical astrologers. There was hardly a royal or ecclesiastical court without its resident astrologer. The *Policraticus* of John of Salisbury (1120-1180) considers the influx of astrological ideas on political practice so serious that it devotes Bks. I and II to its critique. Maimonides's 'Letter on Astrology' (1194), points out the political dangers inherent in astrology: he traces the cause for the fall of ancient Israel to its addiction to astrology; the penchant for predictions gradually corrupted civic virtues, and nurtured the illusion that chance or Fortune is caused by the heavens.[31] Henry Langenstein's *Tractatus contra astrologos conjunctionistas* (Treatise Against Conjunctionist Astrologers) sounds the alarm bells against the growing influence of political astrology in the fourteenth century.[32] Nicole Oresme translated Aristotle's *Politics* and *Ethics* into French in part to counteract the influence of astrology at the French court. His *Livre de divinations* (known in Latin under the title *Tractatus contra judiciarios astronomos*), written between 1361 and 1365, is a trenchant critique of contemporary astrological practices and beliefs as applied to politics. In general, it was believed in European courts that Alexander the Great and the kings of ancient Egypt possessed knowledge of astrology, that Abraham, 'that noble prince and patriarch', taught astrology to the Egyptians, and that Moses, King Solomon, Numa Pompilius, and Scipio were all well versed in astrology. Charles V of France had in his library several works on astrology, and his court astrologer, Thomas of Pisa, was 'always consulted and obeyed' (*toujours consulté et toujours obéi*).[33] The case in England was not any different.[34] In Italy, Biagio Pelacani of Parma taught an astrologico-political naturalism rejecting the Aristotelian view of politics: happiness was no longer thought to consist in the virtuous life; it was thought to be found in the satisfaction of material needs for security, power, and glory. Clearly, astrological politics had a negative impact on Aristotelian politics.[35]

The courts of Alexander VI, Julius II and Leo X also had their resident astrologers. In 1501, Agostino Vespucci informed Machiavelli that there were 'five or six doctors' in the Borgia court who were fond of discussing poetry and astrology ('*ragionando et di poesia et astrologia*'). One of these was Alexander VI's favourite astrologer. When Alexander was still a cardinal, he had correctly predicted that he would one day be pope. But the stingy and ungrateful Alexander did not reward him adequately, and so the unfortunate astrologer experienced ill health and great poverty. Vespucci even sent along to Machiavelli a three-line verse which this astrologer-poet had composed and which was circulating in Rome.[36] Bonatus de Latis and Gaspar Torrella were Cesare Borgia's astrologers.[37] Machiavelli himself reports that Borgia believed 1502 would be a bad year for subjects to rebel.[38] Julius II's coronation was postponed, it was known in diplomatic circles in

Rome, on the advice of astrologers.[39] Charles VIII consulted his astrologer, Simon Phares, before he decided to invade Italy in 1494.[40] In Florence, astrologers normally participated in the deliberations of the Signoria.[41] The installation of Florentine military officers took place at the astrologically propitious point in time, the so-called *punto di astrologia*. Ficino himself determined the *punto* for laying the foundation of the Strozzi palace.[42] In his military campaigns, Julius II normally took advice from his astrologers.[43] As Burckhardt has pointed out, 'Nothing that depended upon the stars was more important than decisions in times of war.'[44] In his 1509 campaign against Pisa, Machiavelli himself was advised by his friend Lattanzio Tedaldi as to the *punto* to take possession of that city. 'Thursday being the day to take possession of Pisa, under no circumstances should the Florentines enter the city before 12.30. A little after 13.00 would be the most propitious for us. If Thursday is not suitable, Friday will be the next best, again after 13.00, but not before 12.30; and the same applies to Saturday, if Friday is not suitable. And if it is not possible to keep either to the day or to the hour, take a suitable time in nomine Domini.'[45] The same Tedaldi had previously written to Machiavelli informing him of what he had said on the subject in public council ('. . . *similiter quid de cometa publice in consilio locutus fuerim*').[46] So much for the astrological practice of political predictions.

Another issue related to the role of the heavens in human affairs is that of celestial signs. Storms, tempests, thunderbolts and the like were often looked upon as 'signs' sent from the heavens to warn humans of impending calamities. Even Guicciardini believed that the 1494 invasion of Italy was preceded by such signs and the prognostications and predictions relating to it. The heavens (*consentimento de' cieli*) concurred, he wrote, with the predictions about the future woes of Italy. Astrologers predicted that more frequent and great changes were in store, and that stranger and more horrible events were about to occur. Thus in Puglia one night, three suns appeared in the sky, surrounded by clouds, accompanied by frightful thunder and lightning. In the territory of Arezzo, an infinite number of armed men on enormous horses were seen for many days passing through the air with a terrible clamour of drums and trumpets. People were only surprised that amidst so many prodigies there did not appear a comet, which the ancients believed to be an unfailing messenger of 'the mutation of kingdoms and states'.[47] Guicciardini also held the belief that 'the influxes of the heavens and other occult dispositions' were causal factors in bringing about changes in civilizational cycles.[48]

Did Machiavelli himself personally believe in celestial signs? His most sympathetic biographer, Roberto Ridolfi, thinks so. For example, a thunderbolt that hit the Signoria in 1511 frightened him so much that he decided immediately to write his will. The thunderbolt had gone right through the chancery destroying three golden lilies over the door. This he immediately interpreted as a bad sign, both for the French King and for the Florentine

government. As Ridolfi writes, 'Machiavelli, like other great men, believed
in celestial omens and was filled with foreboding. On the 22nd of November
[1511] in the presence of his colleagues he made his first will.'[49]

A Sense of Crisis

Widespread astrological practices and a growing belief in the occult powers
of the heavens naturally caused deep concern in many quarters. The notion
that there could be an efficacious occult order existing side by side with the
efficacious natural and the revealed supernatural orders, went against all the
postulates of orthodox philosophy and theology. From the philosophical
side, opposition to astrology and the alleged occult causality of the heavens
often appeared in the various treatises written on the subject of Fortune.
This was as true of Petrarch's *De remediis utriusque fortunae*, Salutati's *De fato
et fortuna*, Bracciolini's *De varietate fortunae*, Aeneas Piccolomini's *Somnium de
fortuna*, Alberti's *De fato et fortuna*, as of Pontano's *De fortuna*. But, as Cassirer
reminds us, 'as we move further into the Renaissance, we feel more and
more that the advancement of the worldly spirit and of worldly culture
strengthens the tendency towards the basic doctrines of astrology.'[50] 'The basic
magical-astrological view of causality comes to be interwoven in the whole
Renaissance philosophy of nature . . . A transcendent bond is replaced by an
immanent bond; a religious and theological bond is replaced by a naturalistic bond. And the latter was a harder one to surmount and surpass.'[51] Yet
attempts to surmount and surpass the new bonds of astrological naturalism
did take place, particularly in the spheres of visual arts, moral philosophy
and moral theology. There is, it was said, an anti-astrological intent in the
works of some of the great painters of the period; and there is also, of
course, an open hostility towards astrology in the works of Pico della
Mirandola and Savonarola. In Pico's *Disputations Against Astrology*, problems
posed by astrology receive their most serious criticism.

Aby Warburg has raised the question of the significance of the presence
of astrological imagery in Renaissance art. Is this presence a sign of a
capitulation to astrology, or of a victory over it? Warburg sees a deeper
significance of the use of astrological imagery in terms of the internal
struggles between reason and magic, between mythopoeic imagination and
reflective reason, or between the assumed causality from the external world
of the stars and the human causality of reason – or, as he puts it metaphori-
cally, in terms of a struggle between Athens and Alexandria (Alexandria
being the birthplace of Ptolemaic astrology), or between Athens and
Baghdad (Baghdad being the birthplace of Abu Ma'shar's astrology). Athens
must always be conquered afresh from Alexandria: 'the liberation of Athens
from the clutches of Baghdad' must periodically be brought about. These,
according to Warburg, are the deeper concerns which explain a painting
such as Dürer's '*Melancholia*', or Botticelli's '*Venus*'.[52] In this view, the artist

transfigures the images of the planets by using them 'as instruments of his quest for the perfect classical proportions of man'.[53] According to Gombrich, what we witness in Renaissance art is not the elimination of astrological motifs, but their 'reform' or humanization. Thus, in the '*Melancholia*' of Dürer 'the astrological belief in the evil power of Saturn has been reformed through the Aristotelian interpretation of Saturnian temperament as the one best suited to contemplation . . .'[54] The influence of Jupiter can, to a certain extent, 'neutralize the malignant effects of Saturn's melancholy and turn it into the lighter form which is really the complexion (temperament) of genius.'[55] To Warburg it also suggests that the emergence of rationality is not a matter of evolution or progress, but one of constant reconquest from forces which threaten it. Good and evil alternate in human affairs; the evil is never eliminated, as the alleged theory of progress implies. Images can either 'enlighten' or 'mislead' us.[56]

The polemic against astrology reaches its critical stage, however, with the publication of Pico's *Disputations Against Astrology*,[57] and with Savonarola's *Treatise Against Divinatory Astrology*.[58] Pico's Preface gives an indication of the perceived threat from astrology: it was corrupting philosophy, adulterating medicine, weakening religion, engendering and encouraging superstition, favouring idolatry, destroying prudence, sacrificing mores, making people anxious, miserable and restless, and transforming free beings into unfortunate slaves.[59] A massive volume divided into 12 books, it presents an analysis of all the astrological doctrines to be found in the available writings of the day in Greek, Latin, Hebrew and Arabic. In Burckhardt's view, the book makes 'an epoch in the subject',[60] and Garin is disposed to compare its importance to that of *Novum Organum* or *Discours de la Méthode*.[61] Savonarola's work, by comparison, looks like a pamphlet, though size and appearance in no way undermine its significance. For, as he states in the Preface, he does not attempt to improve on Pico but only to make his (Pico's) ideas intelligible to the 'average' (*mediocri*) reader of Florence. Pico's work, written in Latin, involved deep and complicated philosophical analysis, and was too learned to be understood by the ordinary citizens of Florence. Savonarola, therefore, felt that he should write something simple and in the vernacular, in order to reach a more popular audience. For our purpose here, which is to establish the intellectual context of Machiavelli's thought on the heavens and the humours, it is important that these two books be read in tandem, for only then will we be able to understand the content of astrological thought in Florence in the last decade of the fifteenth century and the first decades of the sixteenth century, in both the learned and in the ordinary circles. In this respect, Savonarola's work may offer an advantage of its own, for it gives us an understanding of what the ordinary persons in Florence thought of astrology; it is a good index to their heuristic structure as far as this topic is concerned. Thus we learn that Florence was being inundated with astrological ideas of many different writers at this time. He mentions eleven of them by name – Albumasar (Abu Ma'shar), Haly, Abenzagel, Aboasar, Avenagea, Aoniar, Petosiris, Avenrodan, Azerchel, Adarbaraba, and, of course, Ptolemy himself, 'the prince of these astrologers' (*il principe di questi astrologi*) – an impressive list indeed in a book intended for the ordinary reader.[62] In any case, the ultimate purpose of both Pico and Savonarola was the same – firstly, to demonstrate that astrology was neither a science nor an art, but a system of errors contrary to reason and revelation, and injurious to faith and morals, civil life and human dignity; and secondly, to establish that apart from the natural and the supernatural order, there is no such thing as the occult order.[63]

The most important focus of the attack is fixed on the nature of the causality exercised by the heavens. The heavens, though not composed of elemental matter, are nevertheless corporeal entities; as such, their effects on sublunar entities can only be of a corporeal or physical nature. And these effects can be nothing more than physical motion, heat and light; the motions of the heavens possess no qualitative effects whatsoever: 'Apart from the influence of common motion and light, there is no power specific to the heavens.'[64] This undermined in one stroke the basis of the theory of the 'occult virtue' of the heavens.[65] Though the heavens may be the 'general cause' of all motions in the sublunar world (and Pico concedes this), this still in no way explains the behaviour of specific sublunar agents. To understand the actions of such agents, one must study the specific agent involved in its particular nature. Only such knowledge can properly be called scientific knowledge. 'Neither specific nor individual differences of things can depend on celestial motion.'[66] As for the astrological doctrine that a heavenly 'sign' can be a 'cause' of terrestrial happenings, Pico delivers an equally decisive blow. No sign can causally effect physical change in physical entities; physical changes require physical causes. The heavens can indicate that they are causing something only if they are its actual physical cause, otherwise they indicate nothing real. In other words, signs cannot be causes.[67]

Applying the principles he has established so far to the theory of humours, Pico is able to argue that fluctuations in human temperament and humours cannot be attributed to the motions of the heavenly bodies.[68] Nor can differences in 'natural talent' (*ingenium*) and in moral 'character' (*mores*) have anything to do with the four primary qualities of elemental matter and their four corresponding humours, nor with the motions of the planets.[69] The de-linking of the humours and the heavens also lays to rest the theory that wars, civil discords, and factions can be explained in terms of the humours of princes and peoples. It is ridiculous to think that wars, seditions, conspiracies, the fall of empires and the like might be caused by changes in the qualities of the stars or in the bile of princes and kings. 'O happy Italy, would that questions of war and peace be settled by the pharmacist who administers the right pills.'[70] And the use of the Abu Ma'sharian theory of conjunction to explain changes in empires is also rejected; for 'neither good regimes nor bad regimes are subject to the heavens.'[71]

These criticisms also go a long way towards undermining the foundations of astrological medicine, as they emphasized the inadequacy of a purely somatic conception of human well-being. The most distinguishing characteristics of a mature human being, Pico argues, are his/her reason and natural talent (*ingenium*), acquired virtues and philosophic wisdom. In the acquisition of these, it is the non-somatic faculties which play the decisive role. Pico illustrates this point through his celebrated analysis of the achievements of Aristotle and Alexander, the symbols, respectively of intellectual and political virtues.

The heavens cannot explain Aristotle's accomplishments in philosophy and science, neither by the trite argument that many others who were also born under the same star did not attain his eminence, nor by the equally trite argument that both the swine of Boeotia and Aristotle were born under the same heavens. The pivot of Pico's reasoning is that astrologers failed to consider the particular causes explaining particular human beings: in the case of Aristotle, his soul which, being immaterial, could not have come from the heavens, his good body, which he received from his parents, not the heavens, his decision to study philosophy, which he freely made, his industry, which explains his progress, his teacher, who was responsible for the particular direction he took, his natural talent (*ingenium*) which, being immaterial, came from God, not the heavens – these and other particulars are decisive in accounting for Aristotle as an individual.[72]

The same principle is applied to Alexander: Alexander's greatness cannot be explained in terms of the constellation under which he was born, nor in terms of what the 'vulgar' call Fortune. Alexander's greatness became intelligible only in terms of the particularities surrounding him: his virtues of courage, liberality and industriousness, which he cultivated assiduously, his knowledge of military science as well as of letters, the encouragement received from his father, and the warlike region in which he was raised. This is how one should understand the character of an Alexander or a Caesar, a Sulla or an Augustus.[73]

In other words, according to Pico, the explanation of what is specifically great in human beings escapes the grasp of astrology; in fact, what is specific to human beings lies outside the chain of natural causality as astrology conceives of it. The dignity of humans lies in the fact that we have souls and minds; the mind enables freedom of choice, even though with respect to the body we are subject to the bonds of natural causation. But humans are not just phenomena of nature; in important respects – in the acts of willing and knowing – we transcend nature. The 'great miracle' of human beings is our soul, which has the power to break the cycle of necessity allegedly imposed by the heavens or fate. 'Nothing is greater on earth than humans, nothing is greater in humans than their mind and soul; if you scale their heights, you will transcend the heavens; if you incline towards the body and only just look up at the heavens, you will only see yourself as a moth, indeed even something less than that.'[74]

One of the major achievements of the *Disputations* is the final invalidation of the conjunctionist basis of astrological historiography. Bk. V is devoted entirely to this purpose. History, says Pico, is a specifically human creation. Historical time, or 'time of things' (*tempus rerum*) and astrological time, i.e. the time taken by planets to complete their curriculum, are not the same.[75] History is the true 'mistress' of human time, and the knowledge of the motions of the heavens and the stars contributes nothing towards acquiring a true knowledge of history. In other words, astrology has no competence in matters relating to history. For this reason, astrology cannot be considered to be its true 'mistress'.[76] The mistake of conjunctionists such as Roger Bacon and Cardinal D'Ailly is that they too readily followed the 'tale-bearing' (*fabulosissimi*) Arab writers, instead of following the sober Greek and Latin historians.[77]

Given the specifically human character of history, the basis of the notion of a 'fatal hour' of conception according to the Ptolemaic theory of the horoscopes of individuals, and that of the Albumasarian theory of the horoscopes of religions and states, collapse. Astrology claimed that the first 'fatal' hour of the existence of individuals, religions and states had a magical, efficient causality which affects them for the rest of their lives. Pico finds no reason why a special status should be attached to the so-called 'first hour' of historical entities. For such entities fulfil their being and achieve their purpose only through activities which involve duration and a succession of hours. The 'first hour', therefore, does not have any special efficient causal power that can override the efficient causal power of all other hours.[78] Besides, there is no way of knowing the exact time of the first hour of 'cities, kingdoms, factions, and religions', and there is nothing in astrology that enables one to investigate this point.[79]

Pico's critical rejection of the astrological notion of Fortune is no less important than his rejection of astrological historiography. Astrology, particularly the non–philosophical varieties of it, misleads its followers regarding the nature of Fortune. For it speaks of Fortune as if it were a power of the heavens, as if it were a causal agent. According to Pico, Fortune is neither of these. It has nothing to do with the heavens, since the heavens represent only the universal, necessary laws by which the universe operates. Hence, 'when one said fortune, one did not say heaven.'[80] Nor is the 'fortuitous caused by heaven's causality.'[81] For, strictly speaking, the fortuitous are things that happen only to human beings who act for a purpose, i.e. according to a final cause. Yet the fortuitous are precisely those things which do not have a final cause. The correct understanding of what Fortune is, as Pico and Savonarola argue, can be obtained only from a 'right' philosophy such as that of Aristotle or Boethius, and from a 'right' theology such as that of Augustine or Aquinas.[82] In other words, both Pico and Savonarola oppose and reject the position of astrology on fate and Fortune, and they do so with the aid of both Aristotle and Aquinas. In fact, the orthodox principle of both philosophy and theology is that although necessary laws emanating from the heavens rule the sublunar world, there also exists a vast field for chance or the fortuitous in a world so ruled. From the point of view of the human agent, chance or fortuitous events are events that are not intended by the human agent. In this sense, they lack a final cause – but this does not mean that they lack an efficient cause. Thus, in the case of A meeting B by chance in the market-place, the walking of A and B to the market-place (assuming they were walking) constitutes the efficient cause of the chance meeting. But the meeting lacks a final cause or intention, since a meeting was not intended when A and B proceeded to the market-place. This is what Aristotle means when he says that 'luck and the automatic' are caused only 'by virtue of concurrence', and not 'by nature'. For it is not in the 'nature' of either A or B to meet each other whenever they go to the market-place. Yet their accidental meeting is not a 'non-event' either. It is something, and it needs to be explained. All that Aristotle, and for that matter Pico and Savonarola, are concerned to say is that in actual life, fortuitous events do occur, but these do not come from the actions of a 'nature' (in this case the 'nature' of A and B) intending the event in question. In other words, not everything that happens in the world has its causal explanation in the intended activity of intelligent agents. Aristotle is content to leave the matter there, refusing to accept both the Democritean position that everything happens by chance, and the popular position which ascribes chance events to a goddess called Fortune.[83] Astrology, however, vacillating between philosophical and popular parlance, at times attributes chance events to the motions of the heavens, and at times to an assumed entity called Fortune. In the first case, it veers towards absolute determinism or fate, and in the second case it veers towards the popular view that all chance events are caused by the goddess Fortune. The latter view becomes even more complicated when Fortune is identified by some with the powers of the heavens. In the minds of both Pico and Savonarola, the position of contemporary astrology is incompatible with both orthodox philosophy and orthodox theology. The reason why it is incompatible with theology is that, in effect, it substitutes divine Providence with the quasi-'providence' of the heavens, or, alternately, it attributes all chance events to Fortune, which is assumed to be indifferent to human well-being. Such a view goes against the Christian view of Providence, according to which nothing that happens in the world happens by chance; everything – whether the human mind understands it or not – is accounted for by divine wisdom. Thus Pico's critique of astrology's stand on Fortune tends to reaffirm the Aristotelian and Thomistic views on the heavens, fate, Providence, and Fortune. At the very least, Pico's position gives us a benchmark by which to evaluate the position that Machiavelli, as we shall see, takes on these very issues.

Pico's attack on astrology is not based on any empirical or mathematical principles. It is based primarily on his insight into the nature of moral action: human beings cannot act as true moral agents unless they are truly independent of all constraints, especially constraints coming from fate, or natural necessity. His moral theory allows sufficient room for free choice, unencumbered even by the pressures of humours or temperament. Pico is able to conceive of the human agent, at least in this one significant respect, as transcending the macrocosm of the universe. In effect, he denies any strict and complete correspondence between the human world and the macrocosm of the universe. As Cassirer writes, 'the astrological vision of the world had always been bound to the idea of the microcosm. Indeed, astrology seemed to be nothing other than the simple consequence and carrying out of that idea.'[84] And, as Garin rightly points out, 'Pico's glorification of man is, in the last analysis, nothing but an attack upon the idea of the microcosm, *tritum in scholis*.'[85]

As can well be imagined, Pico's attack on astrology provoked counterattacks from a number of different quarters. His own premature death deprives us of any answers that he might have given to them. In any case, the attack came primarily from those who conceded Pico's position on ethics and Providence, but who still wanted to defend astrology on a purely natural science basis. Lucio Bellanti (the Bellanti of *Discourses* III.6) was one of these: his *Defensio Astrologiae*, dedicated to Catherine Sforza de Riario Forli e Imola, appeared in 1498. He still believed a defence of astrology to be possible and desirable, on the basis of both the theory of humours and the general causality alleged to be exercised by the heavens. The latter exercise their power not only through light and motion, but also through 'influence' (*influentia*) and 'signs' (*figura*). Particular agents are the 'instruments' of the primary, heavenly causes. And if the heavens did not move each particular entity, all life on earth would cease to function. He was particularly insistent in maintaining that humours respond to climatic and astral influences.[86] On the whole a passionate, though ineffective, defence, Bellanti's response did not win many followers. Still, he wanted to make clear that he did not espouse unorthodox views. He believed that astrological 'science' and Christian faith could be reconciled. This is why we see him enhancing his arguments with quotations from Aquinas, Duns Scotus and others. As he colourfully put it in his Preface, Duns Scotus and Thomas Aquinas were his 'navigators'.[87]

Pontano also, in his *De Fortuna* and *De Rebus Coelestibus*, responded to Pico, but rather gently, hoping that some compromise between astrological ethics, historiography, Aristotelian philosophy and Christian theology could be worked out. There is no incompatibility, he believed, between the Providence of God and the natural causality exercised by the heavens, provided the heavens are thought to be subject to Providence. He still adhered to the notion that God leaves all matters concerning wealth and power to the domain of Fortune, as He himself does not want to be blamed for disappointments in these spheres. 'The goods of wealth and power were not the outcome of moral virtue but of Fortune.'[88] Pontano preferred to see three kinds of things in the world – the necessary, the possible, and what he called the 'eventual' (*eventitia*).[89] Goods of Fortune, i.e. those pursued in politics and 'economics', belong to the *eventitia*. In other words, he could not see how the art of the acquisition of such things as wealth, honour, and success could be explained without appealing to some such 'principle' as Fortune. 'Economics' and politics had not yet developed a theory of how princes and rulers acquire or lose power, or how merchants and traders gain or lose wealth. In the absence of an acceptable science, Pontano was prepared to adhere to a theory according to which things happened *ex eventitia*.

From the aforegoing, it should be apparent that the debate on astrology brought into the open a number of important issues. Garin identifies three in particular: those concerning 'the order of the world', 'the conception of the self', and 'the *res publica*, or the state'. The first involves the question of the relationship of human beings to the physical universe, the second, the question of the soul and its immortality, and the third, the nature of human society and the state, 'dramatically expressed by Machiavelli'.[90] A proper discussion of any one of these necessarily involves the discussion of the other two. This might explain why it is that, in attempting to reason about the state, Machiavelli felt it necessary to concern himself with the heavens and the humours, and with the non-political question of how 'things of the world' are governed, whether by God or by Fortune. For, contrary to Savonarola and Pico, he still believed that the heavens did exert their causality on human things through motion, power, and signs.

CHAPTER 2

Heaven, History, and Politics

Heaven and the Machiavellian Project

The Preface to *Discourses* I occupies a special place in Machiavelli's writings. Apart from the fact that it is the only portion of the work which has come down to us in his autograph, it also gives us an overall view of the work, and even perhaps of the entire Machiavellian project. The corrections and revisions of the text show the care with which he prepared this Preface.[1] In it, among other things, he complains that his contemporaries are sadly lacking in the knowledge of true history. They read history for amusement rather than for instruction. One gets the true flavour of history only if one sees it as the record of *virtù*. If the present age lacks *virtù*, as he thinks it does, it is all the more necessary for contemporaries to read history, and to imitate those who possessed *virtù* in antiquity. The erroneous attitude of his contemporaries towards ancient history stands in sharp contrast to their attitude towards ancient art, jurisprudence, and medicine. For they patronize artists who seek inspiration from ancient art, and spend large sums of money to buy even a fragment of ancient statues. Likewise, contemporary jurists cultivate ancient jurisprudence, and study the judgements of the ancients as a means to understand the principles of their own laws. The same is true of contemporary doctors of medicine, who study the medicine of Hippocrates and Galen. 'For the civil laws are nothing else than judgements given by the ancient jurists, which, brought into order, teach our present jurists to judge. And medicine too is nothing other than the experiments made by the ancient physicians, on which present physicians base their judgements.'[2] Yet neither contemporary kings nor leaders of republics, neither generals nor lawgivers, pay any attention to the virtuous practices of ancient times: 'in ordering republics, in maintaining states, in governing kingdoms, in organizing armies, in managing wars, in executing laws among subjects, in expanding empires, not a single prince or republic now resorts to the example of the ancients.'[3]

The reason why contemporary political science lags behind contemporary art, jurisprudence and medicine is because of a lack of knowledge of how history operates. And this lack is due, in turn, to the weakness into which Christianity, 'the present religion', has led the European world. 'This I believe comes not so much from the weakness into which the present religion has brought the world, or from the harm done to many Christian provinces and cities by an ambitious leisure as from not having a true knowledge of the histories, for in reading them we do not get that sense or taste that flavour which they have in them.'[4] Christians have interpreted their religion according to *ozio* (leisure) not *virtù*, and in doing so they have been influenced by their own particular view of history, which in turn has been influenced by their cosmology. They read pagan history not to learn moral lessons but merely to enjoy the aesthetic pleasure of its literary qualities. They get the moral lessons they need from 'sacred history'. Acting according to the moral lessons of pagan history would be tantamount to renouncing Christianity. And because of this, Christians consider the imitation of ancient *virtù* to be not only difficult but also morally impossible. The explanation of why Christians consider the imitation of pagan *virtù* morally impossible and why they have, however, to imitate it if they want to be politically virtuous, is the crucial issue of the Preface, if not of the entire *Discourses*. And at the root of the explanation of these issues lies Machiavelli's theory of the role that heaven plays in history and in the governance of the 'things of the world'.

It is, of course, Machiavelli's intention to correct the 'error' of the Christian interpretation of history. That is why he undertakes to write the *Discourses*. 'Wishing, then, to get men away from this error, I have decided that on all the books by Titus Livy which the malice of time has not taken away from us, it is necessary that I write what, according to my knowledge of ancient and modern things, I judge necessary for the better understanding of them, in order that those who read these explanations of mine may more easily get from them that profit for which they should seek knowledge of histories.'[5] It becomes clear by now that the acceptance of what he proposes as the true knowledge of history is a precondition for the acceptance of his 'new modes and orders'. That is to say, his philosophy of history is, so to speak, the foundation on which he will build the edifice of his new political science.

But what is Machiavelli's philosophy of history? He states it with such finesse and economy of words that a modern reader not familiar with the nuances of an astrological view of history is likely to miss his point. His contemporaries judge, he says, 'that imitation is not only difficult but also impossible, as if the heaven, the sun, the elements, men were changed in motion, order, and power from what they were in antiquity'.[6] To appreciate the importance of this passage one is advised to compare it with the draft. The relevant portion of the draft is as follows: 'senza pensare altrimenti di imitarle, giudicando la imitatione non solo difficile ma impossibile, come se il cielo, il sole, li elementi, l'anima, li uomini fussino variati di substantia, di moti, d'ordine et di potenza da quelli, ch'egli erono antiquamente.'[7] Two words have been omitted from the original draft: *anima* (soul) and *substantia* (substance). Pincin speculates that the omission of the word 'soul' is perhaps due to the similarity it has to the word following it, viz. *li uomini* (men); maybe so. But it could also be that the soul, as Strauss never tires of insisting, has no place in Machiavelli's historiography. In orthodox historiography, the soul, as Pico points out, is capable of transcending astral determinism. Anyone who wishes to adopt a naturalistic philosophy of history would do well to omit the soul from the picture altogether. The omission of the word *substantia* is less crucial; Machiavelli leaves it out, Pincin thinks, simply because it was the first word that came to his mind as he was drafting the Preface.[8] In any case, the draft enables us to infer that the text as it now stands has received Machiavelli's fullest attention, and that every word is there because he wants it to be there. But such an inference leads to a further question: what about words that are not there but would have been there had he adopted a Christian theory of history? What I have in mind is the word 'God'. It might be said that he does not include God in the list of causal agents for the obvious reason that nobody would suppose God has changed since antiquity. But such an explanation is not convincing because he *does* include another unchanging causal agent – heaven – in the list in question. It may be remembered that according to pre-modern physics, heaven is an eternal principle of motion. The point is that omitting God from the list of causal agents is essential for Machiavelli's argument. Only by doing so can he safeguard his own 'true' naturalistic theory of history. One cannot have an ethic of Machiavellian *virtù* and at the same time accept a Christian cosmology, a Christian historiography, and a Christian ethical system. For there is a connection between the last three. If one does not accept the theory that the universe is created by God and governed by Providence, a Christian conception of changes in secular time and a Christian conception of political action cannot be validly and con- sistently maintained. Briefly, the omission of God from Machiavelli's list gives us a preliminary clue to the precise intellectual context of his naturalistic political theory.

According to the 'true' conception of history, then, the motions of heaven and the planets (*il sole* here stands for the planets as a group) affect all human motions, collective as well as individual. The 'order' that human history follows – of rise and fall, corruption and renewal – and the 'power' which makes such 'order' possible, are received from the motions of the heavens and the planets. This is the 'truth' which Christianity rejects. According to the latter, history does not move in such cycles; God has intervened in history through the Incarnation, and He continues to inter- vene through Providence. As such, history is not tied to the motions of nature. Its order, power, and motions are derived partly from God and partly from humans themselves. This is why Christianity rejects any notion of human virtue which is tied to astral destiny and astral motions. This is also the reason why it objects to the imitation of Machiavellian *virtù*.

I have suggested that the omission of 'God' from the list of causal agents is significant. Yet Machiavelli is not ignorant of the orthodox Christian view of history. For his poem 'On Ambition' introduces the Christian idea of God as the creator of heaven and earth, even though he misrepresents it by introducing the notion of an occult power 'sustaining itself in heaven', and interfering in human affairs:

> Hardly had God made the stars, the heaven, the light, the elements, and
> man – master over so many things of beauty –
> and had quelled the pride of the angels, and from Paradise had banished
> Adam with his wife for their tasting of the apple,
> when (after the birth of Cain and Abel, as with their father and their
> labour they were living happy in their poor dwelling)
> an occult power which sustains itself in the heaven, among stars which
> heaven as it whirls encloses, to man's being by no means friendly –
> To deprive us of peace and to set us at war, to take away from us all quiet
> and all good, sent two Furies to dwell on the earth.[9]

The mention of an occult power associated with heaven is found elsewhere in his writings. *Discourses* I.3 mentions an occult cause (*occulta cagione*) operating in nature,[10] which one presumes is similar in character to the 'occult power' mentioned in 'On Ambition'. If this is correct, it follows that in general, for Machiavelli, heaven is the source of the occult operations in nature – a point hotly contested, as we have seen in the previous chapter, by the opponents of astrological historiography.

The Preface of *Discourses* II builds on the foundations laid down in the Preface of *Discourses* I. It clarifies the grounds and conditions under which the imitation of *virtù* should take place. The most important of these conditions is that one should have a more or less objective understanding of how one is situated in history: by no means an easy task to achieve. For, says Machiavelli, when it comes to judging 'the things that pertain to the life and customs of men', as opposed to 'the things that pertain to the arts', humans are generally self-serving. They tend to praise themselves and their times more than they should, and this tendency gives them a distorted view of history. But if one knew the laws of history, one would be less prone to partiality and more disposed to a critical self-appraisal. These laws of history tell us that 'human things are always in motion, either falling or rising'.[11] It follows that each state has its period of rise and its period of decline, its period of virtue and its period of corruption. If one is born in the virtuous period, then to praise the past would be wrong; likewise, if one is born in the period of corruption, then to praise the present would be wrong. For only if *virtù* is present may one rightly praise any epoch of history. 'So a city or province can be organized for free government by some excellent man, and for a time, through that organizer's *virtù*, it can keep on always growing better. He who then is born in such a state and praises ancient times more than modern ones deceives himself . . . But they who are born later in that city or province, when the time has come for it to descend towards a corrupt period, do not then deceive themselves.'[12]

To clarify this idea further, Machiavelli falls back once more on his naturalistic conception of history. Considering how human things move, 'I judge,' says Machiavelli emphatically, that the world has always gone on in the same way and that there has been 'as much good as bad' (*tanto di buono quanto di cattivo*) in it, but that this bad and this good have moved from country to country. Though the world remains the same, 'customs' have changed from country to country. Thus, *virtù* was first found in Assyria, it then moved successively to Media, Persia, Rome, France, Turkey, the kingdom of the Sultan, and to the peoples of Germany.[13]

How are we to understand this apparently puzzling view that there is a certain, constant 'amount' of good and bad in the world which is distributed differently at different times? Surely Machiavelli is not propounding some pseudo-Manichaean doctrine of good and evil. Nor could he be referring to good and evil in the moral sense, since moral goodness and moral evil are not susceptible to any quantitative measure. This leaves us with the supposition that he might be talking about good and evil in the sense of astrological natural science, according to which the good and/or evil of countries follow the movements of the beneficent and the maleficent planets. In *Tetrabiblos* I. 5, as we have seen, Ptolemy had already propounded such a theory. Nations undergo the cycle of rise and fall, corruption and renewal, accordingly as they come under the influence of favourable or unfavourable planets. In this sense, one might speak of the 'amount' of good and evil being equal in the world; each nation will undergo good times as well as bad times. In the absence of a better explanation, there is nothing absurd in considering this interpretation, bearing in mind that this was the sort of notion that astrological naturalism was commonly propounding on 'scientific' grounds.

Machiavelli is now in a position to explain why he is impartial in praising the Roman past and blaming the Christian present, for there was *virtù* in the one while there is only corruption in the other.

And truly, if the *virtù* that then prevailed and the corruption that now prevails were not clearer than the sun, I would keep my speech more cautious, fearing to bring upon to myself the very deception of which I accuse others. But since the thing is so clear that everybody sees it, I shall be bold in saying clearly what I learn about Roman times and the present, in order that the spirits of the young who read these writings of mine may flee the present and be prepared to imitate the past, whenever Fortune gives them the occasion.[14]

The motions of heaven explain the course of history; they have something to do with the presence of good and evil in the world. But the role of heaven does not end there; it extends beyond countries to reach each individual too, insofar as the latter is supposed to need the opportunity (*occasione*) which only the heaven can give. This is not to say that Machiavelli propounds some form of fatalism. Far from it. Humans have to do their indispensable share. Heaven and humans are the co-causes of all human achievements, analogous to the Christian doctrine of God and humans being the co-causes of human achievement. As he writes in one of his early discourses, 'the heavens do not wish nor are they able to sustain an undertaking if those involved in it are determined to ruin it.'[15] All this being said, humans still need that one necessary thing, the *occasione*, if they are to succeed. And for this they need the favour of heaven or Fortune. Machiavelli himself feels that he is not so favoured. This is why he feels that 'someone more loved by heaven' than he is would be needed to ensure the success of his innovative project.[16] In other words, heaven's favour is needed even in the practical order. Thus, the two Prefaces reveal both the theory underlying Machiavelli's conception of history, and the necessary, minimum practical conditions under which this theory can be put into practice. In both instances, the role of heaven seems irreplaceable.

Motions of Countries

In the foregoing section we saw how motions emanating from heaven and the planets affected history and politics generally. We shall now attempt to see how this natural motion of universal necessity affects countries or states, or, as Machiavelli is sometimes fond of calling them, 'provinces'. While natural motion functions irresistibly, human motion is also a key factor in determining the character of the regime. Thus, military and political activities bring countries to *virtù* and order, while the practice of philosophy and religious contemplation (but not religion) brings them to 'leisure', disorder and decadence. Neither civic *virtù* nor decadence, however, is immune to the natural motion to which all countries are subject. While this 'circular' motion is not the same as the famous theory of *anacyclosis* (discussed in *Discourses* I. 2), the latter theory must also be seen as falling within the general law of motion affecting countries, and not as a wholly independent phenomenon. For all motions in the world, whether of countries or of regimes, must occur within the context of the order of motion and power, i.e. the sequence of 'heaven, the planets, the elements, and men'. In the *anacyclosis* of regimes, it is the human passion and appetite for luxury and domination which act as their immediate, human cause. In this sense, *anacyclosis* is open to human modification, or 'chance'. A stronger regime may either absorb a weak foreign regime or keep it permanently under its control. These instances of 'chance', or human modifications, certainly affect *anacyclosis* as Machiavelli understands it. But the human passions so crucial for *anacyclosis* are not crucial for the natural motions that affect countries. Natural motion, in other words, functions independently of human passions and appetites.

The clearest and most comprehensive account of natural motion as it affects countries is found in *Florentine Histories* V. 1. As a rule, countries go through a cycle of *virtù*. When they reach their utmost perfection in one direction, they necessarily turn back in the opposite direction. For nothing in the elemental world can be permanent, and everything is subject to the motions received from heaven. Thus:

> In their normal variations, provinces generally go from order to disorder and then from disorder move back to order, because – since nature does not allow worldly things to remain fixed – when they come to their utmost perfection and have no further possibility for rising, they must go down. Likewise, when they have gone down and through their defects have reached the lowest depths, they necessarily rise, since they cannot go lower. So always from good they go down to bad, and from bad they rise up to good. Because virtue brings forth quiet; quiet, leisure; leisure, disorder; disorder, ruin; and likewise from ruin comes order; from order, virtue; from the last glory and good fortune.[17]

The idea that countries reach their utmost perfection and that, when this happens, they necessarily decline, was a commonplace of contemporary astrological natural philosophy. Perhaps Ficino's view on how the 'four causes' work in the world can help to clarify Machiavelli's own position. For Ficino, the motions of countries are the result of four causes: Providence, heaven, elements, and men.[18] Ficino says that there are four causes operating in the human world. Of these, the first is Providence, which, as we have seen, Machiavelli rejects. The second is 'the fateful law of heavenly bodies' which, according to Ficino (but not according to Machiavelli), operates under the guidance of Providence; in Ficino's view, the fateful law of heavenly bodies is so regulated by divine Providence that the planets, in their everlasting and unresting course through the heavens, turn back as soon as they have reached their highest or furthest point. Moreover, they glide very swiftly from the sextile or trine aspects, which are considered favourable, into square or opposing aspects, which are considered harmful. The other two causes (the elemental and the human) operate subject to the 'fateful law of the heavenly bodies'. For Ficino, as for Machiavelli, the elemental cause is the causality exercised by the four elements: earth, water, air, and fire. The four elements are so disposed in natural order under the heavens that when any or all are stretched to the utmost limits of their own natures – when their finite natures do not allow them to go any further, nor their condition of perpetual motion allow them to remain at rest – they are naturally caused to turn back. The four bodily humours and their combinations undergo a similar change. In Nature, says Ficino, descent quite uninterruptedly follows ascent. As for the human cause, or human motion, this too, being subject to heaven, follows the cycle of virtue and corruption. Prosperity inflates mortals, making them swollen and sick. As if diseased, they forget their 'selves', thinking that anything is permissible. But all others grows envious of them, and plot against them, and their fall is as certain as the fall of a stone thrown into the air. Alexander the Great was inflated in this way by his great successes, and so came to an unfortunate end. Excesses of power and luxury are thus seen to have a natural basis. The rise and decline of countries also have a natural cause. Yet, whereas for Ficino, moral, philosophic, and theological virtues must act to remedy the natural tendency to moral decline, for Machiavelli, as we shall see, only periodic renovations through law and punishment can act as a remedy.

A revised version of the motions of countries under the law of heaven is found in Machiavelli's incomplete poem, 'The Golden Ass'. Chapter 3 of this work highlights the connection between the heavens, fate, the humours, the times, politics, war, and peace.

> You see the stars and the heaven, you see the moon, you see the other planets go wandering, now high, now low, without any rest;
> sometimes you see the heaven cloudy, sometimes shining and clear, and likewise nothing on earth remains in the same condition always.
> From this result peace and war; on this depend the hatreds among those whom one wall and one moat shut up together.
> From this came your first suffering; this was altogether the cause of your toils without reward.
> Not yet has heaven altered its opinion, nor will it alter it, while the fates keep toward you their hard purpose.
> And those humours which you have found so hostile and adverse are not yet, not yet purged; but when their roots are dry, and the heaven shows itself gracious, times happier than ever before will return.[19]

And chapter 5 of the same work gives a somewhat more detailed account of how natural motions affect countries.

> That kingdom which is pushed on to action by *virtù* or by necessity will always go upward.
> And on the contrary that city will be full of thickets and thorn bushes – changing her officials from winter to summer,
> until at the end she will of necessity be destroyed and will in her aim be always mistaken – that city which has good laws and bad customs.
> He who reads past events knows that empires begin with Ninus and end at last with Sardanapalus.
> The first was held a man divine; that other was found among the serving maids like a woman who distributes flax.

Virtue makes countries tranquil, and from Tranquillity, Leisure next
emerges, and Leisure burns the towns and villages.
Then, after a country has for a time been subject to lawlessness, Virtue
often returns to live there once again.
Such a course she who governs us permits and requires, so that nothing
beneath the sun ever will or can be firm. And it is and always has been
and always will be, that evil follows after good, good after evil.[20]

The idea that celestial causality or fate affects the history and politics of
countries is applied to the analysis of Italian history specifically. The
underlying assumption of 'The First Decennale', a poetical work dealing
with the history of Florence and Italy in the period 1494–1504, is that
Italian politics work according to the law of fate. This is made explicit both
in the Dedicatory Letter and in the opening lines. Interestingly enough,
there are two versions of the Dedicatory Letter, one in Latin and the other
in Italian. The Latin version is sharper than the Italian version in its
articulation of the link between fate and history. The latter states that Italy,
for the decade in question (which includes the fateful invasion of 1494 and
the change of regimes in Florence), has been oppressed by many misfortunes 'under the necessity of fate' (*colla necessità del fato*). The Latin version
adds a significant qualification to this: Italy has been exposed to such perils
because of 'the necessity of fate, *whose power could not be checked*' (*necessitudine
fati, cuius vis refringi non potest*).[21]

The opening lines of the poem, as mentioned already, are couched in
astrological language: 'I shall sing Italian hardships for those two lustres now
just over, under planets hostile to her good.'[22]

The idea that heaven has intervened or would intervene in the affairs of
Florence and Italy appears elsewhere in his writings. Thus, in *Florentine
Histories* the heavens are thought to have been instrumental in raising up the
'fated' families of Rome: the Colonna and the Orsini. 'The heavens (*i cieli*)
(knowing a time would have to come when the French and the Germans
would abandon Italy and that land would remain entirely in the hands of
the Italians) in order that the Pope, when he lacked opposition from
beyond the Alps, might not make his power solid or enjoy it, raised up in
Rome two very powerful families, the Colonna and the Orsini; with their
power and their proximity these two were to keep the papacy weak.'[23] The
implications of heavenly intervention in the case of these two families are
most interesting, considering the impact they actually have on the fortunes
of the papacy. For even the papacy, it would seem, is subject to the will of
heaven. Likewise, Machiavelli attributes the notorious factionalism of Florence to heavenly causes: 'It is given from on high (*è dato di sopra*, meaning
heaven), in order that in human things (*cose umane*) there may be nothing
either lasting or at rest, that in all republics there are fated families (*famiglie
fatali*), born for their ruin.'[24] The way he states the problem implies that all

'republics' have their fated families; only Florence had more than her share. That is to say, the feuds between the Buondelmonti and the Uberti, the Donati and the Cerchi, the Ricci and the Albizzi, not to mention the Pazzi and the Medici, can and should be seen from the perspective of astral or celestial causes. And, again, Machiavelli's assessment of how the dreadful Duke of Athens came to be the tyrant of Florence is couched in the language of astrological naturalism. He came to Florence because 'the heavens were preparing her for her future evils, that is, the tyranny under his rule.'[25] Finally, in the 'Discursus' on the reform of Florence, he reminds Leo X that heaven can give no better gift to any human being than that of the opportunity to found or reform a society.[26]

Heaven and Periodic Renewal

Turning now to the famous Machiavellian idea of going back to the beginnings or self-renewal, we notice that it too is firmly grounded in his cosmological theory. The preamble to *Discourses* III. 1 clearly connects the idea of the self-renewal of republics, kingdoms and churches to the motions of heaven: 'all things in the world have a finite existence and they follow the course ordained for them by heaven.'[27] This is especially true of 'mixed bodies' such as states and religions. If self-renewal does not occur in them, such bodies will perish; if it does, they will be able to prolong their life-span. For, while every corporate body starts out with some initial goodness (*bontà*) in it, the process of time (which is but a function of the motions of the planets) necessarily corrupts even the best of them, be they political or ecclesiastical. Reinforcing astrological naturalism, Machiavelli employs the naturalism of medical science. If an organism such as the human body does not undergo thorough cleansing regularly, it will perish. 'As the doctors of medicine say, speaking of the bodies of men, "what is accumulated daily, needs daily purgation".'[28]

A striking aspect of the theory of renewal is that it is a joint achievement of both the heavenly and human causes. First of all, self-renewal must occur in states according to the course ordained for them by heaven. And the immediate occasion for such beginnings comes about either because of some external accident or because of internal prudence. Three examples are cited to illustrate the point – those of the early Roman Republic, the contemporary French monarchy, and the thirteenth-century reforms in the Catholic Church.

Rome came to renew herself because of the external accident of the Gallic War of 390 BC. The early reverses in this war made Rome careful about observance of religion and justice. But Rome also renewed herself on account of her internal prudence. The examples cited are those of the terrible punishments meted out to the violators of law, the most inhumane of which being the spectacle of Junius Brutus presiding over the execution of his own sons, whom he himself had earlier condemned to death. Machiavelli feels that human beings need the terror of severe punishment if they are to be kept on the straight and narrow path. He even goes so far as to say that unless a state is prepared to carry out such notable executions as those of the sons of Brutus, at intervals of every ten years, self-renewal is not likely to be successful.[29]

As for the French monarchy, its self-renewal was achieved through the effective use of the institution of the 'parliament', especially that of Paris. Thanks to this institution, the king was able to keep the unruly barons in check and to give protection to the people. This use of the 'parliament' assured the longevity of the French monarchy.

The example of reforms in the Catholic Church is even more interesting, given Machiavelli's premise of astrological naturalism. The Franciscan and the Dominican reforms, he says, rescued the Church from decay, if not demise. Is the inference here that St Francis and St Dominic followed the course ordained for them by heaven? Orthodox theology would interpret renewal in the church as being caused by God and humans, not by heaven and humans. To take the latter view would be to equate the church with a natural institution, and to treat it purely as a *corpo misto*, subject to the occult power of heaven. Yet it seems that Machiavelli certainly allows room for this kind of naturalistic interpretation of the church. Such an interpretation gains plausibility when we take into consideration the astrological claims of Cardinal D'Ailly, who believed that the Franciscan and Dominican orders had for their heavenly cause the planetary conjunction of 1226.[30]

Turning now to the question of war and peace – not an insignificant one for Machiavelli – it is noteworthy that here, too, one is reminded of the operations of heavenly causality. We saw in the last chapter how Pico had ridiculed the astrological interpretations of wars, seditions, and factions. But we also saw that astrology concerned itself very seriously with decisions taken in times of war. Machiavelli himself was given instructions, based on astrological calculations, as to when to lead the army against Pisa. But in *Discourses* I.6 we see a general, more theoretical statement on the issue of the relationship between war, peace, and heaven. All states, we are reminded, are subject to the laws of motion, heavenly as well as elemental. Given this, the question of whether states should remain small and stationary, or become big and expanding, is crucial for Machiavelli. The case for each alternative is examined, and, ultimately, his favour falls on the side of big and powerful states.

> But since all human affairs are in motion and cannot remain fixed, they must rise up or sink down; to many things to which reason does not bring you, you are brought by necessity. Hence if a republic is so organized that she is adapted to maintaining herself provided she does not grow, and necessity then forces her to grow, the process will remove her

foundations and make her fall more speedily. Thus, on the other side, if heaven is so kind to her that she does not have to make war, the effect might be that ease would make her effeminate or divided . . . Therefore, since I believe it impossible to balance these affairs or to keep exactly this middle way, it is essential in organizing cities to think of the most honourable courses, and to organize them in such a way that if necessity causes them to grow, they can keep what they have taken.[31]

A state, for very laudable reasons, may choose the path of peace and quiet; its constitution may even forbid war. But this will not guarantee peace because all states are in motion. It is difficult for states to 'stand still': even if a state has no desire to molest other states, other states could molest it, and from being molested will rise the wish and the necessity to expand.[32] Nor does heaven's 'kindness' promise perpetual peace. It can dispose one to war as well as to peace. Indeed, in astrological natural philosophy, a long peace is not desirable; even if it were granted, it would cause either indolence or internal divisions, either of which could so weaken the country as to expose it as possible prey for a stronger country. Thus, the conclusion that Machiavelli draws is that states ought to remain strong and powerful as long as they can. According to Machiavelli's theory of history, there can be no permanent peace between states.

Is There a Naturalistic Providence?

Machiavelli sometimes appears to attribute to heaven a naturalistic providence or *pronoia* over humankind. He often uses language that indicates that heaven has the power of 'giving', 'willing', 'judging', 'directing', 'testing', etc. Nowhere does he give a formal justification for his use of such language. But this is to be expected from a thinker who is not a formal philosopher, but who nevertheless freely uses concepts and terminology belonging to the astrological tradition of his day. His language regarding heaven situates him firmly within that tradition of astrological natural science which tended to fudge the sharp distinction between physical causation and moral causation. The very attribution of qualities of 'good' and 'bad' to the physical motions of the planets is a sign of such a tendency on his part. As far as I can see, there is no suggestion in Machiavelli that the universe is run by 'blind' forces. At the same time, the motion that runs the universe does not emanate from a wholly transcendent Good or, for that matter, from a wholly transcendent Mind. Confusingly enough, the motion from heaven has both physical and non-physical occult attributes; so much so that one could almost speak of a quasi-providence exercised by the heavens. There are a number of instances supporting this view.

Heaven seems to be concerned to ensure that certain human communities live in relative well-being. One of the threats to such well-being is thought to be overpopulation. Accordingly, it is said that heaven causes plagues, famines, and floods as means of effective population control. Once again, as in *Discourses* III. 1, the analogy between human bodies and corporate bodies is invoked to make the point. Just as the human body maintains itself in good health through regular purgations, so also the human species maintains itself by periodic demographic purges. Such purges, it is said, are caused by heaven: 'As to the causes that come from heaven, they are those that wipe out the race of men and bring down to a few the inhabitants of part of the world, either through plagues or through famine or through a flood.'[33] That such natural calamities occur is not to be doubted, he says, since histories are full of accounts of them. Besides, it stands to reason that this should be so, given the analogy between human body and mixed body:

> Just as in the instance of simple bodies when a great deal of superfluous matter is brought together in them, nature many times moves of herself and makes a purgation for the health of those bodies, the same process appears in this mixed body of the human race. When all the lands are full of inhabitants, so that men cannot live where they are and cannot go elsewhere, since all places are settled and filled full, and when human craft and malice have gone as far as they can go, of necessity the world is purged in one of the three ways mentioned, so that becoming few and humble, men can live more comfortably and grow better.[34]

These ideas concerning the causality of heaven accord well with Ptolemy. He too, in *Tetrabiblos* II. 1, associates heaven with wars, famines, pestilence, earthquakes, floods, and the like. Astrology in Machiavelli's own day took particular interest in the conjunctions forecast for 1503, 1504, and 1524. As Thorndike has pointed out, astrological predictions about the consequences of these much dreaded events abounded in the first two decades of the sixteenth century. These events were thought to be capable of bringing about 'changes in sects and religions, vicissitudes of kingdoms, inundations of waters and rivers, fear of war and contradiction, diverse states of mortal affairs in this inferior world'.[35] According to Thorndike, in anticipation of the 1524 conjunction, as many as fifty-six authors published one hundred and thirty-three editions of various works on the subject.[36] It is very likely that Machiavelli had read some of these works, which may explain his reference to 'histories' being full of accounts of such impending calamities.[37]

Related to the idea of naturalistic providence is the idea that heaven intervenes in human affairs through natural prophecy, revelations, prodigies, and other celestial signs. Machiavelli endorses the opinion that nothing important happens in politics unless it has been preceded by some such signs: 'Before great events occur in a city or a province, there are signs that presage them or men who predict them. What causes it I do not know, but both ancient and modern instances indicate that nothing important ever happens in a city or a province that has not been foretold by diviners or by revelations or by prodigies or by other celestial signs.'[38] He knows that a proper understanding of these signs involves philosophical issues and that philosophers have given different interpretations of them. The 'cause' of these signs, he says, 'should be discussed and interpreted by a man who has knowledge of things natural and supernatural, which we do not have'.[39] This is as good a piece of *direct* evidence as we are likely to get of Machiavelli's awareness of the contemporary debates on astrological natural philosophy. The causes of 'things natural' mentioned here no doubt refer to the motions governing elemental entities, while the causes of 'things supernatural' refer to the motions governing heavenly bodies.

The 'signs' mentioned in *Discourses* I. 56 are Savonarola's prophecies, the 'voice' heard by Marcus Cedicius in the streets of ancient Rome, the thunderbolts that hit the Cathedral and the Signoria in Florence, and the 'apparitions' which people in Tuscany were alleged to have seen above Arezzo. And the four 'important' political events to which these 'signs' are linked, are the invasion of Italy by Charles VIII, the invasion of ancient Rome by the Gauls, the death of Lorenzo de Medici, and the fall of Soderini. What Machiavelli claims here on behalf of astrological natural philosophy, is that these 'signs' actually signify or could signify those four important, but nevertheless contingent human events. That is to say, he wants us to agree that these 'signs' could presage those contingent events because of the alleged relationship they (the 'signs') have with the course of the motions of the heavenly bodies. This is clearly to present the position of astrological natural philosophy – a position which, as we have already seen, is hotly contested by philosophers such as Pico. The latter denies the possibility that the course of the planets could signify future contingent events, for the reason that the course of planets follows necessary laws, whereas future contingent events do not. But the value of *Discourses* I. 56 is that it shows us which side Machiavelli is on; he clearly defends the position of astrological natural philosophers.

In addition to celestial signs, Machiavelli introduces the further problem of 'intelligences' inhabiting the air above us. 'Yet it could be that since, as some philosopher holds, the air about us is full of intelligences – and these through their natural *virtù* foreseeing future things and having compassion on men – these spirits warn men with such signs, so that they can prepare for resistance.'[40] The belief in 'intelligences' of the air being agents of the heavens was also part of contemporary neo-Platonic and astrological speculations. Besides the heavenly bodies, the air was believed to contain spirits, or 'intelligences'. These 'intelligences' belonged to the celestial hierarchy, and as such they were thought to know what was above them and what was beneath them. According to Averroes, for example, the knowledge of these intelligences was greater in proportion to their nearness to the *primum mobile*. Even the least celestial of these intelligences possessed knowledge of the sensible and corruptible sublunar world, including knowledge of human affairs. The astrological hypothesis underlying all this speculation is that there is nothing in the condition of inferior bodies which is not caused by the agitation of celestial motion.[41] It is undeniable that, in the astrological polemics concerning the connection between heavenly signs and political events, Machiavelli is not neutral. He sides with the astrological position: 'However it is, so the truth seems to be; and always after such events strange and new things happen to provinces.'[42]

It appears that Machiavelli considers prophecy to be a heavenly sign, intended to be used in politics. Prophecy is one of the ways in which heaven intervenes in political affairs. True, he makes fun of the 'street' prophets who abound in Florence. But he seems to have great respect for 'serious' prophets. In a letter to Francesco Guicciardini written only a few months before his own death, Machiavelli reports how he spent two days with a prophet discussing Italian politics. 'I remained in Modena two days and conversed with a prophet who said, with witnesses, that he had foretold the flight of the Pope [Clement VII] and the uselessness of the enterprise, and again he says that not yet are we through with all the bad times, in which the Pope and we [Florence] will suffer a great deal.'[43]

Heaven is also presented as a tester of human *virtù*. In this case, the underlying principle is stated in universal terms: 'If we consider well how human affairs proceed, many times we see that things come up and events take place against which the heavens do not wish any provisions to be made.'[44] And this was exactly what the heavens were doing with Rome in the Gallic War of 390 BC; they were testing her *virtù*. This is explicitly stated in *Discourses* II. 29: what happened to Rome happens or could happen to all states, especially to those not as virtuous as she. In other words, heaven contributes its share to the successes and/or failures of human achievements. History is not a totally human-made process. That is why, in a manner of speaking, humans should not take total credit or accept total blame for what they accomplish: 'most of the time we see that they have been led into greatness or into ruin depending on the opportunity that the heavens had either given or withheld.'[45] Even to act virtuously, one needs the 'providential' assistance of heaven.

The analysis of the Gallic War, then, is premised on the theory of naturalistic providence. It demonstrated how much power heaven has over human affairs. Rome made so many errors in strategy and diplomacy in that war – Machiavelli recounts some ten of them – simply because the heavens were unfavourable to her acting virtuously. Livy's account of this episode, which is Machiavelli's starting point, underlines the astrological context of the entire discussion. 'Urged on by the evil star which even then had risen over Rome, they [the Romans] broke the law of nations and took up arms,' is the way that Livy's account begins.[46] Ultimately, the effects of the evil star subsided, and Rome regained her normal composure and won the war. Machiavelli is certain that Rome possessed extraordinary and exemplary *virtù*; at the same time, however, he is equally certain that she enjoyed the naturalistic providence of the heavens.[47]

Sometimes heaven is also spoken of as the giver of the opportunity (*occasione*) to do well. This too is an astrological concept; not only has each moment of time a special quality which can affect the outcome of human action, but it is also a 'gift' of the heavens. In the affairs of state, the importance of *occasione* is fundamental. The heavens cannot give a greater gift to human beings than the *occasione* to found or innovate states.[48] And they to whom heaven has given such opportunity should remember that two roads are open before them: one that will lead them to glory, and the other that will lead them to infamy. As noted earlier, Machiavelli is sadly concerned that his own project might end in failure because of heaven's disregard for him; he hopes that someone 'more loved' by heaven might appear in the future to carry out what he has left incomplete.

Heaven plays one further role in history and politics: it 'guarantees' the regularity with which one cycle of history succeeds another. It is not enough to say that the same passions and the same humours exist in all human beings at all times.[49] For Machiavelli's theory of imitation to work there must be a 'guarantee' that there will be suitable correspondence between the relevant epochs of history. Thus, if the present-day Italians are to imitate the *virtù* of the ancient Romans, there must be support for it from the laws of history. That the present-day Italians should imitate the *virtù* of their ancestors is a duty based on objective reasoning, and not just on subjective preference. Thanks to heaven, there is order in history. This is emphatically asserted in *Discourses* I. 11, with a pointed cross-reference to the ideas raised earlier in the Preface regarding the order of sequence present in history. 'No one should therefore forget that he cannot carry out what has been carried out by others, because, as I have said in our preface, men are born, live and die, always in the same order.'[50]

Some Interpretative Issues

With regard to Machiavelli's position on heaven, history, and politics, there are three issues that have given rise to differences in interpretation. The first concerns the biblical and the philosophic meanings of heaven, the second Machiavelli's meaning of history, and the third the relationship between heaven and Fortune.

Concerning the first, some have thought that *il cielo* in Machiavelli refers to the philosophic concept of heaven, while *i cieli* refers to the biblical concept.[51] But there seems to be no convincing evidence that such a distinction exists in Machiavelli's texts. In our view, he uses the two forms interchangeably, to convey the same philosophical or astrological meaning. Technically, 'heavens' were the seven 'spheres' in which the seven planets moved. But in the common usage of the times, 'heavens' meant either one planet or all the planets taken as a whole.[52]

This is not to say that Machiavelli ignores the distinction between the theological and the philosophical/astrological meanings of heaven/s. Far from it. He is quite aware of the distinction, and he makes it very clear where it matters most: in *Discourses* II. 2. This fact is all the more remarkable since both uses occur in the same paragraph. The context is his criticism of Christianity: it has made the world weak, and it encourages Christians to suffer injuries rather than to avenge them. In general, wanting to go to 'Paradise', Christians tend to neglect their civil duties here on earth. This attitude is, Machiavelli speculates, partly due to the fact that 'the world has become effeminate and the heaven become disarmed' and partly also because Christians have given a pacific interpretation to their religion. The words he uses to draw this contrast are *Paradiso* and *Cielo*.[53]

The meaning of *Paradiso* requires no comment. But the use of *Cielo* here is at first puzzling. In what sense can one say that heaven is either armed or unarmed? To find an answer to this question one has to go back to the language of astrological natural philosophy, according to which certain planets, such as Mars, are thought to promote warlike qualities, while certain others, such as Mercury, are thought to promote contemplative qualities. The point that Machiavelli hints at here, I think, is that there may well be astrological reasons to explain why Christians are more pacific and not as bloodthirsty as some others. According to astrological natural philosophy, Christianity is the outcome of the conjunction between Jupiter and Mercury, which may explain why heaven has been 'disarmed', the world has gone 'effeminate', and Christians are pacific. However this may be, Machiavelli knows the difference between the theological and the philosophic meanings of the concept, i.e. the difference between paradise and heaven. But he does not use *i cieli* and *il cielo* to convey this difference.

The second issue concerns the interpretation of what Machiavelli means by history. It appears from our examination of the source, that history for him is both an account of what humans do, and, as Harvey C. Mansfield, Jr. has pointed out, an 'enquiry' into what they do.[54] The causality of heaven is as necessary for the carrying out of human activity as is human causality itself. In this sense, history is a product of the joint activity of heaven and humans. Heaven's role here is indispensable. According to Machiavelli, celestial motion, elemental motion (including the motions of the humours), and human motion belong to a hierarchical order of motions. Here, one must agree with Felix Gilbert, who says that 'the course of history (for Machiavelli) is not a man-made process. It moves in its own predestined direction which is beyond human control. Man's role consists in the strength with which he can promote this process or with which he can retard it by resisting.'[55]

Harvey C. Mansfield, Jr. sees the relationship between history and nature differently. The reason for his doing so, I believe, is because he thinks Machiavelli reduces nature to Fortune. He does not seem to think that, according to Machiavelli, heaven has any role to play in history. Historical change for Machiavelli, Mansfield writes, 'is either the motion of nature – not perhaps random but not intended by men – or the order and ordering . . . that men intend'.[56] Since nature's motion does not make humans feel safe or grateful, it appears to them to be fortune; and because it looks to them this way, 'it is in effect reducible to fortune.' Finally, neither nature nor fortune can be trusted. And human order and human action are meant to overcome the lack of support from nature and fortune. It follows, then, that 'the context of history must be understood as a contest between virtue and fortune.'[57]

The difficulty with this interpretation is the claim that Machiavelli reduces nature to Fortune. Such a claim allows no room for the role of heaven. Or is heaven also to be reduced to Fortune? As I have argued, in the Machiavellian cosmos there is room for both heaven and Fortune. Heaven gives it its order, power, and motion, and the basis for regularity and predictability. Fortune accounts for the occurrence of chance events within it. It is true that heaven is not *especially* friendly to humans, although it exercises a naturalistic providence. The notion of good and evil which accompanies Machiavelli's notion of heaven is an amalgam of the physical and the ethical, satisfactory to neither physics nor ethics. For this, one must blame astrological natural philosophy, and Machiavelli's reliance on it. And clearly, there is no sovereign Good in the Machiavellian cosmos. Yet this still does not make *everything* that occurs in history the result of a contest between humans and 'nature'. No doubt, those things that occur fortuitously do pose problems to humans; dealing with them may appear to have the character of a 'contest' or struggle with Fortune. But even here, the basis or 'rules' of the contest are said to be laid down by Fortune. Briefly, there is order in history coming from the motion and power exercised by the heaven. There is room for contest in history because many things happen unexpectedly or fortuitously, and *against* these humans have to make effective provisions on their own motion.

The third issue concerns the relationship between heaven and Fortune. At times, as in *Discourses* II. 29, Machiavelli speaks of the two interchangeably. More frequently, however, he speaks of them as though they are distinct. To solve this problem Leo Strauss has insisted that, ultimately, Machiavelli replaces heaven with Fortune.[58]

Whether Machiavelli in fact does this or not can be settled only after we have investigated his treatment of Fortune. Until that is done, we can only say provisionally that as far as this matter is concerned, there appear to be two lines of discourse present in Machiavelli: one proceeding from the concept of heaven, and the other from that of Fortune. These lines sometimes intersect and sometimes do not. This is not surprising, since what is happening here is the inattentive use of two modes of treating the subject – the philosophical and the popular. The philosophical mode sees heaven as the source of motion, order, and power in the universe, and Fortune as the cause of the fortuitous events that happen to humans. In the popular mode, however, the fortuitous is attributed to a goddess called Fortune. We find mention of the existence of such a mode in Aristotle's discussion of Fortune: 'There are also some who think that fortune is indeed a cause, but one inscrutable to human thought, because it is divine or supernatural in character.'[59] This tradition continued through the Middle Ages and the Renaissance, so it is not at all surprising that we find it in Machiavelli as well. The reader, therefore, must be aware enough to be able to discern which mode of discourse Machiavelli is engaged in. In the meantime, our hypothesis that for Machiavelli heaven is the principle of motion, order, and power, stands.

CHAPTER 3

Heaven, Religion, and Politics

The hypothesis we have employed in this book prompts us to ask whether a concept of religion forms an integral part of Machiavelli's political theory; and if it does, what that concept is, and whether it has anything to do with his cosmology. The secondary literature on Machiavelli's thoughts on religion tends to pose the question differently: instead of first establishing the ultimate or cosmological basis of his religious thought, critics begin by asking whether he is a Christian or a pagan or an atheist, and so exhaust themselves in the process. It is not that these questions are irrelevant. They are indeed relevant; but they become so only when set against the background of his fundamental concept of religion as such. And it is our hypothesis that his concept is derived from his cosmology.

According to Machiavelli's cosmology, religion is part of the cosmic phenomena unfolding in time and place in the sublunar world. In this unfolding, the heavens play an indispensable role: they 'inspire' humans to establish religion and to use it exclusively for political ends. This is not to ignore the functions that religion performs at the psychological level, where it is often seen as responding to emotions arising from ignorance and fear of unseen causes and existential human helplessness in general. But Machiavelli appears to be dissatisfied with this limited psychological explanation of religion. He seems to be convinced that forces external to the human psyche also account for the religious phenomena. And such a view is entirely consistent with his cosmology. For just as the heavens control the general laws governing the movement of history and politics, so also, according to him, do they control the movement governing the rise, renewal, and fall of religions. Religions come and go according to the same laws which allegedly govern the motions of celestial bodies. According to this manifestly astrological approach to religion, the heavens are thought to 'judge' that religion should be given to particular societies as a means of reinforcing their politics. This is the root of Machiavelli's view that religion should be an instrument of policy. For as far as Machiavelli's cosmology is concerned, religion has no other justification than that of reinforcing the

political order. The heavens exert their influence differently on different
regions of the sublunar world. The nature of the religion varies according to
the specific influence of the heavens on a specific territory at a given time.
Under these circumstances, the general rule is that one should follow the
religion of 'the place where one is born'.[1]

The Rise, Renewal, and Fall of Religions

According to Machiavelli, the heavens have a role to play at three crucial
points in the historical development of religions – at the time of their rise,
renewal, and fall. He is quite explicit about the heavens' role in the rise of
the pagan religion of Rome: it arose, he says, because of a 'judgement' of
the heavens. Anyone familiar with the astrological debate in Machiavelli's
Florence will have little difficulty in recognizing the significance of the
phrase 'the heavens judging' (*giudicando i cieli*). It has a decidedly Abu
Ma'sharian, conjunctionist connotation. 'Since the heavens judged that the
laws of Romulus would not be sufficient for so great an empire, they
inspired in the breast of the Roman Senate to elect Numa Pompilius as
Romulus's successor, so that Numa might establish the things he had
omitted.'[2]

The difference between Livy and Machiavelli on the question of the
origin of Roman religion is noteworthy; the astrological tone is stronger in
Machiavelli's language than it is in Livy's. Livy does not speak of the
'judgement' of the heavens as being the cause of the origin of the pagan
religion. Rather he says that the Romans had a belief that 'the celestial
numen was interested in human affairs'.[3] In Livy's account the Senate ap-
points Numa without having received any direction from the heavens, and
only after the appointment is made without any religious sanction does it
ask the augurs to see if the heavens approved of the appointment. 'Father
Jupiter, the augur prayed, if it is heaven's will that this man, Numa
Pompilius, whose head I touch, should reign in the city of Rome, make
clear to us sure signs within the limits I have determined. Then he named
precisely the nature of the signs he hoped would be sent. Sent they were,
and Numa, duly proclaimed King, went down from the hill where the
auspices were taken.'[4] Livy begins from a subjective aspect of religion,
namely from the antecedent belief of the Romans that the celestial numen
was interested in human affairs, whereas Machiavelli begins from an objective
or naturalitic standpoint, namely that it was the 'judgement' of the heavens
that the Romans should have their own religion. According to Machiavelli
the heavens take the first initiative, whereas according to Livy the first
initiative comes from the Senate, and that too without any inspiration from
the heavens. The heavens are requested only to confirm what the Senate
wanted to do in the first place. Note also that in Machiavelli's account the
subject of the heavenly inspiration is the Senate, not Numa. From his

account we are not sure if Numa had any inspiration from the heavens even after his appointment. In any case, the founder of the Roman religion is a Senate appointee. For Machiavelli, the instrumental character of religion and the heavens' role in giving it that character, can hardly find a better example. So much, then, for Machiavelli's account of the rise of pagan religion.

Regarding the question of the rise of Christianity, Machiavelli's language seems less explicit. In *Discourses* I. 12 he does speak of the founder (*datore*) of Christianity and of His original intention. He says in effect that the founder of Christianity had allegedly intended Christianity to be a religion similar to the pagan religion. Had Christians carried out this alleged original intent of Christ, Christian states would have been more united and powerful than they are now. 'If religion of this (pagan) sort had been maintained by the princes of the Christian republic, according as its giver had established it, the Christian states and republics would have been more united and more prosperous than they are now.'[5] This is an important passage for understanding Machiavelli's views of religion in general, and of Christianity in particular. Unfortunately, not all English translations of this passage are accurate. Christian Detmold, whose translation the Modern Library College Edition uses, renders the passage quite inaccurately: 'And certainly, if the Christian religion had from the beginning been maintained according to the principles of its founder, the Christian states and republics would have been much more united and happy than what they are.'[6] As Walker rightly points out, *la quale religione* 'clearly refers to the pagan religion about which he has just been speaking', and not to the Christian religion.[7] In fact Machiavelli is saying that while Christ allegedly founded a naturalistic religion, His followers turned it into an otherworldly, supernatural religion. Presumably, Christ intended it to be a religion of *virtù*, an instrument of politics. However, His followers – popes and emperors – somehow interpreted it as a religion of *ozio* instead. They distinguished between the realm of Church and State, religion and politics, and in doing so made 'Christian states and republics' weak. However that may be, there is still no explicit mention in *Discourses* I. 12 of any intervention on the part of the heavens at the time of the rise of Christianity.

The tone changes significantly in *Discourses* II. 2, where we detect an allusion to astrology and to the horoscope of Christianity. Apparently there is a connection between the alleged 'weakness' that historical Christianity has introduced into the world and the heavens becoming disarmed and the earth becoming effeminate. 'This way of living, then,' Machiavelli writes, 'has made the world weak and turned it over as prey to wicked men, who can in security control it, since the generality of men, in order to go to Paradise, think more about enduring their injuries than about avenging them. Though it may appear that the world has grown effeminate, and Heaven disarmed, this without doubt comes chiefly from the worthlessness of men, who have interpreted our religion according to *ozio* and not according to *virtù*.'[8] What is the reader to make of the strange notions of 'the heaven becoming disarmed' and 'the earth becoming effeminate'? The proper context of understanding them, I argue, is supplied by Machiavelli's astrological conception of religion. According to the horoscope of religions, as we saw earlier, Christianity originated at the time of the conjunction between the peace-loving, contemplation-promoting Mercury and Jupiter. Indeed, as Savonarola and Pico della Mirandola often pointed out, such 'scientific' or naturalistic beliefs about the origin of Christianity were actually prevalent in certain circles in Machiavelli's Florence. Machiavelli, then, is saying that, given Christianity's horoscope, Christians have the obligation to interpret their religion politically: i.e. according to *virtù*. What they have done instead, however, is to interpret it theologically, as a means of becoming liberated from sin and of attaining beatific vision. Such 'distortions', as he sees it, have more to do with the worthlessness of the interpreters than with the horoscope of Christianity.[9]

Turning now to the celebrated Machiavellian notion of renewal, the crucial point to be noted here is that renewal occurs according to the *corso* ordained by the heavens. This, he says, is a thing 'very true' (*cosa verissima*). That is to say, his concept of renewal, whether of states or of religions, is set within a cosmological framework, and as far as he is concerned, the truth of this matter is beyond dispute. Religions, like kingdoms and republics, are mixed bodies; they are subject to 'the process of time', viz. birth, renewal, and death. Thus, the heavens account not only for the origin of religion but also for its renovation and final demise. 'It is very true that there is a limit for the existence of all things in the world; but they generally move through the entire course ordained for them by heaven without getting their bodies into confusion but keeping them in the way ordained; this way either does not change or, if it does, the change is to their advantage, not to their harm. And because I am speaking of mixed bodies, such as republics and religions, I say that those changes are to their advantage that take them back toward their beginnings.'[10]

The naturalistic dimension of religious renewal could not have been better brought out than by the analogy drawn between religions and natural bodies. What medical purges are to natural bodies, periodic renewal is to religious bodies. 'Since in the process of time the original goodness is corrupted, if something does not happen that takes it back to the right position, such corruption necessarily kills that body. The doctors of medicine say, speaking of the bodies of men, that "daily something is added that now and then needs cure".'[11] That all mixed bodies are subject to the naturalistic law of 'corruption' and renewal is the underlying assumption in *Discourses* II. 5 as well: 'Just as in the instance of simple bodies when a great deal of superfluous matter is brought together in them, nature many times moves of herself and makes purgation for the health of those bodies, the same process appears in the mixed body of the human race.' Thus the original goodness which religions embody cannot endure in time without the laws of time being applied to it. And it is a law of time, ordained by the heavens, that all religious goodness which comes into existence in time is subject to the law of growth and decay, moral as well as physical. In other words, religious decay has a dual basis: in the psyche as well as in nature. The need for renewal is as much a moral need as it is a need required by the process of time. In the Machiavellian cosmos, religions, including Christianity, have no privileged status among historical phenomena. Like empires and civilizations, they too come and go. They do, however, have a chance of prolonging their existence, should human agents be found who are capable of initiating internal reforms in accordance with the cosmic law of renewal.

The example that Machiavelli uses to illustrate his point regarding religious renewal is taken from what he calls 'our religion', i.e. Christianity. Had the Franciscan and the Dominican movements not occurred, he says, Christianity would have disappeared from the face of the earth. 'In religious bodies these renewals are also necessary, as we see through the example of our religion, which, if St Francis and St Dominic had not brought it back to its beginnings, would have entirely disappeared.'[12] And while saints do initiate religious renewal, for Machiavelli that is not the whole story, for they still must act within a given cosmological framework. This is his distinct teaching. Yet he is not alone, nor is he being particularly anti-Christian in saying this about Christianity. For as we noted earlier, those who subscribed to an astrological philosophy of religion, including Cardinal D'Ailly, had said almost the same thing before him: they had linked, for example, the Franciscan and the Dominican reforms to the conjunction of 1226. Machiavelli does not mention this specific point regarding the Franciscans and the Dominicans, but his general assessment of their works is consistent with a naturalistic interpretation of religious renewal. Indeed, it is obvious that in the Machiavellian cosmos there is more to religious reform than preaching, hearing of confessions, and setting good examples. The reforms in question are also part of the process of time, over which the heavens necessarily exercise their general causality.

Regarding the third issue, viz. the fall of religions, here too the heavens are considered as having a key role to play. Already in *Discourses* III. 1 we see that the 'truth' regarding the disintegration of all mixed bodies is one of the certainties of Machiavelli's political thought. In *Discourses* I. 12 also we see that the present corruption of Christianity had reached a critical point where it faced either a 'scourge' or a total 'ruination'. But it is in *Discourses* II. 5 that the most explicit statement concerning the role of the heavens in the fall of religions appears. Here Machiavelli discusses the causes that bring about 'changes' in religions and languages. These changes, he says, are the product of the conjoint causation of man and heaven: 'part of these causes come from men, and part from heaven' (*parte vengono dagli uomini, parte dal cielo*). Human causality takes the form of religious persecution. This is particularly true of the religions he discusses in *Discourses* II. 5 – the religions of the Etruscans, the Romans and the Christians. But what needs to be emphasized is that, for Machiavelli, human causality is always placed within a cosmological frame of analysis. This is implicit when he invokes the astrological doctrine that 'these religions change two or three times in five or six thousand years' (*queste sette in cinque o in sei mila anni variano due o tre volte*). According to this doctrine, as Strauss points out, each religion would have a life-span of between 1,666 and 3,000 years.[13] Needless to say, the life-span in question is allotted by cosmic causes. That religions, including Christianity, have a 'limit to their existence' was widely believed by those in Florence who adhered to an astrological theory of religion. It is because of such beliefs that there was so much speculation in Florence about the impending fall of Christianity and about the appearance of a counter-Christian religion, the religion of the anti-Christ. Savonarola, for example, reports that Abu Ma'shar had predicted the date of 1460, and Haabraz the date of 1444, as the dates for the fall of Christianity.[14] That Christianity would be replaced by a new astral religion, 'not different from ancient paganism' (*non a gentilitate differentem*), was an opinion said to have been held even by George Gemisthus Plethon, a Greek 'father' of the Ecumenical Council of Florence (1438–45).[15] Given such speculations, it is not surprising that Machiavelli should have spoken of the life-span of religions in general and of the impending 'scourge' or 'ruination' of Christianity in particular.

There is yet another idea in Machiavelli's religious thought which corroborates his astrological view of religion. It concerns his notion of 'natural things' (*cose naturali*) and their alleged relationship to religion. The claim is that the political use of religion depends on a sound prudential knowledge of natural things. In the preceding chapter we saw that knowledge of 'natural and supernatural things' is for him indispensable for the interpretation of prophecy and other 'signs' from heaven. We also saw that 'natural things' refers to 'elemental' things, one of the three things in the chain of 'the heaven, the elements, and men' that constitute the Machiavellian cosmos. A knowledge of how these things are related to one another in their motion, order, and power is thus a prerequisite for judging how 'things of the world' and 'human things' are governed. Now we are told that expertise in 'natural things' is especially necessary for the political use of religion. Only those with such expertise – astrologers, augurs, *pullarii*, et al. – know how to interpret 'natural things' which sometimes at heavens' behest act as 'signs' sent by them. In other words, for him, the political use of religion presupposes an astrologically functioning universe. As such, since the universe is governed astrologically, and since certain 'experts' know how such a universe functions, it is possible for these experts to use religion politically. Political leaders could quite legitimately require the 'experts' to interpret the 'evidence' in a manner suitable to their political agenda. Seen in this context, miracles are thought to be occurrences which some people imagine seeing or hearing in the realm of 'natural things', but which the 'wise' know to be false. But popular belief in such miracles could be enormously useful in the hands of skilled rulers. Indeed, such beliefs, says Machiavelli, should be 'accepted and magnified' by them. This is exactly what Camillus and others like him did with the pagan religion. Thus the soldiers who fought in the Veientian war believed that a statue of Juno performed miracles, and this belief in turn fortified their spirits. And Machiavelli speaks approvingly of the prudential use the Roman augurs and generals made of such beliefs. But in order to be experts in the political use of religion, rulers had to be experts in 'natural things' as well. Thus, 'Whatever comes up in favour of religion, even though they [the augurs] think it false, they are to accept and magnify. And so much the more they are going to do it as they are prudent and as they have better understanding of natural things.'[16] From the point of view of our present concern, the operative concept here is, of course, that of *cose naturali*. As explained above, it is used by Machiavelli in a highly technical sense, a sense, which, unfortunately, many of his translators and interpreters seem to have missed. The words *cose naturali* have been translated as diversely as 'natural course of things',[17] 'natural causes',[18] 'natural laws',[19] 'worldly affairs',[20] and *'la nature humaine'*.[21] But Machiavelli's use of this concept can be correctly grasped, I think, only if we locate it within the context of his cosmology.

Paganism and Christianity

Given Machiavelli's general concept of religion, it is not surprising that he prefers paganism to Christianity. The former easily complies with the basic norms of his cosmology while the latter does not. The life of pagan religion, Machiavelli informs us, was connected to astral divinities and astral signs. It was founded on the responses of the oracles and on the cult of diviners and augurs. Paganism attributed divinity to astral bodies – Jupiter, Mercury, Venus, Mars, etc. These 'gods' were thought to know and control one's future; as such, belief in and devotion to them were encouraged. Thus astrological religion skilfully exploited the common ignorance and fear of invisible causes. The pagans 'easily believed that any god who was able to foretell your future good and future ill was also able to grant it to you.'[22]

Obviously, these beliefs constituted the basis of the pagan concept of the virtue of religion. Paganism saw no difficulty in merging religious virtues and civic virtues. Indeed, religious virtues could be counted as true virtues only if they contributed to civic health. Given this, paganism offered no resistance to the practice of pretended religious virtue, or even to acts opposed to religion, if such acts were needed to maintain the health of the state. Such, more or less, was the ancient Roman practice of the virtue of religion. Their consuls and religious 'experts' used religion 'according to necessity, and prudently made a show of religion even when they were forced not to observe it . . .'[23] Moreover, the pagan religion did not have to contend with anything called theological virtues, and therefore did not have to face the prospects of any possible conflict between these and civic virtues. Furthermore, it did not have the concept of two fatherlands, one temporal and the other eternal. It could therefore concentrate all its energies on the earthly fatherland. Loving the fatherland more than one's soul was, therefore, according to Machiavelli, quite a proper disposition to cultivate.

Machiavelli viewed religion as a form of political 'education'.[24] And pagan religion was perfectly capable of fulfilling this pedagogical function. As a pedagogical device, religion 'caused' the well-being of the Roman Republic.[25] Thus there existed a causal connection between the virtue of pagan religion, civic virtues, law-abidingness, success in war, and imperial power.[26] The point of our argument is that the pagan religion was able to carry out its political mandate – the only mandate it ever had – precisely because this was the original intent of the heavens in inspiring religion in the minds of the people in the first place. Clearly, it is impossible to understand Machiavelli's analysis of the excellence of pagan religion except in the cosmological context in which it takes place. His elaboration of the psychology and sociology of pagan religion, insightful as it is, can make sense only when it is seen within this context. If we overlook the cosmological roots of his political theology we are likely to make him look something which he is not – a sort of enlightenment *philosophe*, who allegedly believes that religion is only a human invention, and a harmful invention at that. To make him such a modern would be to do violence to the data that he himself provides regarding the nature and function of religion.

Machiavelli's criticism of Christianity, as mentioned already, is based on the supposition that Christians have misinterpreted their religion. He is careful, however, not to put the blame for this on Christ; instead he puts the blame squarely on the shoulders of His followers. This, at least, is the burden of his statement in *Discourses* I. 12: if historical Christianity had carried out Christ's original intent, Christianity would have evolved into a political religion. But that did not happen. The first outcome of this development is that Christianity became a source of political disunity and instability. Positive religious beliefs tended to produce schismatics and heretics, and religious disputes became political disputes. Machiavelli remarks with bitterness that the divisions between the Roman, the Greek, the Ravennan, and the Arian factions resulted in much bloodshed and internal persecution, causing more human suffering than anything 'the avarice and natural cruelty' of human beings could ever cause.[27] Had historical Christianity emerged as a national, instead of an ecumenical religion, such religio-political evils would probably have been averted.

Christianity's tendency to produce political disunity took a peculiar form in peninsular Italy. In this case, Christianity fell short of becoming the national religion of the land, remaining instead merely a political irritant. It was not strong enough to make the whole of Italy into either a monarchy or a republic, nor was it weak enough to let another state unify Italy. The outcome of the historical development of Italian Christianity, according to him, was twofold: first, the bad example of the 'court of Rome' made Italians irreligious, and second, the temporal power of the Church made Italy politically weak.[28]

But Machiavelli's criticism goes even deeper than this: from historical analysis it proceeds to theological analysis. To begin with, Christianity introduced the distinction between civic *virtù* and the theological virtues. It further held that beatific vision, not temporal felicity, was the *summum bonum* of humans. It taught that humans had two, not one, fatherlands. In Machiavelli's eyes, the partition of loyalties that this teaching entailed had a debilitating impact on Christian politics; according to him, a fruitful relationship between civic virtues and theological virtues was not possible. Here his naturalistic conception of religion virtually prevented him from appreciating the Christian elements in Florentine civic humanism. Moreover, according to the Christian tradition, humble but saintly human beings were better role models for humans than were warriors and statesmen. When informed by theological virtues, courage had to find room for forgiveness, self-esteem for proper humility. But Machiavelli could not understand any of this. He chides St Francis and St Dominic for teaching 'that it is evil to speak evil of what is evil, and that it is good to live under prelates' control and, if prelates make errors, to leave them to God for punishment. So the prelates do the worst they can, because they do not fear the punishment which they do not see and do not believe in.'[29] The general conclusion that his criticism reaches is that historical Christianity has made the Christian world 'weak': 'Our religion has glorified humble and contemplative men rather than active ones. It has, then, set up as the greatest good humility, abjectness and contempt for human things; the other put it in grandeur of spirit, in strength of body, and in the other things apt to make men exceedingly vigorous. Though our religion asks that you have courage within you, it prefers that you be adapted to suffering rather than to doing something vigorous. This way of living then has made the world weak and turned over as prey to wicked men, who can in security control it, since the generality of men, in order to go to Paradise, think more about enduring their injuries than about avenging them.'[30]

The difficulty of harmonizing civic virtues with theological virtues is called to our attention again in 'The Golden Ass'. The reference there is to Savonarola's Christian politics, according to which prayer, fasting, and devotions are thought to be more important for civic health than is the practice of civic virtues. Machiavelli does not dispute the importance of these expressions of the virtue of religion. What he disputes, however, is that they could be effective without merging into civic virtues in the pagan manner. For he seems to think that while theological virtues may perfect the soul, they cannot perfect the city; they may lead to spiritual salvation, but they cannot procure political salvation:

> One man, it is true, believes that a deadly thing for kingdoms – what brings about their destruction – is usury or some sin of the flesh,
> and that the causes of their greatness, which keep them lofty and powerful, are fasting, alms and prayers.
> Another more discreet and wise, holds that to ruin them such evil is not enough, and not enough to preserve them is such good.
> To believe that without your effort on your part God fights for you while you are idle and on your knees, has ruined many kingdoms and many states.
> There is assuredly need for prayers; and altogether mad is he who forbids people their ceremonies and their devotions;
> because in fact it seems that from them may be reaped union and good order; and on them in turn rests good and happy fortune.
> But there should be no one with so small a brain that he will believe, if his house is falling, that God will save it without any other prop,
> because he will die beneath that ruin.[31]

Our main concern here is not to dispute whether Machiavelli is correct in his criticism of historical Christianity; whether for example he is right in arguing that Christianity is necessarily a religion of *ozio*. We are not even concerned here to enquire whether in singling out 'humility' as the chief moral virtue of the Christians he was being unduly, if understandably, influenced by contemporary trends in ascetical theology. Savonarola's writings on humility, including the short pamphlet, 'Tractato della Humilità' ('A Tract on Humility'), [32] restating St Bernard's famous 'Twelve Steps' in humility, could easily have come to his attention. However that might be, our chief concern here is to point out that his criticism of Christianity gets its sting from his astrological conception of religion.

God in Machiavelli's Philosophy of Religion

The name of God occurs throughout Machiavelli's writings, and it is important to know in what sense it is being used. Does it have a pagan or a Christian reference? And if it has both, which is the predominant one? If the Christian sense predominates, it would obviously pose serious difficulties for the thesis advanced in this book. If, on the other hand, the pagan sense predominates, our argument would be further vindicated.

There is no question that the Christian meaning of God is clearly present in several of his works, including 'The Exhortation to Penitence', 'The Allocution Made to a Magistrate', in sections of the poems 'On Ambition',

'The Golden Ass', and 'The Blessed Spirits'. Thus 'The Exhortation to Penitence' presents God as creator, redeemer, and provident. The created cosmos is good until sin introduces moral disorder into it. According to divine wisdom, everything below humanity is for the 'glory and good of man', and humanity finds its final *telos* in attaining the fellowship of God through Christ. But because of the weakness deriving from sin, human beings tend to turn away from God and turn towards 'thoughts about the world'. Through sin, 'man changes himself from a rational animal into a brute animal. Man changes therefore by practising this ingratitude to God from angel to devil, from master to slave, from man to beast.'[33] The God of Christianity, however, is not a God of vengeance, but rather of forgiveness. The repentant sinner will find divine justice transforming itself into mercy. Graced penitence can 'annul all the sins of men'. The models of such fall and redemption are David, king and prophet, St Peter, St Francis and St Jerome.[34]

'The Allocution Made to a Magistrate', an oration in praise of the virtue of justice, presents justice not only as a principle of order in the city and in the soul, but also as a proxy for divine grace itself. 'This virtue alone, among all other virtues, pleases God the most.'[35] Those who for one reason or another do not discover Christ as the mediator between sinners and God, can nevertheless obtain their eternal salvation through the practice of the virtue of justice. The model *par excellence* of those who obtain their salvation in this way is the Emperor Trajan.[36]

The poem 'On Ambition' clearly presupposes a biblical cosmology:

Hardly had God made the stars, the heavens, the light, the elements, and man – master over so many things of beauty –
and had quelled the pride of the angels, and from Paradise had banished Adam and his wife for their tasting of the apple,
when (after the birth of Cain and Abel, as with their father and by their labour they were living happy in their poor dwelling) . . .
sin entered the world . . .[37]

'The Golden Ass' speaks approvingly of the Christian doctrine that in human action both the agency of Providence as the first cause and the agency of humans as the immediate cause, are active.[38]

If one adds to the aforegoing the evidence from some of his private letters, it is not difficult to draw the conclusion that Machiavelli had a sound understanding of orthodox Christian theology. The question, however, is whether such an understanding implies or requires their incorporation in his political theory. For when we examine his major writings, a different picture of God clearly emerges, which leads us to wonder whether a Christian God is a necessary hypothesis of his political thought.

To begin with, the God who appears in the pages of Machiavelli's major works is a God who is interested only in the political well-being of humans.

The 'greatest good' to be done and that which is most 'pleasing to God', he writes in the 'Discursus', is 'that which one does for one's fatherland'. He reminds the vicar of Christ (Leo X) that no man is so much exalted 'by any act of his' as are those who have innovated republics and kingdoms: 'these are, after those who have been gods (*quegli che sono stati Iddii*), the first to be praised.' The highest glory that is open to humans is not beatific vision but the glory that comes from political achievements. Of all the gifts that heaven and God have given to the Medici family, the greatest is the glorious immortality that would flow from reforming Florence.[39] Now this is a thoroughly pagan norm, consistent with that invoked for the criticism of Christianity in *Discourses* II. 2. The 'Discursus' urges that the pope himself should emulate the pagan ideal of glory and immortality.

Again, God, as found in Machiavelli's theoretical works, is a sort of titular, 'tribal' or 'national' God of the pagan type, a god who always takes sides in political disputes. Thus in *The Prince* God is supposed to be on the side of the Italians, against the barbarians – the Spaniards, the French, and the Swiss. God, through 'marvellous unexampled signs', is directing Lorenzo de Medici, Junior: 'the sea is divided; a cloud shows you the road; the rock pours out water; manna rains down; everything united for your greatness.'[40] God aids Italy against Spain.[41] He sends a terrible storm to Tuscany as a warning to the Florentines.[42] He is said to be the cause of the city's temporary unity.[43] A just God is sure to punish any pope who would act against Florence.[44] God saves Florence from the pope, Venice and Naples by causing the Turks to attack Italy.[45] Leo X's election to the papacy is interpreted as bringing not only political glory to the family, but also as a 'special sign of God's alleged desire for Italian unification'.[46]

Furthermore, the God of Machiavelli's major works is a God who 'speaks' to political innovators. Moses, Numa Pompilius, and Savonarola are specifically mentioned; Lycurgus, Solon and 'many others' also are said to have had the same privilege. 'And truly no one who did not have recourse to God ever gave to a people unusual laws, because without that they would not be accepted.'[47] But 'speaking to God' in the sense in which Machiavelli intends it, is nothing more than a political ruse to gain acceptance from unwilling followers. There is no guarantee of the truth of the alleged conversations. This is clear enough in the case of Numa, who satisfied the requirements of 'speaking to God' by allegedly speaking to the Nymph Egeria. Savonarola is reported to have 'prayed' to God to send him 'a clear sign' approving his political programmes for Florence. But Machiavelli is of the opinion that the friar is actually wearing a political 'cloak' here, and that his claims to being close to God are nothing more than a means of 'making his lies plausible'.[48] Savonarola's programmes met with some initial success only because he was able to persuade the sophisticated people of Florence that he spoke with God. But Machiavelli remains sceptical. 'I do not intend to decide whether it was true or not, because so great a man ought to be spoken of with reverence, but I do say that countless numbers believed him without having seen anything extraordinary to make them believe him . . .'[49] And Machiavelli's reference to Moses's reported conversation with God is also hedged with some caution: 'And though Moses should not be discussed, since he was a mere executor of things laid down for him by God, nevertheless he ought to be exalted, if only for the grace that made him worthy to speak with God.'[50] Machiavelli's point about 'talking with God', then, is not to say that one can speak with the biblical God or even with a superhuman entity, but rather to say that there are people who will believe that such 'talk' can de facto take place.

Along the lines of this discussion, the issue arises of God being friends with new princes, an issue to which Sebastian De Grazia devotes much thought.[51] Thus God's friendship is available to the elder Lorenzo de Medici,[52] to Lorenzo de Medici, Junior, Moses, Cyrus, and Theseus: 'nor was God more friendly to them than to you' (*nè fu a loro Dio più amico che a voi*).[53] But what is the criterion of such alleged friendship? Political success. God is 'friends' only with the winners, not the losers: hardly a Christian idea of God. This point is made in the *Florentine Histories*, where Machiavelli analyses the behaviour of one of his favourite new princes, Francesco Sforza of Milan. He became the new prince of Milan through the very unChristian vice of treachery. After leading the Milanese forces against Venice at Caravaggio in 1448, he changed sides and treacherously joined Venice, with whose help he came back to usurp power in Milan in 1450. The Milanese wondered how such a wicked man as Sforza could be God's friend. To these, he explains that only the outcome of events can tell on whose side God will be. He (God) was on his side, Sforza argues, precisely because he won the war and was able to usurp power in Milan.[54] The same point is made by another of Machiavelli's new princes, Castruccio Castracani: 'God is the lover of strong men because we see that He always punishes the powerless by means of the powerful.'[55]

Besides, Machiavelli himself is not sure whether what is needed for success is God's love, heaven's love, or Fortune's love, since he considers them to be equivalent in value. His own hoped-for success in introducing 'new modes and orders', he feels, is dependent on the love of heaven – in fact, of someone 'more loved by heaven' (*più amato dal Cielo*) than he apparently feels himself to be.[56] In the case of Lorenzo de Medici the Elder, his success depended on the love of both God and Fortune. Briefly, the qualifications attached to the love of God suggest that the God in question cannot be the biblical or Christian God. The latter does not favour winners and abandon losers, nor is the latter's love in any need of being supplemented by the love of heaven and/or Fortune. The idea of God being 'friends' of new princes appears in Machiavelli's use of it to be a pagan, rather than a Christian idea.

Then again there is the question of Machiavelli's conception of God's relationship to Fortune. How does God govern 'the things of the world' and 'human things'? Three schools of thought on this question are identifiable in Machiavelli's Florence. The first held that God alone governs these affairs through His Providence. This is the orthodox Christian position, held for instance by Savonarola and Pico della Mirandola. The second school contended that God governs both natural and human affairs through heaven and Fortune. This heterodox position was held by Pontano and Bellanti, and possibly by Ficino and Pomponazzi as well. The third school maintained that the heavens and/or Fortune govern both natural and human affairs without any reference to God. This is a non-Christian, libertine position, and, as we have seen, Machiavelli's own grandson attributed this position to his grandfather: Niccolò tried to explain everything through natural and fortuitous causes. We find adequate evidence of the third position in *The Prince* and the *Discourses*. In *The Prince* he first reports the view held by others that God and Fortune govern the things of the world: 'It is not unknown to me that many have held and hold the view that things of the world are so governed by Fortune and by God that men cannot correct them by their prudence . . .'[57] He does not identify himself with this position, and he does not leave us in any doubt as to where he stands: 'I judge that it might be true that Fortune is the arbiter of half of our actions, but also that she leaves the other half, or close to it, for us to govern.'[58] In the *Discourses* he supports the view that human affairs are subject to the power of heaven.[59] Briefly, while he is certain that some extra-terrestrial, extra-human force has a share in the governance of the world, he is equally certain that that force is not the biblical God.

Sometimes Machiavelli casts God in a supporting role to Fortune. Thus the new princes, and even Moses, receive their *occasione*, the indispensable condition for success, from Fortune, not from the Christian God.[60] And it is even possible that Fortune can 'cancel' God's ordinances. This, he feels, is what happened to Cesare Borgia. 'And though up to now various gleams have appeared in someone from which we might judge that he had been ordered by God for her redemption, nevertheless we have seen later, that in the highest course of his actions, he was repulsed by Fortune.'[61] The fate of Cesare Borgia contains a salutary warning for all new princes: God's help is useless unless endorsed by Fortune. Now a God who is not independent of Fortune is not the Christian God. Clearly, Machiavelli expresses God's relationship to Fortune in pagan terms.

Finally, Machiavelli's endorsement of the new princes' (God's 'friends') 'entering into evil' is quite incompatible with the Christian conception of rulership and God's Providence. For Machiavelli, the key to the success of such new princes as David of the Old Testament and Philip of Macedon is their willingness to enter into evil. This willingness allowed David to make 'the rich poor and the poor rich', and Philip to move his subjects from place to place as cattlemen move their cattle. Such conduct, however, Machiavelli readily recognizes as 'contrary to every decent form of government, not only Christian but also human'. In fact, such conduct is so inhuman and unChristian that it is better, he says, for a human being to live a private life than 'to be king who brings such ruin on men'. 'Nevertheless,' he adds quickly, 'a ruler who does not wish to take that first good way of governing, if he wishes to maintain himself, must enter upon this evil one.'[62] In the final analysis, then, there is no room in Machiavelli's political philosophy for a typically Christian conception of good governance. The hypothesis of God's intervention in things of the world and human things is neither necessary nor compatible with Machiavelli's political theory. On the other hand, the hypothesis of the intervention of the heavens and Fortune is not only compatible with but also necessary for it. Though a close analysis of available evidence on the subject of God suggests that Machiavelli is not a systematic theologian, there is nevertheless enough evidence to suggest that there is an overall coherence in his thoughts on God. That is to say, his political philosophy has no need for a Creator God any more than for the Platonic Good or the Aristotelian Mind. All it requires is the heavens and Fortune. By replacing 'the God of Abraham, Isaac and Jacob', as well as the God of the philosophers, with astral and planetary gods and the goddess Fortune, he embraces a form of neopaganism, which seems to go even beyond the boundaries set by Paduan Averroism. His God is God only in name. While he might use, as the context requires, a doctrine of Christian theology to prove his own point, the point in question has nothing to do with Christian theology as such, (and often it has everything to do with what is opposed to it). Under no circumstances does his use of Christian themes and metaphors imply that he endorses the political teachings of Christianity. At the same time, it needs to be added that his position on God is not a neat esoteric trick played on the ignorant masses, nor a new type of apology for Christianity. All it means is that he is not a Democritean/ Lucretian materialist. In Machiavelli's cosmos the heavens do remain the source of religion, and Fortune the presiding deity.

Some Interpretative Issues

In recent critical literature, Machiavelli's conception of religion has been given serious consideration. Leo Strauss and Sebastian De Grazia agree that a correct understanding of Machiavelli's position on religion is a precondition for a correct understanding of his political philosophy taken as a whole. But there the agreement ends. Strauss thinks that Machiavelli is basically an atheist, and a clever one, while De Grazia considers him a Christian apologist, though of a peculiar kind.

According to Strauss, Machiavelli pays great attention to religion for an entirely negative reason, namely to argue that religion, including Christianity, is a purely human invention,[63] to be manipulated by an unscrupulous, often irreligious political élite. The basis of all religion, pagan as well as Christian, is a belief in the power and intelligence of gods. This belief itself need not be true, i.e. 'based on firm or reliable experience'; in fact it is caused by self-deception, if not by pure deception.[64] However that may be, Machiavelli is an astute atheist who, unlike modern atheists, does not make atheism a militant creed. Being wiser, he is quite content to leave the 'people' to their religion so long as it makes them good, patriotic, and law-abiding citizens. According to Strauss, Machiavelli wants to leave not only God, but also the heavens and Fortune as well, out of his politics.[65]

In our view Strauss is moved to take the position described above because he seeks to maintain at all costs his position that Machiavelli is the bearer of modernity. And he cannot be that if he still subscribes to the alleged divinity of the heavens and Fortune. Ignoring Machiavelli's astro-logical approach to religion, Strauss attributes to him what appear to be principles of biblical criticism of a much later date, viz. that the Bible is to Jews and Christians what Livy's *History* is to Romans – a piece of *historical*, not theological, writing, having no supernatural inspiration at all. Any inspiration it has comes from the human authors themselves. The Bible stands or falls on the basis of the *historical* accuracy of the truths claimed in it. Such accuracy can be verified only in reference to other non-biblical, even anti-biblical, but most importantly, *historical* sources. The following exam-ples may illustrate my point:

'. . . the critical student of the Bible must rely on potentially or actually anti-Biblical literature in order to discern the truth about the Biblical religion.'[66]

'The crucial importance of miracles in the Biblical records compels Machiavelli to adopt as a provisional canon the rule that very extraordi-nary events reported in the Bible for which there is no evidence stemming from men not believing in the Bible are not to be believed.'[67]

'. . . according to him [Machiavelli], the Bible is of human origin, consists to a considerable extent of poetic fables, and must be read "judiciously", i.e. in the light of non-Biblical or even anti-Biblical thought.'[68]

'We may try to express his [Machiavelli's] thought as follows: the Biblical writers present themselves as historians, as human beings who report what God said and did, while in fact they make God say and do what in their opinion a most perfect being would say and do; the ground of what presents itself as the experience of the Biblical writers is their notion of a most perfect being; that notion is so compelling that the "Ought" comes to sight as "Is"; this connection is articulated by the ontological proof; there is no way which leads from "the things of the world" (i.e. the cosmological proof) to the biblical God; the only proof which commands respect, although it is not a genuine proof, is the ontological proof.'[69]

If our argument in this chapter is valid, however, what Machiavelli really wants to do is to attack Christianity on the basis of the principles of sixteenth-century astrological historiography, not on the basis of those assumed by nineteenth-century higher criticism. Given Machiavelli's cosmology, he cannot eliminate the heavens and Fortune from his analysis of religion. They are as necessary a presupposition of his theory of religion as they are of his theory of politics.

De Grazia, too, rightly recognizes that religion is an essential component of Machiavelli's political theory. 'The references to the divine in *The Prince*', he says, 'comprise significant metaphysical and theological statements, with political bearings just as significant.'[70] And the phrase 'God more a friend to them than to you', occurring in *The Prince*, ch. 26 (about whose contextual meaning De Grazia has very enlightening things to say), affects the basis of Machiavelli's political and moral philosophy.[71] As for the *Discourses*, it is 'a fundamental work in the political theory of religion.'[72] Machiavelli's religious thought supposes that there is a hierarchy of what De Grazia calls 'teleological beings' – God, heaven or heavens ('usually a weak, paganized variant of God'), Fortune, and astral forces – beings who 'interrupt natural events'.[73] 'Niccolò's God,' we are told, 'is the creator, the master deity, providential, real, universal, one of many names, personal, invokable, thankable, to be revered, a judge, just and forgiving, rewarding and punishing, awesome, a force transcendent, separate from but operative in the world.'[74] According to De Grazia, Machiavelli believes that all religions except Christianity are false; the latter alone is 'the true faith'.[75] As for his attitude towards Italian Christianity, he is 'reform clerical', not anticlerical.[76] Though Machiavelli's hell is not as horrible a 'place' as Dante's, and though it may be an alternative to Christianity's paradise, De Grazia feels that on the whole Machiavelli can be accommodated within the Christian fold.

What is troublesome in such an interpretation of Machiavelli's religious thought is the absence of a viable distinction between his pagan theology and Christian theology. De Grazia seems to conflate the two. One explanation for this confusion, in our view, is the lack of attention paid to Machiavelli's own basic theory of religion and deity which, as I have argued, is definitely pagan, and not Christian. A Christian conception of God cannot support the view that Machiavellian new princes are God's favourites, but the pagan view of God definitely can. Similarly, a pagan view of religion can hold that Machiavellian *virtù* is the highest fulfilment of religion, whereas the Christian view of religion cannot. The God of Christianity does not depend on the heavens, Fortune, and astral forces for governing 'the things of the world'. The 'gods' of Machiavelli's religion (the heavens and Fortune), on the other hand, do in fact govern the world without any assistance from God.

Likewise, the view that Machiavelli holds special brief for Christianity can hardly be sustained. The fact that he knows Christian doctrines well does not mean that he endorses them, nor that he uses them constructively in his own political philosophy. He is, no doubt, a cultural Christian who considers Christianity as 'our religion'. But his cultural commitment to Christianity does not involve any theological/philosophical commitment to the doctrines of Christianity. Perhaps one example may suffice to illustrate this point. In the *Art of War*, he reports that pagan generals were in the habit of exploiting the superstitious beliefs of their soldiers. Christian generals, on the other hand, he notes, are 'almost free' (*quasi liberi*) from such habits because of Christianity's opposition to superstition. Nevertheless, he says, should the need arise, Christian generals should ignore Christianity and follow the example of their pagan counterparts. In other words, Christianity or no Christianity, Christians must be prepared to use superstition if that will be politically useful. De Grazia uses a part of the passage in which Machiavelli makes this point, but uses it only to argue that he (Machiavelli) 'gives Christianity credit for its war on superstition'.[77] But he leaves out the crucial section of the passage which advises that Christian generals should ignore Christianity and follow the example of paganism when necessary. The passage is worth quoting in full despite its length:

> Moreover, the ancient captains had one worry from which the present ones are almost free, which was the interpreting to their advantage of unfavourable auguries: if a bolt of lightning fell in the army, if there was an eclipse of the sun or the moon, if there was an earthquake, if in mounting or dismounting from his horse the captain fell, the soldiers interpreted it unfavourably and became so fearful that if they entered battle they easily lost. And for this reason the ancient captains, as soon as an accident happened, either showed that it resulted from some natural causes or interpreted it to their advantage. Caesar, falling in Africa as he left his ship, said: 'Africa, I seize you.' And many have explained the cause of an eclipse of the moon and of earthquakes. Such things cannot happen in our times, both because our men are not so superstitious (*tanto superstiziosi*) and because our religion keeps itself far from such opinions. *Nevertheless whenever they do come up, we must imitate the methods (ordini) of the ancients.*[78]

A fair assessment of the passage cited above would show that, however correct Christianity's position on astrological superstition might be, Machiavelli is not prepared to endorse it. On the contrary, he was quite prepared to endorse the opposite pagan position. Taking all available data into consideration, then, one is obliged to conclude that Machiavelli is a neopagan whose aim is to paganize rather than to secularize Christianity.

CHAPTER 4

Fortune

The concept of Fortune occupies a prominent place in Machiavelli's political philosophy.[1] It raises a number of issues fundamental to his thought. Does Fortune have a share in the governance of the 'things of the world'? Do the fortuitous events that occur in life have a cause? If so, are they caused by a superhuman agent? Is that agent the heavens or Fortune? If it is Fortune, what impact does 'she' have on human action and human autonomy? How does Fortune relate to free will, chance, fate, and determinism? If the causality of heaven, as we saw earlier, explains the motion, order, and power operating in history, politics, and religion, why introduce another supposed causal agent such as Fortune? What is it that Fortune explains that heaven does not?

We are not sure that Machiavelli answers these and related questions to the satisfaction of everyone. Whatever his answers, they are set within the framework of his cosmology. And to the extent that this is so, his thoughts on Fortune have a coherence of their own. Thus the fortuitous, he believes, are not chance happenings, though they may appear to be so to the unwise. For they have a cause, viz. Fortune. Heaven is thought to govern mainly or only those things in the sublunar world which occur with regularity and predictability, while Fortune is thought to govern mainly or only those things which occur by chance or accident.

It follows that we cannot explain human destiny solely in terms of human autonomy. The empires of heaven and Fortune set a limit to what human autonomy can accomplish. The quality of the times and the nature of the temperament or humours of each individual emerge as issues connected with human action as well as with Fortune. Human action, faced with the fortuitous, takes on the features of a 'struggle' with Fortune. Though often presented as a goddess, she is not a goddess to be revered, but one with whom one has to struggle and from whom one has to wrest, as it were, our successes and achievements. But there is a twist to the struggle in question: for although we may have the impression of being successful in the struggle, it is Fortune who sets the precise terms of the struggle, and in that sense it is she who ultimately determines whether we will be successful or not. Such, in brief, is the scope of his discussion of the concept of Fortune.

Machiavelli inherits different traditions of thought on Fortune and the weight of this inheritance presses rather heavily on him. This explains why he uses the concept differently in different contexts, and why not all his meanings are compatible with one another. Thus sometimes we find the use of the notion of Fortune in the sense of a causal agent superior to humans. At other times we find that fortune refers to the fortuitous events which occur in life and which affect the outcomes of our actions. Here the treatment may resemble somewhat the traditional treatment of *tyche* in philosophical literature, as, for example, in Aristotle's *Physics* II.4. And again, we find the term Fortune referring to a favourable or unfavourable condition of life, or a favourable or unfavourable relationship one has with others. Had Machiavelli spoken of Fortune only in the last two senses, there would have been comparatively little difficulty in explaining his position on the subject. But the fact is that he often speaks of Fortune in the first sense, i.e. as a superior causal agent, and this way of speaking presupposes his cosmology in a special way.

On Fortune considered as a superior agent, both philosophy and popular religion had taken their respective positions. Certain branches of natural philosophy, especially the Ptolemaic one, had identified the superior causal agent responsible for the fortuitous with the motions or the 'will' of heaven.[2] According to these thinkers, it was not enough to explain the fortuitous in terms of its immanent and proximate causes. They wanted to explain it in terms of its ultimate cause as well. And this ultimate cause, according to them, was, of course, the heavenly bodies. It is because of such explanations that the question of Fortune came to be connected with heaven and fate, and with astrological determinism. This in turn connected Fortune with questions of free will and freedom of choice. We can hear clear echoes of these philosophical utterances in the pages of the 'Ghiribizzi' and *The Prince* 25.

Christian philosophy, in its turn, had taken a different stand on the question of Fortune considered as a superior causal agent. From Boethius to Aquinas, Pico and Savonarola, Christian thinkers found no difficulty in accepting the Aristotelian explanation as a starting point in their attempt to explain the proximate causes of chance and the fortuitous. However, because of the Christian notion of Providence, they felt it necessary to go beyond Aristotle, to link chance and fortuitous events to Providence as their ultimate cause. Providence, according to Boethius' famous dictum, is divine reason governing all things, the necessary as well as the fortuitous. Chance in this view is 'an unexpected event brought about by a concurrence of causes which had other purposes in view. These causes come together because of that order which proceeds from inevitable connection of things, the order which flows from the source which is Providence and which disposes all things, each in its proper time and place.'[3] As will become apparent later, Machiavelli did not see the fortuitous in terms of Providence, and therefore in terms of Christian philosophy.

Popular pagan religion, in its turn, gave an entirely different account of the nature of fortune as a higher cause. It identified 'her' as a goddess, one of the many divinities inhabiting the heavens. The Romans, as Machiavelli reminds us in *Discourses* II. 1, built more temples in honour of the goddess of Fortune than in honour of any other divinity. For obvious theological reasons, Christianity could not accept this popular pagan view of Fortune. However, we do find the Christian poet Dante giving Fortune an intermediary status between God and humans, below God but superior to humans. Dante reconciles Providence and Fortune by making the latter an agent of God in charge of all mutable earthly things such as kingdoms and republics, wealth and glory. Dante's influence on Machiavelli on this point, as in others, is considerable. Thus in the *Inferno*, Fortune is identified as 'the general minister and leader' (*general ministra e duce*), put in charge of the fate of nations and peoples. Her will and purpose (according to Dante she has will and purpose) transcends human understanding, and her actions remain inscrutable. It is because of her 'decision' that one people rule while another languishes. She 'foresees and judges and maintains her kingdom as the other gods do theirs.' For Dante, Fortune, though inscrutable, is not malignant. His explanation is plain enough: a 'minister' of God acting according to His Providence cannot be hostile to humans. In other words, according to Dante, God and Fortune together govern the fortunes of countries.[4] One can hear an echo of this Dantean concept in Machiavelli, as in *The Prince* 25 where Machiavelli reports others as saying that 'things of the world are governed by fortune and by God'; or as in *Florentine Histories* VIII. 36, where he remarks that Lorenzo the Magnificent 'was greatly loved by Fortune and by God'.

But the comparison between Dante and Machiavelli ends there. For in Machiavelli's view, as we shall see, Fortune is a malignant goddess, or at least a goddess indifferent to human well-being. The reason for this is not difficult to discern: the Machiavellian universe is not governed by Providence; nor do humans have a special status in it; the human end is dictated by the cyclical motions of the planets. In the Machiavellian universe, there is only cyclical motion, order and power. There is no mention of love nor of any self-disclosing communication between humans and any transcosmic entity. Moreover, his world is governed not only by natural motion, but also by the occult qualities supposed to be inherent in natural motion. And in this occult order, Fortune governs supreme. Instead of being a *ministra* of God, she is the mistress of human destiny, and that destiny, thought to be tied to the motions of the planets, is subject to chance, not to reason. Briefly, in the Machiavellian cosmos, there is no room for God's Providence, although there is room in it for both heaven and Fortune; he makes room for these, because they address two different causal issues, the one pertaining to the necessary and the other pertaining to the fortuitous.

Yet another image of Fortune emerges from the pages of Machiavelli. He somewhat inconsistently considers the fortuitous without theological imagery. Fortune is considered as a woman who allows herself to be challenged, and who can be challenged and struggled with. Fortune, considered in this way, is without any cosmic or divine trappings. Even so, she plays a role in human existence. The unforeseen and the unexpected, even when understood in strictly immanentistic terms, can potentially have a paralysing effect on human initiative and endeavour. Florentine merchants and traders are able to attain the great successes they attain because they are able to look upon Fortune in strictly immanentistic terms, as controllable by foresight, the technical know-how of commerce, and economic risk-taking. With good bookkeeping and sound fiscal management, a good deal of the terror that Fortune would otherwise cause in the human imagination might be nullified. Thus, with prudence and calculations, humans can keep the fickle goddess of wealth within reasonable human control.[5]

Machiavelli also insists that with foresight and boldness humans can attempt to master the fortuitous element of political life. The key to success here is, of course, *virtù*. What might frustrate them, however, is the attitude of resignation to fate. They can, however, at least attempt to escape this frustration by looking upon political life as a constant struggle against the unforeseen and the fortuitous. And they may even succeed in the struggle, if they are prepared to exercise their *virtù* in its maximum degree. Thus Machiavellian *virtù* is directed against Fortune understood as the personified symbol of the fortuitous. The most famous of all Machiavelli's metaphors, 'Fortune is a woman', conveys this posture of struggle between humans and the fortuitous. *Virtù* is to be exerted in the maximum degree if humans are to win in this struggle.

But what defines the limits of *virtù*? This is a question underlying all discussions of Fortune. And it is in attempting to determine the limits of *virtù* that we discover Fortune's real power over humans. If humans are to win, we find, Fortune herself must allow them to win. To understand the thought conveyed by Machiavelli's metaphor we must go to his cosmology and to his anthropology in which it is reflected. For Fortune determines the limiting conditions of achieving success through *virtù* – the times of birth and death, the humour and the temperament with which one is born, and the quality of the times through which one's life passes. And without control over these conditions, humans find themselves at a 'metaphysical' disadvantage in their struggle against Fortune.

Thus, under the rubric of Fortune, Machiavelli covers a number of issues – Providence, chance, fate, astrological determinism, free will, humours, temperament, and the quality of times. Apart from this broad range of issues, what is most striking in his approach to Fortune is the two-fold way in which he treats the subject. When we look closely at the relevant texts, we find that they are concerned either with Fortune as she affects countries or with fortune as she affects individuals. For Fortune affects countries and individuals differently. When one has to struggle against Fortune, one must make sure which aspect of Fortune it is that one is struggling against. For what will be good in the struggle against Fortune as she affects countries will not be good in the struggle against Fortune as she affects individuals.

But how may we account for this two-fold pattern of treating Fortune? In searching for an answer we find a curious similarity between Ptolemy's treatment of the causality exercised by the heavenly bodies and Machiavelli's treatment of the causality exercised by Fortune. Ptolemy, as we noted earlier, divided astrology into two kinds, the 'universal' and the 'particular.'[6] Universal astrology considers the causality of the heavens over countries and peoples, while particular astrology considers the causality of the heavens over individuals, especially with respect to their humour, temperament, and times.[7] Machiavelli also distinguished between Fortune affecting countries and Fortune affecting individuals, and in *The Prince*, as we shall see in detail below, he uses the words 'universal' and 'particular' to convey this distinction. In the 'Ghiribizzi' also the universal-particular distinction appears with respect to 'things' and 'times': 'times and things often change universally and particularly.'[8] I maintain that this distinction has a Ptolemaic-astrological tone. According to astrological natural philosophy, universal time – the time consequent upon the motions of the planets – moves on its own, producing its appropriate qualitative effects on nations and peoples, while particular time – the time affecting the life of each individual – moves on its own, producing effects on the humour and temperament of each individual human being. Humans, though 'free', are nevertheless subject, both collectively and individually, to the natural qualitative mutations which occur in things and times. It is with this hypothesis in mind that we propose to examine Machiavelli's treatment of Fortune in the two-fold way.

Fortune and Countries

Throughout his writings, Machiavelli speaks of Fortune as she affects countries – for example, the Roman Republic, Italy, Florence, Venice, the Papal states. In *The Prince*, the *Discourses*, and the poem 'On Fortune', the discussion of the fortunes of countries becomes very crucial for his argument. The most pertinent example is chapter 25 of *The Prince*, for it is here that the distinction between universal and particular Fortune is made explicit. The preamble of this chapter raises certain philosophical issues: How are things of the world governed? What is the nature of the debate on this issue? Is human prudence of any help here? Should humans 'sweat' over things or should they resign themselves to chance? He then calls the reader's attention to 'the great changes' (*variazione grande delle cose*) that have occurred in Italy in 'our times', meaning largely, but by no means only, the humiliating foreign invasion of 1494. These 'great changes', he avers, have persuaded many people that human prudence is of no avail. And he himself is 'sometimes' inclined to agree with them. He is not, however, quite prepared to deny freedom of choice, and accordingly, he is prepared to admit that 'Fortune is the arbiter of half of our actions' and that 'the other half, or almost that, she leaves for us to govern'.[9]

What has set these philosophical reflections in motion are the misfortunes of Italy. In other words, the focus of the first part of *The Prince* 25 is fortune as she affects countries. And it is to illustrate the problem raised by the Fortune of countries that he introduces the first of the two metaphors used in this chapter, viz. the metaphor of the raging river. 'And I liken her [Fortune] to one of these violent rivers which, when they become enraged, flood the plains, ruin the trees and the buildings, lift the earth from this part, and drop it in another; each person flees before them, everyone yields to their impetus without being able to hinder them in any regard.'[10] There is no question in Machiavelli's mind that countries are subject to Fortune. Fortune affects them as floods affect soil, trees, buildings, and human populations. The point of the metaphor is to enlighten us about both the nature of Fortune as she affects countries, and about the nature of the remedies against these effects that human prudence can produce. The nature of the Fortune of countries is such that it will necessarily affect them adversely from time to time. The nature of the remedies is such that their prescription requires great foresight; with foresight the adverse effects of Fortune can be minimized. Although rivers are potentially damaging, he points out, it is possible for humans to build dams and dykes to control an otherwise unruly river. And just as only unruly rivers cause damage to the environment, so also Fortune causes damage to countries only when they are not militarily protected. Her power is stronger in countries where *virtù* is weaker. The dams and dykes of the river metaphor stand for military power and effective diplomacy. These constitute the proper human response to the Fortunes of countries. Italy, in contrast to Germany, Spain, and France, has been without their 'dams' and 'dykes'. It does not, for instance, have an efficient citizen army. 'If it had been dyked by suitable *virtù*,' Machiavelli writes, 'this flood would not have caused the great changes that it has, or it would not have come here at all.'[11] The mention of Italy, Germany, Spain and France, makes it very clear that Machiavelli is referring to the Fortune of countries, or 'general Fortune' as Ptolemy would have called it. The remedies implied here – military strength, a citizen army, sound diplomacy – are remedies against collective misfortunes. They do nothing to solve the personal misfortunes of particular individuals, or, to use Ptolemaic language, 'particular Fortune'. Personal misfortunes, as we shall see later, will require altogether different remedies. But in the first part of chapter 25, Machiavelli is not concerned to discuss them.

At this point, Machiavelli's argument takes a sudden turn: it moves from consideration of Fortune as she affects countries to Fortune as she affects individuals. As Gennaro Sasso points out, the passage in question is of great importance. Clearly, Machiavelli alerts the reader that at this point one part of the treatment of the subject ends and another begins: an analysis of the 'particular' follows the analysis of the 'general'. In the relationship between these two parts lies the interpretative key of the chapter.[12] The passages in question as found in the Burd edition of *The Prince* are as follows: '*E questo voglio basti avere detto quanto all'opporsi alla fortuna in universale. Ma ristringendomi più al particolare, dico, come si vede oggi questo principe felicitare, e domani rovinare, senza avergli veduto mutare natura o qualità alcuna.*'[13] These sentences have posed some difficulty for both their editors and translators. And the difficulty has to do with the 'general'-'particular' distinction they contain. We find three different editorial arrangements of the two crucial sentences.

The first, as given above, is Burd's, who follows the original text, which, as is well known, does not divide chapters into paragraphs. As far as we know, the division into paragraphs of the chapters of *The Prince* does not have Machiavelli's authority; it was introduced by various editors. Thus Burd does not make any special editorial effort to draw the reader's attention to the 'general'-'particular' distinction. Note, however, that Burd has 'universale' and 'particolare' in the singular, whereas the other editors, as will be noted immediately below, have them in the plural.

The second arrangement, followed by Martelli and Sasso, keeps the two sentences together, but as forming the beginning of a new paragraph. '*E questo voglio basti avere detto quanto allo opporsi alla fortuna, in universali. Ma, restringendomi più a' particulari, dico come si vede oggi questo principe felicitare, e domani ruinare, senza averli veduto mutare natura o qualità alcuna.*'[14]

The third arrangement, followed by Bertelli, Chabod, and Lisio, places the two sentences into two different paragraphs: the first sentence containing the notion of 'general Fortune' forms the last sentence of one paragraph, and the second sentence containing the notion of 'particular Fortune' forms the first sentence of the succeeding paragraph. Thus: '*E questo voglio basti quanto allo avere detto allo opporsi alla fortuna in universali.*

Ma, restringendomi più a' particulari, dico come si vede oggi questo principe felicitare, e domani ruinare, senza averli veduto mutare natura o qualità alcuna.'[15] Among the English translators, Allan Gilbert, Peter Bondanella, Mark Musa, and Russell Price follow the third arrangement, while Luigi Ricci, E.R.P. Vincent, and Harvey C. Mansfield, Jr. follow the second arrangement. (No modern English translator has followed the first arrangement.) Thus:

Ricci-Vincent: 'This must suffice as regards opposition to fortune in general. But limiting myself more to particular cases . . .'[16]

Mansfield: 'And I wish that this may be enough to have said about opposing fortune in general. But restricting myself more to particulars . . .'[17]

Allan Gilbert: 'I think this is all I need to say in general on resisting fortune.

Limiting myself more to particulars . . .'[18]

Bondanella-Musa: 'And this I consider enough to say about fortune in general terms.

But, limiting myself more to particulars . . .'[19]

Russell Price: 'But I have said enough in general terms about resisting fortune.

Considering the matter in more detail . . .'[20]

These translations tend to imply that Fortune as she affects countries and Fortune as she affects individuals are related to one another in logical terms, as the 'general' is to its 'particular'. A careful scrutiny of the two Fortunes, however, would reveal that this way of considering them is unsatisfactory. Instead, what Machiavelli means, I think, is that there are two distinct ways of considering the problem of Fortune, as there are two ways in which Fortune affects sublunar affairs. The causes of the misfortunes of countries are not the causes of the misfortunes of individuals. Likewise, the remedies suitable for treating the misfortunes of countries are not suitable for treating the misfortunes of individuals. One does not build 'dams' or 'dykes' to avert a personal tragedy. Thus how can an analysis of the causes of the fortunes or misfortunes of Julius II throw light on the causes of the fortunes or misfortunes of Italy? Properly speaking, Julius II's case can be considered only as a particular application of the general thesis regarding Fortune as she affects individuals. Similarly, Italy's case is properly considered as a particular application of the general thesis regarding Fortune as she affects countries. To consider otherwise would be to mix categories that should not be mixed. In other words, by studying why countries succeed or fail, one does not arrive at an understanding of why individuals succeed or fail. Countries and individuals are affected differently by Fortune. If one wants to understand why Germany, France and Spain flourished, one must look at their military power and foreign policy. If one wants to understand why Julius II flourished, one must look at his 'nature', temperament, and the qualities of his times. Personality is more complex than policy. It is not necessary to labour the point: in *The Prince* 25 Machiavelli is discussing the two distinct ways in which Fortune operates, and it is crucial that we adhere to that distinction the way Machiavelli meant it.

The poem 'On Fortune' contains a long descriptive account of the Fortunes of countries. Fortune is the goddess causing the fortuitous things that happen to countries:

By many this goddess is called omnipotent, because whoever comes into this life either late or early feels her power.

She often keeps the good beneath her feet; the wicked she raises up; and if ever she promises you anything, never does she keep her promise.

She turns states and kingdoms upside down as she pleases; she deprives the just of the good that she freely gives to the unjust.

This unstable goddess and fickle deity often sets the undeserving on a throne which the deserving never attains.

She disposes of time as suits her; she raises up, she puts us down without pity, without law or reason.[21]

Machiavelli's most comprehensive review of history – even more comprehensive than that found in *Discourses* II. Preface – is found in this poem. The fortunes of states are due to the actions of this goddess. The metaphor of the raging river occurs here again:

All that realm of hers, within and without, is adorned with narrative paintings of those triumphs from which she gets most honour.

In the first space, painted in vigorous colours, we see that long ago under Egypt's king the world stood subjugated and conquered, and that for long years he held it subject in continuing peace, and that then the beauties of nature were expressed in writing.

Next we see the Assyrians climbing up the lofty sceptre, when Fortune did not permit the king of Egypt to wield authority longer.

Thereafter we see her happy to turn to the Medes; from the Medes to the Persians; and the hair of the Greeks she crowned with the diadem she took away from the Persians.

Here we see Thebes and Memphis subdued, Babylon, Troy, and Carthage too, Jerusalem, Athens, Sparta, and Rome.

Here is represented how splendid they were, noble, rich, and powerful, and how at the end Fortune made them their enemies' booty.

Here we see the noble and god-like deeds of the Roman Empire; then how all the world went to pieces at her fall.

As a rapid torrent, swollen to the utmost, destroys whatever its current anywhere reaches,

and adds to one place and lowers another, shifts banks, shifts its bed and its bottom, and makes earth tremble where it passes,

so Fortune in her furious onrush many times, now here now there shifts and reshifts the world's affairs.[22]

Turning now to the *Discourses*, one of Machiavelli's main concerns in this work is to establish the relative importance of *virtù* and Fortune in the evolution of Rome as a republic and as an imperial power. No doubt, his general thesis is that Rome's greatness and perfection were owed more to *virtù* than to fortune. But the thesis is still based on the premise that Fortune and *virtù* are both causal factors. His aim is only to establish the relative importance of *virtù*. Thus Rome produced a perfect constitution, thanks partly to the favour of Fortune and mostly to the *virtù* of its social 'classes'. 'So favourable to her was Fortune that even though she passed from the government of the king and the aristocrats to that of the people ... yet never, in order to give authority to the aristocrats, did she take all authority of the aristocrats to give it to the people, but continuing her mixed government, she was a perfect state.'[23]

As for the cause of Rome's imperial expansion, Machiavelli presupposes, as the title of *Discourses* II. 1 indicates, that both *virtù* and Fortune were involved. He asks, 'What was more the cause of the empire that the Romans acquired, *virtù* or Fortune?' And although the answer favours *virtù*, it by no means implies that Fortune had no part to play. His polemics against Livy and Plutarch might give the false impression that he ignores Fortune in favour of *virtù*. He only chastises them for attributing too much to Fortune. He readily concedes that it was due to Fortune that Rome did not have to fight two major wars simultaneously, and that she could take on her enemies one by one. At the same time, she used her military power derived from her citizen army, and diplomatic skills derived from her aristocracy, very adeptly. Or, as he puts it, she 'mixed her Fortune with the greatest *virtù* and prudence'.[24] The foundations of her power were 'the Roman people, the Latin name, the associated cities in Italy, the colonies from which she drew her soldiers'.[25] These foundations were the creations of Roman *virtù* rather than of Fortune.

From the analysis of Roman history Machiavelli formulates a general principle regarding how any country can deal with the Fortunes of countries: if a country has a good army, good leadership, and good diplomacy, it can deal with whatever Fortune brings, without any disadvantage to itself. 'Hence I believe that the Fortune the Romans had in this matter would have been enjoyed by all those princes if they had acted like the Romans and had been of the same *virtù* as they.'[26]

It needs to be stressed, however, that the greater importance of *virtù* over the favours of Fortune is only a general principle. For in particular cases, such as the 'accident' of the Gallic War of 390 BC, the favours of Fortune could prove to be the more crucial factor. It is true that Fortune shows her power when countries are poorly organized and militarily weak. 'Where men have little *virtù* Fortune shows her power much; and because she is changeable, republic and states often change.'[27] In particular situations, a sufficiently virtuous leader could 'regulate' his country's Fortune: there is no automatic rule 'that every revolution of the sun' will produce uniform effects upon countries. *Virtù* can modify events even if only up to a point.[28] That is the meaning of the dual causality of humans and Fortune. Even so, Fortune always has the last word. She can help or hinder a country by keeping a virtuous leader alive or by killing him, since questions of health and sickness, life and death, are under Fortune's control.[29]

Machiavelli's analysis of the early reverses which Rome suffered in the

Gallic War (mentioned above) highlights his view that in particular in-stances Fortune is more crucial than *virtù*. For these reverses were due to the disfavour of Fortune, who wanted to 'test' Roman *virtù*. Accordingly, she permitted those accidents to occur in order to make Rome stronger and bring her to the greatness she attained. Machiavelli is so committed to this view that, in a remarkable passage, he attributes a variety of notably different accidents to Fortune:

> And for this reason she had Camillus exiled and not killed, had Rome captured but not the Capitol, arranged that the Romans in order to protect Rome should not plan anything good, and that later to defend the Capitol they should not fail to use any good measure. She arranged, in order that Rome might be taken, to have the greater part of the soldiers defending the city of Rome. Yet in arranging this she prepared everything for its recapture, having brought a Roman army unharmed to Veii, and Camillus to Ardea, in order to be able to make a great muster, under a general not spotted with any ignominy through defeat and unharmed in reputation, for the recapture of their fatherland.[30]

Machiavelli's point, then, is that Fortune controls the destiny of countries. This is as true of Christian countries as it was true of pagan countries. That is to say, Fortune, not Providence, governs the fate of all countries, whether pagan or Christian. Cases analogous to the Gallic War could be brought out from Christian times to prove the point, he says, but he omits doing so since the pagan case is 'enough to satisfy anybody'. In any case, he is unusually emphatic on this matter: 'I affirm, indeed, once again, that it is very true, according to what we see in all the histories, that men are able to second Fortune but not to oppose her. They can weave her designs but cannot destroy them.'[31]

Yet another way in which Fortune affects countries is by controlling the quality of their times. As 'On Fortune' states, 'she disposes of time as suits her'. Thus, the 'good times' and the 'evil times' through which countries pass are the products of Fortune's whims. According to the 'Ghiribizzi', the quality of the times through which a country passes affects the *virtù* of those who govern it or attempt to conquer it. Thus it could come about that cruelty, treachery, and irreligion can be effective in a country where humanity, loyalty and religion had once flourished. Likewise, humanity, loyalty and religion could be effective in a country where cruelty, treachery and irreligion had once flourished. That is why Hannibal succeeded in Italy and Scipio in Spain. To explain this phenomenon, Machiavelli invokes an analogy from nature: 'as bitter things disturb the taste and sweet ones cloy it, so men (taken collectively) get bored with good and complain of ill.'[32] This is how he accounts for the successes of Hannibal (a cruel man) in Italy (a country noted for humanity), and of Scipio (a humane man) in Spain (a country noted for cruelty).[33] In the same way, the early Roman Republic could not be corrupted by a man such as Manlius because her times were favourable to *virtù*, while the late Republic was vulnerable to the corruption perpetrated by men such as Sulla and Marius, because she was passing through times favourable to corruption.[34] The underlying idea here is that the 'matter' of the body politic is subject to the ravages of time, which as noted above, is controlled by Fortune.[35]

Fortune and Individuals

Machiavelli devotes more space to the analysis of Fortune as she affects individuals than he does to Fortune as she affects countries. And the astrological context of his analysis is even more unmistakable here than it is in the previous case. We start with the poem 'On Fortune' which gives an overview of his position.

In this work, Fortune is associated with heaven and its occult power. She is responsible for many things in the sublunar world: leisure (*ozio*), necessity, chance (*caso*), luck (*sorte*), and opportunity (*occasione*). Most notably, she controls time, honour, riches and health as these affect individuals. It is she who endows each one with his/her humour. She prefers men who are aggressive, who 'push and shove' her, but she is fickle; to use one of his own metaphors, only those who can jump from wheel to wheel (wheels which she herself sets up) can be successful. The key issue in considering the Fortune of individuals is success. The examples of Alexander, Caesar, Cyrus, Pompey, Marius, and many others unnamed, prove how she affects the success of individuals. In the final analysis, it is necessary to follow one's star, and to live from moment to moment, hour to hour:

> Power, honour, riches, and health are ready as rewards; as punishment and affliction there are servitude, infamy, sickness, and poverty.
> Fortune displays her mad fury with these distresses; the gifts she offers to those she loves.
> That man most luckily forms his plans, among all the persons in Fortune's palace, who chooses a wheel befitting her wish, since the humours that make you act, so far as they conform with her doings, are the causes of your good and your ill.
> Yet you cannot therefore trust yourself to her or hope to escape her hard bite, her hard blows, violent and cruel, because while you are whirled about by the rim of a wheel that for a moment is lucky and good, she is wont to reverse its course in mid-circle.
> *And since you cannot change your character nor give up the disposition that heaven endows you with*, in the midst of your journey she abandons you.
> Therefore, if this be understood and fixed in his mind, a man who could leap from wheel to wheel would always be happy and fortunate, but because to attain this is denied by the *occult virtue* that rules us, our con-

dition changes with her course.

Not a thing in the world is eternal; Fortune wills it so and makes herself splendid by it, so that her power may be more clearly seen.

Therefore a man should take her for his star and, as far as he can, should every hour adjust himself to her variation.[36]

Though the great men of history have pushed and shoved her, it did not save them from their tragic fate. Alexander the Great and Julius Caesar are the best examples of this:

If then your eyes light on what is beyond, in one panel Caesar and Alexander you see among those who prospered while alive.

From their example we well realize how much he pleases Fortune and how acceptable he is who pushes her, who shoves her, who jostles her.

Yet, nevertheless, the coveted harbour one of the two [Alexander] failed to reach, and the other [Caesar], covered with wounds, in his enemy's shadow was slain.

After this appear countless men who, that they might fall to earth with a heavier crash, with this goddess have climbed to excessive heights.

Among these, captive, dead, mangled, lie Cyrus and Pompey, though Fortune carried both of them up to the heavens.

Have you ever seen anywhere how a raging eagle moves, driven by hunger and fasting?

And how he carries a tortoise on high, that the force of its fall may break it, and he can feed on the dead flesh?

So Fortune not that a man may remain on high carries him up, but that as he plunges down she may delight, and he as he falls may weep.

As we look at those who come next, we see how from the humblest rank men rise to high position and how uncertain life is.

There we see how she afflicts both Tullius and Marius, and the splendid horns of their fame many times now she exalts, now she cuts off.

We see at last that in days gone by few have been successful, and they have died before their wheel reversed itself or in turning carried them down to the bottom.[37]

The fundamental problem which Fortune, as she affects individuals, poses concerns why one might flourish today and fail tomorrow, why moral virtues make no difference in attaining political successes and failures, and why many judge political actions by their outcome, not by their means.[38] Machiavelli's answers to these problems are based on such issues as the quality of the times, the humour and the temperament of the actor, and the consequences these have for free will and the fixity of particular human nature. The astrological character of this approach can hardly be missed. If anyone fails to see it, the references to the well-known astrological aphorism, 'the wise man will overcome the stars', will help open his/her eyes.

We come across three references to it: the first, in the Machiavelli-Vespucci correspondence, the second in the 'Ghiribizzi', and the third in *The Prince*.

The Machiavelli-Vespucci correspondence suggests that Machiavelli's interest in the natural science of astrology goes as far back as 1504. Unfortunately his letter to Vespucci is lost, but we have Vespucci's response to Machiavelli's letter. That letter reveals the kind of issues that Machiavelli is concerned with at this time. Vespucci writes:

> It is better to pass over the praises of astronomy and how it affords usefulness to mankind with a dry foot than to plunge into a deep whirlpool. It is enough that your view should be accepted as very true, since all the ancients with a single voice say that the wise man himself is not able to change the influences of the stars, since in eternal things no change can occur. But in respect to the wise man, this is understood by his changing and varying his course again and again.[39]

Two years later, writing the famous 'Ghiribizzi' to his friend Giovan Baptista Soderini, Machiavelli seems to have changed his opinion on 'the wise man solution' to the problem of the Fortune of individuals. If such a wise man, who understands the times and who can adapt himself to them, could be found, he would always be successful and be able to protect himself from failures. If such a man could be found 'it would come to be true that the wise man would master the stars and the fates.' But because such a man could not be found, because men are in the first place shortsighted, and in the second place unable to master their own nature, Fortune will always master them.[40] *The Prince* 25 confirms the above: 'Nor is a man to be found so prudent that he knows how to accommodate himself to this, both because he cannot deviate from that to which his nature disposes him, and also because always having prospered while walking in one road, he cannot be persuaded to depart from it.'[41]

Although it may appear that Machiavelli has abandoned the classical astrological solution, the appearance here is quite misleading: far from abandoning the astrological mode of understanding, he is adapting it in his own way. The wise man solution was the conscience-saver of classical astrology. With prognostication based on correct knowledge of the motions of the stars, one could take preventive measures, and thereby beat astral determinism, or at least escape its most dangerous effects. But Machiavelli, as we saw above, will have none of it. His own original solution is first formulated in the 'Ghiribizzi' and later refined in *The Prince*. According to the 'Ghiribizzi', humans act according to their individual imagination (*fantasia*) and individual natural talent (*ingegno*). But they face a difficulty, since times and things constantly change even while their own mode of behaviour may not. The key to success is to maintain a harmony between the quality of one's time, the quality of 'general' time, one's temperament and humour, and one's actions. No amount of prognostications and predictions by themselves can bring this harmony about. In fact no human ingenuity can bring it about. For it can only be brought about by Fortune.

Machiavelli insists that his conclusion regarding the conditions of success is not a speculative one. Rather he claims that it is empirically founded in the study of 'the actions of men and their modes of acting'.[42] These men include Julius II, Hannibal, Scipio, Lorenzo de Medici, Giovanni Bentivoglio, Paolo Vitelli, Francesco Sforza, and 'many others'. As he states, 'to verify this opinion, I think these instances on which I have based it, are enough . . .'[43]

The explanation in *The Prince* 25 constitutes Machiavelli's final statement on the subject. Here, in addition to the points he raises in the 'Ghiribizzi', he makes explicit the importance of humour and temperament: in the pursuit of glory and riches (the two universal categories under which all human strivings can be summed up), humans act according to their humour and their temperament: one with caution, another with impetuosity; one with violence, another with art; one with patience, another with its contrary; and each attains his/her end with these diverse modes of acting. Empirically, one sees that persons with the same temperament do not always achieve the same result. For example, of two cautious persons one succeeds while the other fails. On the other hand, two persons with different temperaments may be equally successful. These phenomena reflect the rule that 'the quality of the times' must harmonize with both actions and temperament if an action is to be successful. This rule explains the 'variability of good', that is, why a person who is successful at one point in time can at another point in time fail. If one conducts oneself with caution and patience, and the times and affairs turn in such a way that one's conduct is good, one comes out successful. If, however, when times and things change one does not change one's mode of acting one is ruined. Thus, a cautious person, when required by the quality of the times or by the situation to act impetuously (i.e. contrary to his/her natural humour and temperament), would not know how to act properly. The result is that he/she comes to ruin.[44]

What remains to be stressed is that this famous analysis of the causes of success and failure is inspired by the principles of astrological natural philosophy. For it was such a natural philosophy that spoke of the quality of the times, and especially of the quality of one's own individual time, i.e. astrological time. As Franz Cumont remarks, astrology considered each moment of time as having 'a definite influence, as being endowed with magic potency'; and it codified time 'by placing each division of time under the protection of a star in its system of "chronocratories"'.[45] It was also as- trology which raised time to the status of a 'Supreme Cause'.[46] One can certainly hear an echo of this in *Discourses* I. 3: 'Time, they say, is the father of every truth.'[47] And in *The Prince* Machiavelli writes that 'Time drives all things forward and brings with it good as well as bad, bad as well as good.'[48] 'Times are superior to brains,' he once reported approvingly as having been the opinion of Ferdinand of Aragon; the moral is that one should judge things day to day, hour by hour. The same report mentions why Alviano, a much dreaded Spanish general, succeeded in Italy: 'the times favoured his nature.'[49]

Whereas in the 'Ghiribizzi' Machiavelli uses many cases to verify his hypothesis, in *The Prince* 25 he uses only one, that of Julius II. Julius acted 'impetuously' (i.e. according to his humour and temperament) in all he did. Fortunately, however, he found 'the time' and the 'things' comfortable to his 'way of acting', and this is why he was always successful. He accomplished with his 'impetuosity' what other popes with 'all their prudence' would never have accomplished. Machiavelli makes clear that he is not talking about his military campaigns alone, but indeed about 'all' of his actions, and that if he omits his 'other actions', it is simply because the same rule applies to them as well. It is not the case that Julius II enjoyed some miraculous immunity from failure. However, the reason for his unbroken record of success is that death, or, as Machiavelli puts it, 'the brevity of his life', saved him from having to taste the bitterness of defeat. In fact, if times had required cautious behaviour, Julius, with his impetuous temperament, would have been quite unable to cope with them: 'he would never have deviated from his modes of behaviour to which his nature inclined him.'[50]

Of all his characters, Julius II is the one whom Machiavelli studies in some depth; and in his case also, he applies the principles of astrological natural philosophy. *The Prince* 25 brings out four points not mentioned earlier: the importance of his temperament and humour for understanding his behaviour, the priority of temperament and humour over prudence, the importance of the time of his death, and the practical inability of the will to counteract inclinations based on temperament and humour. Each of these issues is discussed in the context of the underlying astrological natural philosophy at work.

Let us take the case of Julius II's temperament and humour first. In *The Prince*, as well as in several other texts, it is referred to as being 'impetuous'. What is being considered in these contexts is his particular humour, although it is not called by its technical name. The technical names for the four humours, as is well known, are choler or yellow bile, blood, phlegm, and black bile. They produce respectively the four temperaments – choleric, sanguine, phlegmatic, and melancholic. Fortunately for us, Machiavelli does call Julius's humour by its technical name: in a 1503 diplomatic dispatch sent from Rome to Florence, he describes Julius's 'nature' as 'honourable and choleric'.[51] Again, in 'Decennale I', it is identified as 'malignant choleric humour'.[52] In 'Decennale II', he calls it 'natural ire'.[53]

The identification of Julius II's humour with its technical name is extremely important for our whole argument here. For it provides us with an important clue for interpreting Fortune as she affects individuals. In *The Prince* 25 Machiavelli mentions impetuosity, violence, caution, patience, etc., as being the characteristics of human beings. Though he does not use the technical terms here, what he really refers to are the various humoral types. Because he identifies impetuosity with choler, we may reasonably conclude that he would have used technical names to describe the other character traits too, had he found the occasion to do so. In any case, there is hardly any doubt that as far as Julius II is concerned, his humour is choleric.

Regarding the priority of humour and temperament over prudence, here we have the first indication from Machiavelli that the 'old' formula for successful human action, viz. prudence, is no longer acceptable to him. According to the 'old' formula, prudence or *phronesis*, is action according to right reason (*recta ratio agibilium*): right reason enables one to make the final judgement on what is to be done, having taken into account circumstances, persons, character, and the times. The 'new' Machiavellian prudence, on the other hand, casts aside right reason; its sovereignty is taken over by temperament based on humour. As he writes in the *Life of Castruccio Castracani*, it is Fortune, not prudence, which makes men great. The reason, he says, is 'because Fortune, wishing to show the world that she – not prudence – makes men great, first shows her force at a time when prudence can have no share in the matter, but rather everything must be recognized as coming from her.'[54] A sharper astrological point can hardly be made. For it is the teaching of astrological natural philosophy that one acquires one's unchangeable temperament at birth, if not at conception. The functioning of the theory of the quality of times requires the prior acceptance of this principle.

It goes without saying that the time of death is also 'controlled' by Fortune. Hence the significance of the mention in *The Prince* 25 of the 'brevity' of Julius II's life. Elsewhere Machiavelli also speaks of the importance of the time of death of two of his famous characters – Alexander VI and Castruccio Castracani. In 'Decennale I', Alexander VI is said to have been killed by heaven, meaning Fortune as symbolizing the power of heaven.[55] In *The Prince* 7, Alexander VI's death or, as he puts it here too, 'the brevity of Alexander's life', is considered to have been the result of an 'extraordinary and extreme malignity of Fortune'.[56] In Castruccio's case, Machiavelli is not satisfied with the simple medical explanation of his death: i.e. that one evening he caught a fatal chill after being exposed to unhealthy winds. He wants to explain Castruccio's death in terms of its fortuitous cause as well. 'Fortune, hostile to his glory, when it was time to give him life, took it from him and broke off those plans that he for a long time before had been intending to put into effect, nor by anything other than death could he have been impeded.'[57] The conclusion that Machiavelli draws from his analysis of Castruccio's life is that Fortune, who is 'the arbiter of all human things' (here he goes beyond the half-and-half formula of *The Prince* 25), did not give Castruccio enough time to be able to overcome her.[58] The implication here is that one can overcome Fortune only with Fortune's help.

Finally, we must consider the question of the inability to overcome the inclinations of one's temperament. Humour and temperament are the basic constitutive elements of what Machiavelli calls our particular human nature or *natura*. Endowed with such a nature, humans conduct themselves, not according to prudence, but according to their imagination (*fantasia*).[59] The notion of humans as essentially rational and that of humours, temperament, and appetites as being subordinate to reason, finds no support from Machiavelli. That is why he can say with impunity that one cannot go against one's inclinations. He is so committed to this idea that in one chapter alone, *Discourses* III. 9, he repeats it as many as five times. It is stated, first, as a general rule: 'you always act as nature forces you.' Secondly, it is reiterated in connection with his brief analysis of the Fortunes of Fabius Maximus Cunctator. Fabius succeeded against Hannibal because of his 'cautious' temperament, and because his times and Rome's times harmonized. Had he been called to face a situation which required a different temperament, he would have been unable to cope with it; he would still be fighting Hannibal! To make his point absolutely clear, Machiavelli goes out of his way to remark that 'Fabius acted through nature and not through free choice (*elezione*).' He comes back again to the same principle in his brief analysis of the Fortune of Scipio. His temperament was impetuous, and because of this he was able to take the daring step of taking the war to Carthage, which enabled him to win it.[60] The fourth time he invokes the principle is in relation to Julius II: 'of necessity he would have fallen, because he would not have changed either his mode or his order of behaviour.' Finally, the principle is restated in the conclusion of the entire discussion: 'we cannot oppose that to which nature inclines us.'[61]

Indeed, the same principle is invoked again in the analysis of Castruccio's character: he finally chose a military career, we are told, 'by nature more than anything else'.[62] Remirro de Orco, the cruel deputy of Cesare Borgia, who had the misfortune of being cut into two pieces by his master, is called cruel, because of his 'bitter nature'.[63] The reason why Machiavelli himself became a writer on politics, he says in one of his letters, is owed to Fortune. 'Fortune has determined it, that since I do not know how to reason about the silk business or the wool business or about profits and losses, I must reason about the business of politics.'[64] There is something in his particular nature that necessarily disposed him to be a writer on politics, and this is because Fortune had made his nature to be such. The point seems unstated – Fortune distributes humours. A modern reader unaccustomed to the astrological mode of thought of the Renaissance may be inclined to dismiss a statement such as this as nothing more than a manner of speaking, having no theoretical significance, somewhat like someone saying today, 'luckily I am a historian, not a banker.' But the intellectual context from which Machiavelli speaks here does connect this particular statement to a theory of human nature.[65] Pico had severely criticized this tendency in Machiavelli's

Florence to connect humours with professional aptitudes. The astrologers claim, he wrote, that some are born for philosophy, others for poetry, still others for public life or a military career. They believe that this is so because of 'the motions of the stars' (*a stellarum motibus fieri*).[66]

Given Machiavelli's repeated assertion that *elezione* or freedom of choice is inefficacious against the inclinations of particular human nature, how seriously are we to take his support for *libero arbitrio* (which is but another name for *elezione*)? Freedom of choice, being freedom of indifference, means nothing if it is obliged to choose that which particular human nature already predetermines. Yet, as every student of Machiavelli knows, in two well-known passages, he declares his intention to defend *libero arbitrio*. The first is in *The Prince* 25, where he says that lest we sacrifice freedom of choice, we should hold that Fortune controls only half our actions, while the other half, or almost that, is left for us to govern: 'in order not to annul our freedom of choice I judge it true that Fortune may be the arbiter of one half our actions but also that she leaves the other half, or almost, for us to govern.'[67]

This can hardly be seen as a ringing endorsement of the idea of freedom of choice. For one thing, according to this formula, we are not one hundred per cent in charge of our actions – we are not fully autonomous. Half our actions is directly under the control of Fortune, and the other half, or almost that (even that portion which is said to be under our direct control), is still indirectly under her control. This is so because it is she who decides that things be this way. The image of Fortune that underlies this conception is that of the goddess to whom one must submit, and not that of the woman against whom one must struggle.

How, then, are we to understand this formula? Why the qualification of 'almost half' even in the area of autonomy allotted to us? A quantitative division of our action seems to make no sense. How can two causal agents produce the same effect on a half-and-half basis? Machiavelli does not explain. From what he has told us elsewhere, however, we can infer that it is Fortune who endows us with our particular nature, its humours, its temperament, and the quality of the times in which it acts. Do these, then, constitute the first half of our action that is not directly under our control? And can the other half be the ability to take decisions to act within the limits of our particular humour and temperament? If this be the case (what other option is there, given what Machiavelli has told us about particular human nature?), freedom of choice in the traditional sense is not actually being defended here. What is defended, however, is the 'freedom' to act according to one's temperament and fantasy. Freedom of choice, according to Machiavelli, then, does not include the freedom of indifference. We act according as our humour and temperament prompt us to act. There is no room here for the exercise of *phronesis* and for bringing our actions in line with the dictates of moral insights or 'right rule' (*recta ratio*).

Machiavelli's second statement on freedom of choice is found in *The Prince* 26. The position he takes here is in sharp contrast to that taken in the first statement discussed above. It is the orthodox Christian position, according to which Providence and freedom of choice are seen as being compatible. God and the human agent act as co–causes producing the same effect, and God's foreknowledge does not impair our freedom of choice.[68] Our actions are properly our own and the praise we receive for virtue would be meaningless unless freedom of choice was presupposed. Of course Machiavelli does not explain how this happens to be the case. He simply asserts that 'God does not do everything, so as not to take freedom of choice from us and that part of glory which belongs to us.'[69]

What are we to make of Machiavelli's apparent espousal of the orthodox Christian position here? Does it mean that he is abandoning the position he has taken in the first statement? I do not think so. He uses the orthodox Christian position for rhetorical effect rather than for theoretical reasons. He wants Lorenzo de Medici to act and he uses all the means at his disposal to persuade him to act. Insofar as this is true, his rhetorical use of the orthodox Christian position on Providence in no way modified his theoretical position on Fortune and free will.

Given the foregoing considerations of Machiavelli's position on freedom of choice, one does not see how one can count him among the defenders of the notion of freedom of choice. How could freedom of choice for Machiavelli be a sign of human autonomy, if, as he claims, humans cannot deviate from that to which their temperament inclines them? How could they act ethically if they cannot transcend the limitations imposed by their humours? How could they escape being a plaything of cosmic forces if they receive their humours, temperaments, and the quality of the times of their actions from Fortune? His analysis of the success or failure, as the case may be, of Julius II, Cesare Borgia, and Fabius Maximus is based not on their ability to exercise freedom of choice, but on their time and temperament.[70]

Fortune as a Woman

The use of the metaphor of woman marks the high point of Machiavelli's treatment of Fortune as she affects individuals. The immediate context of the use of this metaphor makes it clear which temperament is best suited for dealing with Fortune. The impetuous (i.e. the choleric) temperament is the preferred one. 'I judge this indeed, that it is better to be impetuous than cautious, because Fortune is a woman; and it is necessary, if one wants to hold her down, to beat her and strike her down, and one sees that she lets herself be won more by the impetuous than by those who proceed coldly. And so always, like a woman, she is the friend of the young, because they are less cautious, more ferocious, and command her with more audacity.'[71]

This is perhaps the most famous metaphor that we find in Machiavelli's writings, and it has given rise to many different interpretations. Whatever interpretation one prefers, it is important to adhere to the basic issues which it raises. The first is that it may be applied only to Fortune as she affects individuals, not to Fortune as she affects countries. One remedies the misfortunes of countries, as we have seen already, by building 'dams and dykes', or strong military power. The metaphor of a struggle against woman has no application in international politics. Secondly, what is crucial for success in the struggle of individuals against Fortune is having the right temperament, which takes the whole issue to its astrological cosmology and anthropology. Thirdly, though the advantage of the choleric humour and youth are crucial for success, they are not by themselves decisive, because it is ultimately the woman who lets the youth succeed. In other words, human success depends on human initiatives as well as on Fortune's favour. The youth 'pounds and beats' her, but significantly it is she who allows him to do so. Had she withdrawn her 'consent' the youth would be unable to hold her down. In other words, in an ultimate sense, humans are seen as being the plaything of Fortune, even if they may not be aware of it. Even Julius II, a man of intense activity, and the most successful of Machiavellian characters, depended on Fortune's favour. Hence neither the metaphor nor the thought behind it can justify the notion that 'Fortuna can be vanquished by the right kind of man.'[72]

What Machiavelli is concerned with here is to give an activist rather than a passivist interpretation of human action. Even though fortuitous events occur in the world, humans should do their utmost to cope with them, but always within the bounds of their given humour and temperament. In fact, this is all that they can do. From this perspective, human action appears as a struggle in which success does not depend entirely on human causation. It is a struggle because, in Machiavelli's view, there is no perfect congruence between the faculties of human nature and the ends which humans propose to themselves: 'nature [i.e. one's particular nature] has made man able to crave everything but unable to attain everything.'[73] Again, 'human appetites are insatiable, since man has from nature [i.e. from one's particular nature] the power and the wish to desire everything and from Fortune the power to attain but little; the result is bad discontent and weariness with what is attained.'[74] Given this anthropology, those alone succeed whose efforts take place under conditions of time and temperament set by Fortune.

The motions moving the Machiavellian universe do not emanate from Mind, Reason, or Love. They are natural motions emanating from the heavenly bodies which allegedly have varying qualities as they affect different human beings. Indeed, they are not particularly friendly to humans. Humans have no privileged position in the universe. They are natural creatures, endowed with particular temperament and capable of forming fantasies. The general conclusion which Machiavelli reaches is that humans should be active rather than passive. This is not to say that success is guaranteed.

Freedom of choice is at best freedom to act within one's humoral structure; at worst it is an illusion. Every human achievement is a joint product of human causation and Fortune's causation, of *virtù* and Fortune. Not even Moses is exempted from this rule. For he needed the indispensable *occasione* which Fortune alone gives. Numa, too, owed his success to Fortune and the times.[75] Even Machiavelli's own success, he feels, depends on Fortune's favour.[76] In sum, in the Machiavellian cosmos the stable, uniform events are thought to be caused by heaven, while the fortuitous events are thought to be caused by Fortune. Human action is circumscribed by both heaven and Fortune, but in different ways. They remain factors which political philosophy must take into account.

Some Interpretative Issues

In recent critical literature the Machiavellian notion of Fortune has received its most serious consideration from Leo Strauss and Hanna Pitkin. Strauss's interpretation is guided, I think, by his overwhelming concern to present Machiavelli as the founder of modern political philosophy. He can be presented in this garb, I believe, only if it can be shown that he did not really believe in the pre-modern things he says about the subject. If he says such things about Fortune, it is, according to Strauss, partly for the benefit of the vulgar and partly to go from the concept of nature to that of Fortune. Under no circumstances does Machiavelli endorse a pre-modern view of Fortune. In other words, according to Strauss, Machiavelli's discussion of Fortune is really not a discussion of Fortune at all – it is really a discussion of *accidents* occurring in life. By reducing the discussion of Fortune to a discussion of *accidents*, Strauss is able to dispose of all the inconvenient pre-modern things that Machiavelli says about Fortune. There is a 'movement' of thought in Machiavelli, he says, from God to Fortune, and from Fortune to accidents: 'We conclude that the movement of fundamental thought which finds expression in both books [*The Prince* and the *Discourses*] consists in a movement from God to Fortuna and then from Fortuna via accidents, and accidents occurring to bodies or accidents of bodies, to chance understood as a non-teleological necessity which leaves room for choice and prudence and therefore chance understood as the cause of simply unforeseeable accidents.'[77]

Strauss is quite right in saying that there is a movement in Machiavelli's thought from God to Fortune. But there is no movement from heaven to Fortune. For his theory needs both heaven and Fortune: the heaven to explain why there are stable and uniform laws operating in the universe and why there is astral determinism in it; and Fortune to explain why fortuitous events occur in a cosmos so ordered and so determined. Chance and regularity are both present in the Machiavellian cosmos. Not everything that occurs in it occurs because of chance or *caso*. Strauss makes the Machiavellian notion of chance look like the only causal 'agent' operating in his (Machiavelli's) universe, and he makes it look like an immanent cause at that.

Hanna Pitkin's highly original and rewarding interpretation of Machiavelli's notion of Fortune involves an exploration of the symbolic meaning of the notion. Pitkin's emphasis, therefore, is on human autonomy and manliness, and how these may be secured, supposing that the world is 'mostly run by a large senior, female person, who holds men in her power to a greater or lesser extent, depending on their conduct and specifically on their manliness.'[78] The emphasis in question is justified, as far as it goes. Machiavelli's greater emphasis, however, is on humours, temperament, the quality of the times, and the harmonization of these, not on the sexual maturity or immaturity of the human agent concerned. Machiavelli's emphasis may be a regrettable 'defect' of his pre-modern thought, but that is the way Machiavelli analyses successes and failures. At the same time, the astrological context of Machiavelli's analysis of Fortune is lightly dismissed: it is said that 'there are only one or two passages that support' the case for that context.[79] The same is true of Pitkin's treatment of Fortune as she affects countries ('general' Fortune) and Fortune as she affects individuals ('particular' Fortune).[80] Finally, it is assumed by Pitkin that the woman-metaphor is the pre-eminent metaphor for understanding Machiavelli's 'real' view of the subject of Fortune: 'Which is Machiavelli's real view: the river or the woman?' she asks.[81] Her answer, the latter. But if our distinction between Fortune as she affects countries and Fortune as she affects individuals is correct, then the 'real' view of Machiavelli can be ascertained only if we keep both metaphors before our eyes. The river-metaphor is as important as the woman-metaphor, since they refer to two quite distinct realities.[82]

CHAPTER 5

Virtù

In the preceding chapters we discussed Machiavelli's ideas concerning the causality exercised by heaven and Fortune in history, politics and religion. We shall now turn our attention to an examination of his views concerning human causality in politics. The word which he chooses to describe it is none other than *virtù*. Interestingly enough, he uses the same word in a number of different senses. For example, the quality of an inanimate object such as a bow or a weapon is called its *virtù*. In *The Prince* 6 he speaks of the *virtù* of a new prince and the *virtù* of a bow in the same paragraph.[1] In *Discourses* II. 2, he speaks of the *virtù* of a tyrant and the *virtù* of arms in the same sentence.[2] In *Discourses* I. 56 he speaks of the 'natural *virtù*' of airy intelligences. In *Discourses* I. 58, the voice of the people is referred to as their 'occult *virtù*'.[3] In the poem 'On Fortune', the power of the heavens is described as its 'occult *virtù*'.[4] There is *virtù* of the body just as there is *virtù* of the spirit; there is *virtù* of specific individuals as there is *virtù* of groups – generals, armies, people, citizens, republics.

It is important to be aware of the polyvalent character of this term in Machiavelli's thought. Such awareness, if nothing else, should at least remind us that *virtù* has no affinity with moral virtue. The predominant sense in which *virtù* is used in his writings, however, and for which the term has acquired its importance concerns the area of human causation. Provisionally, then, we may describe *virtù* as the stable disposition or ability of an individual or group by which he, she, or it is enabled to perform acts conducive to the good of the state. It may be possessed by exceptional individuals such as founders or innovators of states – Moses, Romulus, Cesare Borgia – or it may be possessed by ordinary citizens such as those of the ancient Roman Republic or the modern Swiss cantons. It may be the ability of great generals such as Hannibal, Scipio, Julius Caesar, or of saintly kings such as David, but it could just as easily be possessed by vicious tyrants such as Agathocles of Syracuse. In its rarer form, it is the ability which enables a private person to become most public of all persons – the founder or the innovator of a state. While it is compatible with the aggressive behaviour of statesmen towards other states, it is also compatible with their lawful and constitutional behaviour towards their own citizens. Thus the connection between *virtù* and the public good is one of its important aspects. This makes 'ambition' the most vicious of public vices. Ambition, whether found in a faction or in an individual, whether motivated by desire for power or by greed, destroys the virtuous quality of the public good. Yet at the same time, *virtù* is said to be compatible with cruelty, especially when it is 'well used'. A Machiavellian founder could be inhumane yet still be virtuous. Above all, *virtù* when applied to a state is contrasted with its corruption.

Anthropology of Virtù

Part of the peculiarity of Machiavellian *virtù* is due to Machiavelli's cosmological postulates and to the anthropology derived from them. Only when we have situated *virtù* in these contexts can we fully appreciate its ethical implications. For the idea of *virtù* presupposes a certain view of human nature. As the 'Exhortation to Penitence' shows, Machiavelli was quite familiar with the view of human nature underlying the traditional notion of virtue. According to that view, humans are 'rational animals' endowed with 'reason and will'. They are composite beings, made up of soul and body. In them, the nutritive, appetitive and rational powers constitute a hierarchical order. Sensation, imagination, practical and theoretical reason form their epistemological structure. The humours and the appetites are distinct from reason, but nevertheless open to rational guidance. The power of making practical prudential judgement, *phronesis*, enables the moral agent to reconcile the requirements of both what is naturally right and what is circumstantially possible. Virtue is an acquired disposition, rooted in rational nature but concerned with the passions and guided by *phronesis*, thanks to which one is able to satisfy one's appetitive needs in moderation, i.e. according to the rule of reason. This humanism, reinforced by Christian faith, is part of Machiavelli's inherited tradition.

But such humanism does not form the foundation of Machiavelli's notion of *virtù*. He prefers the view that humans are part of material nature like other brutes. The notions of what is right and wrong, good and bad, just and unjust, arise in them only as a result of living in society for the purposes of security. There is nothing in human nature which requires humans to live a life of moral rectitude. The only requirement of their nature is that they should live in security for the purpose of satisfying their needs for glory and riches. Thus, while he frequently speaks of the *virtù* of body (*corpo*) and spirit (*animo*), he does not speak of the virtue of the soul (*anima*). The soul is not a presupposition of Machiavelli's political anthropology, except perhaps in a negative sense. The famous letter of 16 April 1527 to Francesco Vettori mentions the soul only to stress the point that the love of the soul occupies a lower position in the order of love: 'I love my fatherland more than my soul.'[5] In the *Florentine Histories* also, a similar idea occurs: he speaks approvingly of those who esteem 'their fatherland more than their souls'.[6] Leo Strauss concludes that Machiavelli's silence on the soul is deliberate; he wants to show that it has no place in his political philosophy.[7]

Although the soul has no place in Machiavelli's political anthropology, the body and what he calls *animo*, humours, *ingegno* and *fantasia* do have a place in it. The concept of *animo* is used extensively by Machiavelli. It means 'spirit', 'intention', or 'purpose'. In contemporary usage, *animo* was distinguished from *anima*. In Ficino's thought, for example, spirit constitutes the middle level of human nature, the higher level being the soul, and the lower level, the humours. Of the three – soul, spirit, humours – only the soul is completely free from astral influences, whereas the spirit and the humours are open to them. Imagination was thought to be the vehicle of the spirit.[8] While the soul was considered to be immortal, i.e. capable of surviving the dissolution of the body, the spirit was considered unable to do so. Insofar as this was held to be true, any anthropology that excluded *anima* was *ipso facto* understood to be materialistic.

We have already referred to Machiavelli's famous statement regarding the natural proneness of human beings to evil. Now, this proneness is said to arise from 'the malignity of their spirit'.[9] Agathocles is said to have possessed great '*virtù* of spirit and body'.[10] Cesare Borgia was a man of 'great spirit'.[11] The spirit is the basis of affection and loyalty: thus Borgia is said 'to empty the spirits' of the people of Romagna of 'the affection' for the Orsini and the Colonna factions in order to transfer it to himself. The notorious execution of his deputy, Remirro de Orco, is carried out in order 'to purge the spirits' of the inhabitants of Romagna and to gain them for himself.[12] Machiavelli despised Giovampagolo Baglioni, the tyrant of Perugia, because he lacked 'the spirit' to commit the perfect crime, namely the assassination of Julius II when he was his guest. He was held back, Machiavelli notes in disgust, not because of any moral scruples or conscience (*o per bontà o per conscienza*) but by a lack of courage of spirit.[13] The notorious fratricide of Romulus is spoken of in terms of his *animo*: he committed the deed not for advancing his private interest but for the sake of the common good (*bene commune*).[14] Emperor Commodus was a man of 'cruel and bestial spirit';[15] Ferdinand of Aragon kept the 'spirits' of his subjects in suspense and wonder by carrying out deeds of pious cruelty.[16] A successful prince should have his 'spirit' so disposed as to change with the winds of fortune, so that he would not depart from good (*bene*) when possible but would enter into evil (*male*) when necessary.[17] Virtuous citizens such as Cincinnatus were able to display their civic virtues – obedience, humility, love of poverty, respect for their elders – because of the 'generosity' and the 'nobility' of their 'spirit'. Fame and reputation did not inflate their 'spirit' nor did the obscurity of private life deflate it.[18]

Animo, then, comes closest to being a faculty that enables humans to perform 'virtuous' actions. It is also clear from the examples mentioned that it is a morally neutral faculty in that it enables one to perform both morally good and morally evil actions.

Machiavelli also speaks of the humour of individuals as being significant for 'virtuous' behaviour. Humour defines one's temperament, which prompts one's spirit to act in the way it does. As we saw in the previous chapter, humour basically constitutes one's particular nature. Thus, one is either choleric or sanguine, melancholic or phlegmatic. Machiavelli accepts this reading of human nature quite readily. In fact, in several instances he considers humour to be the most readily identifiable key to personality. This notion underlies the famous 'orations' in the *Florentine Histories*.[19] In the Dedicatory Letter to this work, he explains how he has adapted these fictional orations to the 'humour' of the speaker.[20] The notion of humour underlies his advice to his friend, Raffaello Girolami, the newly appointed Florentine Ambassador to Spain. One of the qualities of a competent ambassador, Machiavelli writes, is the ability to identify correctly the 'humour' of the statesmen he is dealing with.[21] As we have seen in the previous chapter, humour is the key to understanding particular human nature. It determines temperament, which determines inclinations, which in turn determine behaviour. And freedom of choice, according to this reading of human nature, is not able to counteract the demands of humour. The traditional notion of *virtù* was based on the precept of practical reason, which required that good be done and pursued and evil be avoided. A humour-based theory of virtue, as Machiavelli's *virtù* suggests, on the other hand, does not require any such pursuit of the moral good and avoidance of moral evil. The *summum bonum* that particular human nature pursues, according to Machiavelli, is the love of riches and glory within the bounds of the love of the fatherland.[22] And, as the *Art of War* states, 'the love of the fatherland is caused by nature', i.e. one's particular nature.[23]

Ingegno (natural talent) is another element of Machiavellian anthropology. It is mentioned in the 'Ghiribizzi'. It is said to be 'given' by 'nature' to each individual, and it works in tandem with imagination. 'I believe that as nature has made each man an individual face, so she has made him an individual *ingegno* and an individual *fantasia*. From this results that each man conducts himself according to his *ingegno* and imagination.'[24] Its earliest dictionary meaning, that given by the 1611 *Vocabulario della Crusca*, is 'acuteness in inventing or in imagining things without a master's or a guide's help'.[25] The *Discourses* is said to be the fruit of the author's *ingegno*.[26] The new princes are said to possess '*ingegno* and *virtù*'.[27] In duels and small combats, Italians are said to excel in *ingegno*.[28] Lorenzo di Filippo Strozzi, to whom the *Art of War* is dedicated, has few equals in *ingegno*, and Cosimo Rucellai is said to have possessed great 'dexterity of *ingegno*'.[29] Castruccio Castracani, too, displayed 'prudence and *ingegno*'.[30]

The precise nature of *ingegno* or *ingenium*, i.e. whether it is a spiritual or a bodily power, was a subject of debate in Machiavelli's contemporary intellectual circles. Ficino, for example, contrasts *ingenium* and virtue: whereas '*ingenium*' is a gift of God, virtue is something which one acquires by one's own effort. 'A man should be praised not for natural talent (*ingenium*), but for virtue.'[31] Alberti, on the other hand, points out that astrological natural philosophy considers *ingenium* to be a gift of the planet Mercury.[32] Pico della Mirandola specifically attacks this astrological theory of *ingenium*. 'Neither is *ingenium* from a star, since it is incorporeal; it must therefore be from God.'[33]

The question that arises, from the point of view of our present concern, is, What does Machiavelli think the nature of *ingegno* to be? Is it from God or from nature? Since he explicitly states that it is from nature, the presumption is that he thinks of it as a natural power of the material part of the individual's personality. If this is correct, it would follow that *virtù* based on the Machiavellian conception of *ingegno* need not be bound by any strictly supra-corporeal norms, such as the norms of right reason.

Turning now to Machiavelli's idea of imagination (*fantasia*), we find that it is also founded in one's particular nature. The 'Ghiribizzi' states more than once that each human being is 'governed by his or her *ingegno* and imagination'.[34] Michael Oakeshott strains the meaning of *fantasia* when he says that it is a principle whereby one guides oneself by one's *understanding* of oneself. The word closer to Machiavelli's meaning would be 'imagining', not 'understanding'.[35] Machiavelli also believes that *ingegno* and *fantasia* contribute to the relative inflexibility of our nature. They make it difficult for humans to adapt their behaviour to every change in the quality of the times. 'Thus, because times and affairs in general and individually change often, and men do not change their fantasies and their mode of behaviour, it happens that a man at one time has good fortune and at another time bad.'[36]

It is useful to bear in mind here that at about the same time as Machiavelli was writing these thoughts on *fantasia*, a path-breaking re-evaluation of the phenomenon of *fantasia* itself was also taking place. In 1500, a few years before the 'Ghiribizzi' was written, Gianfrancesco Pico della Mirandola, the nephew of Giovanni Pico, published his major work on imagination.[37] Imagination, it seems, was under siege from new enemies, not the least of whom were the astrological natural philosophers. What Gianfrancesco Pico was doing was offering a defence from the orthodox, i.e. the Aristotelian-Thomistic, side. According to the orthodox view, imagination is not an autonomous faculty, i.e. one which is supposed to act against the ends of reason; it takes the middle position between the world of senses and the world of the intellect. It is 'that motion of the soul which actual sensation generates', but also 'a power of the soul which out of itself produces forms'; it 'fashions all the likeness of things, and transmutes the impression of some powers to other powers', and is 'a faculty of assimilating all other things to itself.'[38] Above all, imagination is meant to serve and minister to 'both the discursive reason and contemplative intellect'.[39] At the same time, it can conceive 'what now is no more, but as well what it suspects or believes yet to be, and even what it presumes cannot be created by Mother Nature.'[40]

Inasmuch as imagination has its roots in the humours, however, its health or its disease varies with the health and diseases of the humours. It is the testimony of 'philosophers and medical men', Gianfrancesco Pico writes, that 'one's imagination is determined by the relative supply of blood, phlegm, red bile, or black bile. Thus, in correspondence with the diversity of humours, one's imagination is stimulated to form diverse images: cheerful, dull, grim, sad.'[41] It is precisely here that a potential threat to the proper functioning of imagination arises. When the act of cognizing is 'influenced by these humours', 'the spiritual eye of the soul, the intellect, changes and is deceived, just as the bodily eye experiences illusions through tinted, part-coloured lenses.'[42] Even worse, the influence of the humours on thought can distort truth. Although to the intellect truth is one, of its own nature, pure, and unmixed, yet 'on account of diverse and contrary phantasms, truth appears manifold, corrupted, and mixed.'[43] In other words, our temperament decisively influences our imagination and, through our imagination, our perception of truths, especially practical truths. 'Thus, various images, and often false ones, arise from the varying disposition of the body, which we obtain from our parents, from our native land, and from our manner of living . . .'[44] These, however, are only the 'proximate' causes of our temperament and our fantasies. The universal cause of these is heaven (caelum). Here, Gianfrancesco Pico explicitly takes issue with astrological natural philosophy, and denies that heaven is a particular cause of the operations of the humours: 'Heaven, however, is a universal and remote cause, not, as the astrologers say, a particular cause.'[45]

From the point of view of our enquiry here, what is striking is the theory that defects of virtue have their basis in the defects of our fantasies, which in turn have their origin in the state of the humours. Diseased humours are the 'nurseries' from which emerge 'almost all the deceptions of phantasies'.[46] Owing to 'the diverse mixture of humours', one is rendered now gloomy, now happy, now keen, now dull. 'The cause of these phenomena must be referred to temperament, in which, to pass over the first and simple qualities, either blood, or phlegm, or red bile, or black bile, predominates; but the cause can also be credited to the functioning of imagination, as it has its starting point in the things, which we call objects, that are subject to the senses.'[47]

There is a correlation between diseased or uncontrolled imagination and decline of moral virtue. Gianfrancesco Pico goes so far as to say that the errors that occur 'as much in civic life as in the philosophic and Christian life take their beginnings from the defect of imagination. The peace of the

State is disturbed by ambition, cruelty, wrath, avarice, and lust.'[48] A depraved imagination, he says, is 'the mother nurse of ambition', which impels one to outstrip others without regard to virtue and nobility. Cruelty is 'born from and nourished by' the imagination of an 'ostensible but deceptive good' which induces one to insult, wound and murder others. Deceitful imagination is also at the root of lust. As for avarice, which makes one unmindful of justice, it is also stimulated by imagination. Diseased imagination, then, lies at the basis of all social and political vices.

Insofar as Gianfracesco Pico represents the traditional response to the crisis in the theory of imagination, we have little option but to place Machiavelli among the opponents of the traditional, and among the supporters of the new view. Machiavelli's anthropology does not have room for reason, intellect, or grace; it is confined to *animo*, *ingegno* and imagination – all of which, according to his non-orthodox view, are subject to the influences of the heavens. Imagination for him is free of intellectual guidance. And insofar as this is the case, Machiavellian *virtù* is deprived of the benefits of rational insights that come from 'right reason' (*recta ratio*, *orthos logos*).

The Cosmological Context of Virtù

Although *virtù* operates according to *animo*, the humours, *ingegno*, and *fantasia*, its effectiveness, according to Machiavelli's thought, depends on certain cosmological factors. The most well-known of these, as we have already seen, is the quality of the times. The need to conform modes of behaviour to the quality of times is a basic presupposition of both *The Prince* and the *Discourses*. Thus the secret of Julius II's successes is that his behaviour was in accord with the quality of his times. The same is true of the successes of Fabius Maximus and Scipio. Manlius Capitolinus, Sulla, and Marius could not have done what they did, unless the times were favourable to their *nature*.[49] Now, as we have mentioned several times before, the notion that time has quality is an astrological notion, and Machiavelli seems to have adopted it as one of his working hypotheses.

One of Machiavelli's well-known ideas, 'opportunity' (*occasione*), is also connected to the idea of time. Indeed, the efficacy of *virtù* depends on both the recognition and the utilization of the opportunity at hand. One of the reasons why he insists that Cesare Borgia and Alexander VI were great men is that they were men skilled in recognizing their *occasione*.[50] *Virtù* can best succeed if heaven also cooperates: and heaven cannot give a better opportunity for '*virtù* and glory' than to give a new prince a city already in a state of corruption.[51] There is also a presumption in Machiavelli's thought that actions should be undertaken simply because the time for their undertaking is sanctioned by heaven. This is how, in *Mandragola*, Lucrezia justifies her illicit liaison with Callimaco: 'So I am forced to judge that it comes from heaven's wish that has ordered it so, and I am not strong enough to refuse what heaven wills me to accept.'[52] In one of his Letters, Machiavelli counsels his friend Francesco Vettori to take his cue from the conditions of the times: 'do not be frightened, show your face to Fortune, and continue to do what the revolutions of the heavens, the conditions of the times and of men bring before you.'[53] A few weeks later he follows this up with the advice: 'I beg you to follow your star, and not to let an iota go for the things of the world, because I believe, have believed, and will always believe that it is true, as Boccaccio said, that it is better to act and repent than not act and repent.'[54] Again, reflecting on their amorous escapades, he writes: 'And this way of proceeding, if to some it may appear censurable, to me seems praiseworthy, because we are imitating nature, who is variable; and he who imitates her cannot be rebuked.'[55]

Perhaps nothing illustrates Machiavelli's idea of the connection between *virtù* and cosmic forces better than his 'Capitolo Patorale', dedicated to Lorenzo de Medici. Lorenzo possesses many virtues because 'heaven was striving to show its *virtù*' when it gave the world a man of Lorenzo's nature. Jupiter gave him his *allegro* temperament, Venus endowed him with many graces, Mars gave him a heart worthy of Caesar, Mercury implanted in him seeds of astuteness, Juno gave him a spirit capable of ruling an empire, and Saturn the basis for a long life.[56] Even allowing for poetic licence, one is still struck by Machiavelli's tendency to assimilate human *virtù* with planetary *virtù*. Had we not understood Machiavelli's naturalism, we would have been tempted to consider these comparisons in terms of poetic fancy and nothing more. Certainly, it is part of his poetic fancy, but it is also something more. For it arises from a *forma mentis* that is alive to the cosmic dimension of *virtù*.

The Ethics of Virtù: Some Interpretative Issues

The ethics of Machiavellian *virtù* has been the subject of endless debate. Jacques Maritain, in one of the most penetrating essays on the subject, accuses Machiavelli of snapping the connection between political ethics and morality, metaphysics and theology, and of mutilating 'the human practical intellect and the organism of practical wisdom'.[57] Given Machiavelli's anthropology, it is easy to agree with this assessment. For Machiavelli endorses as 'normal' the fact of political immorality. According to this endorsement, politicians, when they resort to injustice in establishing order and when they employ 'useful evil' in pursuing their will to power, may proceed with a clear conscience, as though they were discharging a 'duty'. As Maritain writes, 'A plain disregard of good and evil has been considered the rule of human politics.'[58] In the Machiavellian ethics, everything is permitted as long as it serves the power interests of the fatherland. Before Machiavelli, says Maritain, rulers did not hesitate to apply bad faith, perfidy, falsehood, assassination, and the like to the attainment of their ambitions. But in doing so, the presumption was that they felt guilty, or that they ought to feel guilty. After Machiavelli, however, no crime done in the name of the fatherland is admitted to be evil before it is committed, although after it is committed humankind may pronounce judgement on it on the basis of some standards of positive justice. Political crime may be judged as having been a mistake, but no longer as a moral evil. Criminals such as Agathocles, Baglioni, and Cesare Borgia may be unworthy of glory, cowardly, or unlucky by Machiavellian standards, but there is no hint in his judgement that they deserve blame because they did something morally culpable. The worst that can happen to a Machiavellian character is that he or she is unlucky or that he or she is a failure; he or she is immune to a sense of moral tragedy, the sense that an avoidable immoral deed, recognized as such, has been committed.

Then there is the famous thesis of Benedetto Croce in which he argues that Machiavelli's originality lies in his discovery of the autonomy of politics from ethics. 'It is a commonplace that Machiavelli discovered the necessity and the autonomy of politics, which is beyond moral good and evil . . . and has its own laws against which it is vain to rebel, nor can politics itself be exorcized or chased out of the world with holy water.'[59] Croce conceives of the practical as being independent of any moral direction. In this sense, the 'law' of politics has to follow its course, independently of what other laws, pertaining to other spheres of life, might have to say. Machiavelli rather relies instead on the image of the Centaur (an invention of the poets) to convey his understanding of the prince as part man and part beast of prey, 'and it is to the animal element that he ascribes the force of mind'.[60]

Sir Isaiah Berlin questions Croce on this point. Berlin argues that Machiavelli, far from separating politics from morality, introduces a morality of his own. This is to imply that *virtù* entails ethical qualities, if by ethics is meant acting according to some ultimate principle, or in view of some ultimate end. 'For Machiavelli,' writes Berlin, 'the ends which he advocates are those to which he thinks wise human beings who understand reality will dedicate their lives. Ultimate ends in this sense, whether or not they are those of the Judeo-Christian tradition, are what is usually meant by moral values.'[61] Machiavelli prefers as his ultimate end what Berlin calls a 'pagan' ideal of politics, according to which the common good of the fatherland is superior to the good of the individual. 'Since men are beings made by nature to live in communities, their communal purposes are the ultimate values from which the rest are derived or with which their ends as individuals are identified.'[62] According to Berlin, Machiavelli opposes public morality to private morality so radically that there can be no reconciliation between the two. Thus, the analogy between a state and an individual is a fallacy: 'The state and people are governed in a different way from an individual.' 'It is not the well-being of individuals that makes cities great, but of the community.'[63] 'There is more than one world, more than one set of virtues: confusion between them is disastrous.'[64] This, in Berlin's, view, sums up Machiavelli's position on ethics and virtue.

Even though Berlin's aim in his essay is to refute Croce, he actually goes far beyond that purpose. As one reads the essay, it becomes clear that his criticism of Croce is based as much on Machiavellian texts as on the modern liberal notion of the equivalency of all moral ultimates. Morality, it is implied, is a matter of emotional preference, lacking a rational foundation. There is no rational ground for choosing one moral ultimate from another. Rationality can be applied only to means, and not to ends: these by implication, are a matter of preference, taste, or prejudice. Berlin writes: 'if rationality and calculation can be applied only to means or subordinate ends, but never to ultimate ends, then a picture emerges different from that constructed around the ancient principle that there is only one good for men.'[65] The notion that a moral end can be considered valid simply because someone can be found who would make them his or her ultimate value, is an irrational notion. Berlin concludes that Machiavelli, 'despite himself', unintentionally paves the way for modern pluralism in morals and in conceptions of virtue. For although Machiavelli does not explicitly affirm pluralism, after Machiavelli 'doubt is liable to infect all monistic constructions'.[66] The originality of Machiavelli lies, therefore, in his rejection of the Judeo–Christian ethic as the only ethic suited for social and political life. He isolates politics as a field of study, from the theological world picture in terms of which this topic was discussed both before and after him.[67]

Machiavelli may well have eliminated the theological world picture. But what good is it if he replaces it with an astrological world picture? What has he gained by replacing the natural law theory with the astrological theory of the coordinated operations of 'the heaven, the sun, the elements and man'? Berlin does not address these questions. Furthermore, the liberalism that Berlin traces to Machiavelli is hardly to be found in Machiavelli himself. And as for the equivalency of moral ultimates, it is hardly the case that Machiavelli thinks that an astrological world picture is morally equivalent to the theological world picture or the natural law world picture.

Friedrich Meinecke, in his turn, tries to distinguish and combine naturalism and ethical quality in *virtù*. 'Machiavelli concentrated all his real and supreme values in what he called *virtù*', writes Meinecke.[68] It was originally something 'natural and dynamic', something which 'Nature had implanted in Man', an unregulated natural force indifferent to good and evil. But when transformed by political purpose and direction, it can become what Machiavelli calls *ordinata virtù*, a code for both rulers and citizens. It then becomes both a quality that sets apart political leaders, and a characteristic that identifies the good citizens. When transformed in this way, *virtù* preserves and expands states, and in this capacity it uses even religion and morality instrumentally – for the ends of the state.

Finally, Leo Strauss, in what is perhaps one of the most searching critiques of Machiavelli, rightly points out that Machiavelli's teaching is normative and ethical. For his ultimate aim is to replace the classical and Christian ideas of political virtue with those of his own. 'Machiavelli does not oppose to the normative political philosophy of the classics a merely descriptive or analytical political science; he rather opposes to a wrong normative teaching a true normative teaching.'[69] Machiavelli's new and 'true' teaching is that moral virtue has no place in politics except as the instrument of those who seek political power. That is to say, his analysis of virtue is wholly destructive of moral virtue. Strauss writes: 'Moral virtue, wished for by society and required by it, is dependent on society and therefore subject to the primary needs of society. It does not consist in the proper order of the soul. It has no other source than the needs of society; it has no second and higher source in the needs of the mind.'[70] The highest need of society is patriotism, love of the fatherland. The state, whether monarchical or republican, is for him essentially a fatherland. Love of the fatherland defines the limits of our love as political animals. And our love as political animals cannot and does not embrace humanity or the community of fatherlands.[71] As we pointed out in the Introduction, Strauss quite rightly recognized that a cosmology underlies Machiavelli's ethics. The furthest that Strauss would go in this respect, however, was to say that that cosmology was not teleological. If our analysis so far has been valid, on the other hand, we are now in a position to identify that cosmology as being the astrological cosmology widely accepted in Florence in the time of the Renaissance.

At the basis of Machiavelli's ethics, then, lies his astrological world picture. According to that picture, the cosmos is a system of motion which does not originate in the Mind or in the Good. Instead, the motions of the heaven and the planets provide for a fatherland, and our individual temperament or our particular nature generates the necessary love for it. Furthermore, the emphasis in astrological thought is on particular empires, states and regions, not on humanity as a whole. Our love therefore never embraces humanity itself. And the fortunes of states follow the quality of their times. This is the basis of his doctrine of the natural migration of *virtù* from fatherland to fatherland, depending upon the favour of the heavens.

According to such a world picture, then, Machiavelli absolutizes the good of the fatherland in such a way that no ethic embracing all fatherlands is possible. The common good symbolized by the fatherland is a good that does not take into account the claims of natural justice. For while the republican love of self-rule and liberty fosters friendship among citizens, that same love can become a *libido dominandi* as far as non-citizens and aliens are concerned. The good of the fatherland is to be attained at all costs; even the good of the soul may be sacrificed for the sake of fatherland. There is no admission that the interests of the fatherland must be secured within a framework of natural justice which has its source in the nature of the collective human good. In other words, the *virtù* required for attaining liberty, prosperity, empire, and glory is incompatible with moral virtue. Glory and riches are the ultimate ends of individuals; they are also the ultimate ends of fatherlands. Moral virtues have no independent status. They may be tolerated so long as they contribute to empire, glory and prosperity, or they may be sacrificed if they stand in the way.

> One's fatherland is properly defended in whatever way she is defended, whether with disgrace or with glory . . . This idea deserves to be noted and acted upon by any citizen who has occasion to advise his fatherland, because when it is absolutely a question of the safety of one's fatherland, there must be no consideration of just or unjust, of merciful or cruel, of praiseworthy or disgraceful; instead setting aside every scruple, one must follow to the utmost any plan that will save her life and keep her liberty.[72]

And it is the fatherland itself that reveals what constitutes its good here and now; an appeal to a higher court, therefore, is not needed. The distinction between a good citizen and a good person, so basic to the classical and Christian political science, has no place in Machiavelli's. The good citizen is *ipso facto* the good person, insofar as he or she is prompted by the love (*carità*) for the fatherland.[73] This was the case of Rome during its virtuous epoch, when 'the love (*amore*) of the fatherland was more powerful than any other consideration.'[74]

For Machiavelli, the positive element in *virtù* is that, through patriotism, it can make good citizens out of bad individuals. For, says Machiavelli, it is true that 'men never do anything good except by necessity' and that where there is excessive freedom everything leads to disorder.[75] In general, humans are 'ungrateful, fickle, pretenders and dissemblers, evaders of danger, eager for gain'.[76] Humans do not know how to set limits to their desires. When they do not fight from necessity, they fight from ambition, the cause of which is that 'nature has created them able to desire everything but unable to attain anything.'[77] And yet patriotism, combined with the discipline of laws and institutions, can make them virtuous. This is the only 'redemption' that Machiavellian *virtù* promises.

One of the major casualties of Machiavellian *virtù* is moderation (the anchor of the alternative classical and Christian notion of virtue), in desires, assertions, and expectations. Lack of virtuous moderation is congruent with an astrological outlook. Machiavelli writes: 'since all human things are in motion, and cannot remain at rest, they must rise or they must fall; to many things to which reason does not bring you, you are brought by necessity.'[78] Given this cosmic and psychological pressure, one is not advised to take a middle course, 'because our nature does not consent to it'.[79] It then becomes part of *virtù* to assert itself excessively. The desire for limitless growth, limitless expansion, and limitless consumption is integral to Machiavellian *virtù*: the only thing that can make up for existential insecurity, both political and economic, is the pursuit of more power and more goods. Hence Machiavelli's paradoxical statement that one can mitigate these limitless desires only by an excessive *virtù*.[80]

J. H. Whitfield makes a spirited defence of Machiavelli on this point, arguing that Machiavelli has a sound understanding of the need for self-knowledge, for measuring one's forces against reality, for restraining one's appetites, and for the wisdom of half-victory.[81] While Whitfield is right on strictly pragmatic grounds, it is doubtful whether his argument is compelling on the basis of Machiavelli's theoretical principles. For as we noticed earlier, according to Machiavelli's theoretical principles, one must act according to one's humour: the question of moderation hardly arises at all as a principle. Julius II and Fabius Maximus succeeded not because they exercised moderation, but because they acted according to their humours, and in times propitious to them. And if some have acquired a temperament and a habit for excessive consumption, excessive desires, and limitless expectations, for Machiavelli this would be understandable. For such is the price they have to pay for being virtuous in the Machiavellian sense of *virtù*.

In order to exercise Machiavellian *virtù*, then, one necessarily acts according to one's humour. And Machiavellian *virtù* produces the external good of the fatherland understood as riches and glory; in other words, *virtù* does nothing to perfect the good internal to the soul. The soul and its needs have no place in Machiavelli's politics. While classical and Christian conceptions of political virtue never radically separated the health of the soul from the health of the state, the private good from the public good, in Machiavelli's notion of the public good, such a separation is mandatory. The common good must always prevail over the good of the individual. Nor is there any need to bring the two realms – the private and the public – into fruitful contact with each other. This is why he asserts that morally virtuous actions and morally reprehensible actions can contribute equally to the public common good. Thus liberality and miserliness, generosity and rapacity, cruelty and mercy, faithfulness and unfaithfulness, chastity and lasciviousness, integrity and deceitfulness, being religious and being irreligious, etc., can be equally effective, depending on how they contribute to the public good. The vices of Hannibal and the virtues of Scipio, in Machiavelli's view, did not make any moral difference as far as their behaviour 'in the public realm' was concerned. Nor did Savonarola's probity do him any good in his hour of need. Romulus's fratricide, on the other hand, did not harm him in any way. The radical separation of politics into public and private realms, without the possibility of any fruitful contact between them, is the dark side of Machiavellian *virtù*.

But even when he opts for the radical separation of the private and the public, Machiavelli still wants those who operate in the public realm to have a reputation for private virtue. Indeed, Machiavellian *virtù* cannot work effectively except in the shadow of such a reputation. For a reputation for private virtue remains important, since humans judge more by appearance than by reality, 'more by their eyes than by their hands'. 'Everyone sees how you appear, few touch what you are, and these few dare not oppose the opinion of many. So let a prince win and maintain his state: the means will always be praised by everyone. For the vulgar are taken in by the appearance and the outcome of a thing, and in the world there is no one but the vulgar . . .'[82] In the final analysis, *virtù* is a disposition to do whatever is necessary for the good of the fatherland. Such a disposition is not compatible with moral virtue. In the classical and the Christian conceptions of virtue, internal integrity and public life are held to be compatible because the life of the soul and the life in the state are thought to be intimately connected to the notion of the good. It is the task of political prudence to safeguard, cultivate, and bring about that good in all that one does.

Machiavellian *virtù* permits the use of any means for the preservation of the state. It is Machiavelli's insight that if states had at their disposal only the principles of moral virtue, they would not be able to meet their security needs. This is the case especially with respect to war. A state that adheres only to moral virtues will be unevenly matched against one that adheres to *virtù*. The ability to meet security needs by means of moral virtue alone, diminishes in proportion to the prevalence of bad states in the world. The consequence, Machiavelli claims, is that good states are obliged to imitate the ways of bad states. This gives rise to the moral dilemma which he considers in *The Prince* 18: 'If all men were good, then this teaching would not be good; but because they are bad and do not keep faith with you, you also do not have to keep faith with them.'[83]

Thus, international politics expose the alleged inadequacy of moral virtues and the need to replace them with Machiavellian *virtù*. Thus Machiavelli draws a connection between the ethics of *virtù* and the politics of 'reason of state', between the view which claims that statesmen can resort to any means in war and the view which says that states have no higher obligation than self-preservation.

Which ethic, then, has the final validity: the ethic of *virtù* or that of moral virtues? On this question, Maritain and Strauss take differing stands. Maritain says that Machiavelli is obliged to defend *virtù* because of his radical pessimism about human nature, because of his belief that humans are beasts of prey endowed only with intelligence and powers of calculation. According to Maritain, such radical pessimism is not justified; for he insists that human nature remains good 'in its root-tendencies'. This is why humans are able to struggle, despite factual evil in the world, for the realization of potential good.[84] The struggle between those who argue from factual evil and those who argue from the potential for good has been the source of the motive power for human improvement. Machiavelli's view that factual evil presents the whole truth about humankind, and that for this reason *virtù* and 'reason of state' are the only effective bases for security in the international system, thus cannot be accepted as valid. For the motion that moves everything in the human world is the motion towards the good, and evil has no decisive influence here. War, therefore, does not reveal the basis of any intrinsic ethical bankruptcy, since war can be used to defend the potential for good, and as such this type of use of force is a virtuous use of force.[85]

Strauss, on the other hand, claims that the stand which the Machiavellian state is obliged to take on war, the necessity that war imposes on it to accept technology as a tool of war, and the acceptance by the state of the modern notion of science, 'render impossible the good city in the classical sense'.[86] In other words, war, technology, and science have removed the old distinction between good and bad regimes, and with it the distinction between the virtuous city and the corrupt city. Insofar as this is true, all states are obliged to practise Machiavellian *virtù*. The so-called bad states may be said to impose their habits on the so-called good states today. 'Only on this point does Machiavelli's contention that the good cannot be good because there are so many bad ones prove to possess a foundation.'[87]

Maritain's point, however, is that the practice of moral virtues, of prudence and justice in particular, is not so intimately tied to the classical notion of the good city that they cannot be practised under modern conditions. In fact, the adaptation of these virtues to modern conditions is the task of political science today.

CHAPTER 6

Humours

The notion of humours is the second major source of the naturalism
characteristic of Machiavelli's political theory. In the last chapter we saw
how this notion enters into his concept of particular human nature to
account for the fixity of human temperament. It is the humour that prompts
each individual human being to pursue his or her ends, i.e. power, riches,
and glory. But Machiavelli does not limit the use of this notion to the
analysis of particular human nature; he extends it to his analysis of the nature
of the body politic as well. He readily accepts the parallelism between the
human body and the body politic: each has its own humours. As we shall be
seeing in subsequent chapters, the theory of humours is fundamental to the
arguments of four of his major works – *The Prince*, the *Discourses*, the *Florentine
Histories*, and the 'Discursus'. The basic idea is that just as the human body is
composed of the four humours, so also the body politic is composed of its
particular political humours.

Machiavelli's insight here is derived from the presuppositions of the
Renaissance science of medicine. These go back to Galen and Hippocrates,
and their contemporary commentators. Nothing can better convey the
basic ideas embraced by the theory of humours than the following statement from Hippocrates:

> The human body contains blood, phlegm, yellow bile and black bile.
> These are the things that make up its constitution and cause its pains and
> health. Health is primarily that state in which these constituent substances
> are in correct proportion to each other, both in strength and quality, and
> are well mixed. Pain occurs when one of the substances presents either
> deficiency or an excess. It is inevitable that when one of these is separated
> from the rest and stands by itself, not only the parts from which it has
> come, but also that where it collects and is present in excess, should
> become diseased . . .[1]

The theory of humours, as can be seen from the above text, is fundamentally a theory of the 'constitution' of the human body. It is a unique theory

in that it speaks of the unity of the organism as resulting from the cooperation, not between likes, but between opposites. For each of the four humours, considered individually, is opposed to every other humour. Yet when brought together by nature they can produce a healthy constitution. If one of the humours breaks out of its proper place and seeks to stand alone, however, it will disturb the balance of the whole constitution and thereby produce its 'corruption', or pathology. The key to bodily health is that each humour gets its proper satisfaction. If a body is not able to provide this, its constitution is considered diseased. To seek satisfaction apart from the proper balance of humours is the symptom of sickness. When this occurs, it is the duty of the physicians to restore the proper balance between the constitutive humours.

Another peculiarity of the theory of humours is that it is tied to the theories of ancient physics and cosmology. The contrary properties of the humours were thought to be derived from the primary qualities of elemental matter – heat, coldness, dryness, and wetness. Moreover, the humours were also thought to be subject to the influences of the heavenly bodies, which made astrological medicine an important branch of the medical sciences.

The most important idea that early political theory borrowed from the theory of humours is the notion of satisfaction. Each of the political humours of a body politic has the natural and the legitimate need to be satisfied. This need for satisfaction is a pre-moral need. Political morality not only has to respect it, but must also do everything in its power to meet it. Thus it came to be thought that the function of good government is to satisfy the needs of each of its constituent parts. And, should one political humour seek to dominate the other humours so as to obstruct or nullify their legitimate needs, the resulting situation would be pathological. The healthy satisfaction of the needs of each humour was considered a precondition for the health of the body politic as a whole. In this way, the theory of humours provided a norm for judging what constitutes the good political constitution: i.e. one in which the satisfaction of the basic needs of each humour is possible. It also provided a norm for judging what constitutes the corrupt constitution: i.e. one in which each humour seeks its own individual satisfaction without due regard to the health of the political organism as a whole. The theory also implies that the individual is not the only unit of a political community. Groups, 'classes' or 'humours' are also the natural units of the political community. This means that a good state must satisfy the needs not only of its individuals, but also of its constituent 'classes'.[2]

By the middle of the fifth century BC, medical science had acquired an exemplary status as far as political science was concerned. Medical analogies abound in Plato and Aristotle. Pathologies of political regimes are sometimes called the humoral malignancy of the body politic. Thus Plato speaks of the diseases of oligarchies and democracies caused by idlers and spendthrifts: '. . . when these two come into being in any regime, they cause trouble, like phlegm and bile in a body. And it's against them that the good doctor and lawgiver of a city, no less than a wise bee-keeper, must take long-range precautions, preferably that they not come into being, but if they do come into being, that they be cut out as quickly as possible, cells and all.'[3] And, as Werner Jaeger points out, Aristotle 'parallelized over and again' the similarities between human body and the body politic, between virtues of the body and those of the soul.[4] According to Ernest Barker, Aristotle's doctrine of the 'mean' draws on 'the medical conception of health as a balanced and proportionate state midway between excess and defect'.[5] Plutarch compared the Lycurgan reforms to 'medical regimen': as in the case of a body diseased and full of bad humours, whose temperament is to be corrected and regenerated by medicine, so Lycurgus sought to root out the 'inveterate fatal distempers' of Sparta.[6] According to Alan Wardman, the metaphor of medical balance is central to Plutarch's political thought.[7] Thomas Aquinas is one of many in the Middle Ages who makes use of the analogy of humours for political analysis. Just as the doctor aims at health, which consists in the ordered concordance of the humours, Aquinas writes in *The Summa Contra Gentiles*, so also the ruler of the state aims at peace, which consists in the ordered concord of its citizens. The doctor quite properly and usefully (*bene et utiliter*) cuts off diseased limbs if they threaten the health of the body. Likewise, the ruler of a state kills pestiferous men justly and sinlessly (*juste et absque peccato*) should they disturb the peace of the state.[8] Nicholas of Cusa, in his *De concordantia catholica*, uses a similar mode of analysis. He traces the roots of many of the social and political vices – covetousness, fraud, factionalism, sloth, injustice – to the malignant humours of the body politic; the art of government is manifested above all in the ability to cure the distempers of the body politic.[9]

In Florentine political tracts of Machiavelli's times, we come across several examples of significant uses of the notion of humours. Savonarola's *Trattato del Reggimento degli Stati*, for example, goes beyond the a priori mode of argument. He starts his arguments against tyranny by invoking the classical theory that tyranny is the worst form of government. But he soon abandons or perhaps modifies it, saying that every country should have a government suited to its 'complexion' or nature. The key variables here are 'blood' (*sangue*), signifying courage, and 'natural talent' (*ingegno*), signifying natural genius. Peoples of the northern regions abound in 'blood' but they lack 'natural talent', while peoples of the southern regions abound in 'natural talent' but lack 'blood'. In both instances, a despotic form of government is natural and fitting for them. Since the people of Florence abound in both these qualities, neither monarchy nor aristocracy is suitable for them; a republican form of government alone is natural for them.[10]

For Guicciardini, as L. A. Burd points out, the use of the notion of humours in political analysis marks the end of 'the old reasoning "*alla filosofica"*'.[11] His *Dialogo del Reggimento di Firenze* leaves behind arguments from the authority of philosophers, in favour of a new 'empirical' argument.

> We should not look for an imagined government, which is perhaps more easily found in books such as the Republic of Plato than in actual practice. But taking into account the nature, the quality, the conditions, the inclinations – and to tie all these notions together in one word, the humours – of the city and the citizens, we should look for a government that can be introduced with the support of the citizens and which, once introduced, can be maintained according to their taste. In approaching this the example of medical doctors should be kept in mind. Doctors have the freedom to adapt their knowledge to the nature of the actual malady of the patient. Though in theory they can prescribe any number of remedies to the patient, they do not do so in practice. They do not prescribe a remedy simply because it is in itself good and well regarded. They prescribe only those remedies which the patient's complexion and other conditions can actually accommodate.[12]

Machiavelli's Uses of Umori

Given the intellectual context described above, it is not surprising that Machiavelli makes such significant use of the notion of humours. Critics are familiar with his use of medical themes and, as for the metaphor of the body politic, his use of it, as Quentin Skinner has noted, is 'pervasive'.[13] Machiavelli's use of the notion of *umori* is part and parcel of this new trend. The state is the body politic; its well-being is its health, its lack of well-being its sickness; the prince is the doctor, and political science resembles medical science more than it does moral science: these are ideas fundamental to Machiavelli's political thought. Thus, both *The Prince* and the *Discourses* speak of the need for an early diagnosis of political ills: in the beginning of an illness, it is easy to cure though difficult to diagnose; once the disease has progressed, it is easy to diagnose but difficult to cure: 'so it is in the things of state.'[14] So also, the innovator is often obliged to administer 'strong medicines' in order to rid the political organism of its ills.[15] For Machiavelli, the theory of periodic renewal is buttressed by the medical theory of the daily purging of peccant humours. Corporate bodies necessarily accumulate malignant humours in the process of time and unless they are purged of these the organism itself will die: 'The doctors of medicine say, speaking of the bodies of men, that "daily something is added that now and then needs cure".'[16]   The analogy of the human body – heads and limbs – is invoked in the famous last chapter of *The Prince*: Italy's illness is due to the weakness of its head (*debolezza de' capi*), not its limbs; for 'there is great *virtù* in the limbs, if it were not lacking in the heads'.[17] In his literary works, the humours come up for specific mention. Thus, in 'The Golden Ass' Machiavelli speaks of the need for purging the humours if one is to be happy, and of the role that the planets play in bringing about such purgings.

> And those humours which you have found so hostile and adverse not yet, not yet are purged;
> but when their roots are dry, and the heavens show themselves gracious, times happier than ever before will return.[18]

'On Fortune' reminds one of Machiavelli's belief that the humours and Fortune must work harmoniously if one is to be successful in what one does: 'since the humours that make you act, so far as they conform with her [Fortune's] doings, are the cause of your good and your ill', one's actions must conform to one's humour and to Fortune's wishes.[19] In the *Mandragola*, one of the main characters, Callimaco, is presented as a medical doctor who has recently returned to Florence from Paris. In Act II. Scenes 2 and 6, Callimaco cites several pedantic medical formulae in Latin.[20] The basic theme of this play is, of course, built around a mythical medication called the 'mandrake'. Finally, medical science is given honourable mention in the all-important Preface to the First Book of the *Discourses*, where it is held out as a model for the new science of politics.

In his political analysis, Machiavelli uses the notion of *umori* in a number of different senses. First of all, political humours refer to desires and appetites natural to a social group. Desires are pre-rational in that their satisfaction is a matter of necessity rather than choice. Reason is not so much a restraint upon them as a stimulant, since the political satisfaction of these desires is what constitutes the *summum bonum* of Machiavellian politics. Desires are not acquired, as such; they are constitutive. We find several formulations of more or less the same idea. To begin with, the formulation in *The Prince* reads: 'For in every city these two diverse humours are found, which arises from this: that the people desire neither to be commanded nor oppressed by the *grandi*, and the *grandi* desire to command and oppress the people.'[21] The parallel passage in the *Discourses* is as follows: '. . . in every republic there are two opposed humours, that of the people and that of the *grandi*, and all the laws made in favour of liberty result from their discord.'[22] In *Florentine Histories*, we find the principle stated thus: 'The great and natural enmities that exist between the people and the nobles, caused by the wish of the latter to command and of the former not to obey, are the cause of all evils that arise in cities. From this diversity of humours all other things that agitate republics take their nourishment.'[23] And in the 'Discursus': '. . . nor can we believe a republic fitted to last, in which there is no satisfaction of those humours that must be satisfied; and if they are not satisfied, the republics fall.'[24] Finally, *umori* is described as the universal principle characteristic of political communities always and everywhere: 'He who considers present affairs and ancient ones readily understands that all cities and peoples have the same desires and the same humours and that they always have had them.'[25] Again, 'all the things of the world, in every period, have their individual counterparts in ancient times. This arises because they are carried on by men, who have and always have had the same passions; therefore, of necessity the same results appear.'[26]

At first it appears that there is an ethical difference between the humours of the two groups. The aspirations of the oppressed are said to be 'more honourable' (*più onesto*) than those of the *grandi*.[27] The aspirations of a free people are said to be 'seldom harmful to liberty', since they result either from oppression or from the fear that there will be oppression.[28] On the other hand, the 'great desire' of the *grandi* to dominate is less honourable than the desire of the people not to be dominated.[29] But on closer examination it appears that the oppressed of today always turn out to be the oppressors of tomorrow. It is only the factual inability of the oppressed to usurp power that keeps them from becoming actual oppressors. Had they the opportunity, they would certainly seek to dominate. The oppressed are eager to defend liberty not because they are more virtuous, but because they cannot seize power themselves. In other words, they make a virtue out of necessity. What differentiates the two groups is the actual possession of power by one and the actual lack of power of the other. The difference between the oppressors and the oppressed is thus one of the actual possession of advantage, time and circumstance. For both are driven by the same 'madness' (*furore*) for power, but at any given time only one of them can be successful in their drive.[30] Indeed, for Machiavelli it is natural and normal to desire to dominate, and those who succeed in satisfying this desire will always be praised. Only those are blamed who do not have the ability to dominate others, but who nevertheless attempt to do so.[31]

The notion of humours is used in a second applied sense to designate the social groups of a given body politic. Thus, the patricians and the plebeians of the ancient Roman Republic are sometimes called its humours. In the Roman Principate there were three such humours: the patricians, the plebeians, and the army. When speaking of Florence, Machiavelli normally refers to its three humours: the *grandi*, the *popolo*, and the *popolo minuto*; or the *popolo grasso*, the *popolani*, and the *plebe/plebe infima*; or the *primi*, the *mezzani*, and the *ultimi*. Venice is normally spoken of as having two groups: the gentlemen and the *popolo*. Romagna, Naples, and Lombardi were infested with 'idle' gentlemen who oppressed the 'people' of those regions. The 'people' of the cities of Germany and Switzerland, on the other hand, hated their 'gentlemen', killing them whenever they got the opportunity. France had its barons and its people. Turkey, by contrast, did not have a baronial class; its provincial rulers were temporary court appointees. The army, on the other hand, was the most powerful political humour of that country.

Thirdly, humours are used to describe the activities produced by the interaction between the political groups. Thus, for example, the disturbances produced by the Agrarian Laws of Rome are called the *umore* arising from the conflict between the patricians and the plebeians.[32] Similarly, the factional conflicts of Florence are almost always called the humours of Florence.[33]

Occasionally, humours are used to describe conflicts between states. Thus, the conflicts between the Swiss cantons and the emperor are referred to as 'the contrary humours' (*umori contrari*) of that region.[34]

Elsewhere, the term is used to describe typically Machiavellian conceptions of good and bad. There are healthy and malignant humours, depending on whether the humours in question contribute to the health or the sickness of the body politic. Divisions that lead to factionalism are universally condemned as being bad, while divisions that promote the good of the body politic are praised as being desirable and necessary.

Finally, and most importantly, the term is used to classify political regimes: out of the conflicts between the two opposed humours, states Machiavelli, 'one of three effects occurs in cities, either principality or republic or licence (*licenzia*)'.[35] This is undoubtedly Machiavelli's most original use of the notion of *umori* and its importance for understanding the nature of his political theory cannot be exaggerated. For here he has introduced a new criterion of classifying political regimes. Regimes are the 'effects' of the conflicts between political humours: how they combine or fail to combine is the key issue. Henceforth, political regimes are defined according to the way in which they satisfy the humours of their constitutive groups. For the humours are satisfied differently in each of the three regimes.

In a principality, the humours are satisfied, to the extent that they are satisfied, not by the efforts of the groups themselves, but by the intervention of the prince. The prince maintains his own power by aligning himself with the strongest political humour. Self-government is not possible in a Machiavellian principality. The social groups are too antagonistic to each other for them to resolve their differences by themselves. The traditional classification of monarchy and tyranny now appears meaningless: the basis of the distinction is no longer ethics but rather the notion of 'satisfaction' of the social groups. A monarchical regime no longer requires the prince to realize the common good of the whole realm; the Machiavellian principate requires only that the dominant humour in the monarchy be satisfied, so that the prince will be able to maintain his own power. And this end can be achieved as easily by a tyrant like Septimius Severus as by a good monarch such as David. From the perspective of the theory of humours, the classical distinction between a good king and a tyrant is no longer significant.

In a republic, by contrast, the social groups are capable of resolving their differences through the medium of the constitution and the law. They are, in other words, capable of self-government; they do not need the mediation of a prince. That is why group-equality and group-freedom are possible in a republic. No one group is permitted to dominate the entire state or to hold all instruments of power. There is a sharing of power between the groups. Group conflict remains, to be sure, but it does not degenerate into a struggle in which one group seeks the total elimination of the other. Should such a situation occur, as for example it did in the Roman Republic during the civil war, the republic itself would become diseased and would eventually die. A healthy republic, however, ensures that this will not happen, by providing for the satisfaction of all the relevant groups that constitute it.

A republic encourages the flourishing of citizens of different humours and temperament, whereas a monarchy does not. Because of this, republics are more lively, more flexible, and more successful in their foreign relations than are monarchies. Rome, for example, was able to face the threat from Carthage successfully because she could call upon the talents of men of such diverse humours as Fabius Maximus Cunctator and Scipio Africanus. When Rome needed a man of cautious temperament, she was lucky to find Fabius, and when she needed a man of impetuous temperament, she was lucky to find Scipio. Monarchies, by contrast, have to depend on the temperament of one person alone. In this way, Machiavelli uses the theory of humours to explain the superiority of republics over monarchies: the former can enjoy better fortune and last longer because of the way the humours are treated in each.[36]

In a *licenzia*, on the other hand, there exists neither the order produced by a prince nor the self-government produced by a republic. The groups of a *licenzia* are always at odds with one another, and the antagonism between them is too strong to produce any form of stable government. The reason for this is that each group pursues its own interest without due regard for the interest of the whole, and often at the expense of its rivals. Groups become factions, and the constitution and the law become instruments of factional conflicts. In a *licenzia*, only the interest of the group in power at a given time is satisfied. Thus, a *licenzia* is in a permanent state of political instability or ill health.

It is clear that for all practical purposes, Machiavelli recognizes only three forms of government — the monarchy, the republic, and something in between: the *licenzia*, for him the worst. Whether by accident or by design, his three major works — *The Prince*, *Discourses*, and the *Florentine Histories* — more or less correspond to these forms of government, respectively. There is, then, at least some obvious merit in considering them from the perspective provided us by the theory of political humours.

Once the theory of humours is seen for what it is, it is not difficult to see why Machiavelli has no real use for the 'old' system of classifying governments. The basis of the 'old' system is the ethics of the classical notion of the common good: a government is good if it achieves the common good, and it does not matter much whether it is a government of the one, the few, or the many. Machiavelli mentions the old theory in *Discourses* I. 2, more as a report of it than as though it was his own theory. Somewhat detachedly, he reports that 'some who have written of states say' that those who organize government should make use of one of three kinds of government, called princedom, aristocracy, and popular government. However, 'some others, and according to the opinion of many, wiser men', hold that there are six kinds of government, of which three are bad, and three good, and that they revolve in a cycle of six regimes. Somewhat unexpectedly, however, Machiavelli remarks that he himself considers all these kinds of regimes – the good as well as the bad – to be 'pestiferous' (*pestiferi*) because of the short life of the good and the viciousness of the bad. How can he call even the good forms of government 'pestiferous'? He does so only under the supposition that even these do not guarantee for a sufficient period of time the satisfaction of the various humours of the body politic. As far as he is concerned, a purely ethical differentiation between regimes is of no great interest. What matters is whether or not a given regime can satisfy the humours of its relevant classes. There is no doubt that he accepts the mixed regime as desirable, but he does so neither on Aristotelian nor on Polybian terms, but rather on his own terms, i.e. in terms of the theory of humours. What gave the Roman constitution its 'perfection' – and what will give any constitution its perfection, as we shall see when we examine his proposals for the reform of the government of Florence – is not so much its mixed character as its being founded on its humours. 'To this perfection she came through the discord between the plebeians and the senate.'[37]

It is not difficult to see the connection between Machiavelli's theory of political humours and his emphasis on effective truth. The test of a good Machiavellian regime is whether or not it can provide adequate satisfaction to its constituent groups. Insofar as this is true, the theory of humours is part of his scheme to introduce new modes and orders into political science, and to move away from the view that politics is a branch of moral science or a study of imagined republics and principalities. Clearly, the 'old' ethical standards are not applicable in Machiavellian forms of government. Indeed the theory of humours opens the way for discarding the traditional view that the cultivation of moral virtues and of character built on them are the proper ends of politics. With Machiavelli, the proper end of politics becomes the satisfaction of our needs, but needs as they arise from our group temperament. The differences between principalities, republics and *licenzie* still remain, but these differences stem not from the classical notion of 'form', but rather from the Machiavellian notion of humours and their satisfaction. The unity which the Machiavellian polity requires is ultimately a unity of its constituent groups, whose exemplar is taken from the unity of the four humours in the human body: a unity of opposites.

The notion of humours as an instrument for political analysis does not exist in contemporary political science. We no longer invoke it to explain notions of social conflict, of social class, or of the body politic itself. The notions of class and conflict are seen today in dialectical rather than medical terms; and dialectical notions of conflicts always call for victors and vanquished. The victorious class is supposed to liquidate the vanquished class. Such a state of affairs, for Machiavelli, would be the very sign of political pathology; for him, political health would require the continuation of the unity of the opposites. However that may be, it is useful to remember that as late as the nineteenth century, the notion of the humours is occasionally used to express the older notion of conflict. John Locke's use of it is both interesting and instructive. In the *Second Treatise of Government* he applies it to distinguish the disposition of a social class, namely 'the people'. In chapter 19 of the *Second Treatise of Civil Government* Locke criticizes the view that to base Government on the 'uncertain humour' of the people would be to court political disaster. 'To this perhaps it will be said, that the People being ignorant, and always discontented, to lay the Foundation of Government in the unsteady Opinion, and uncertain Humour of the People, is to expose it to certain ruin; and no Government will be able long to subsist, if the People may set up a new Legislative, whenever they take offence at the old one.'[38]

Even as recently as the early nineteenth century, 'humours' in the political sense is still in use. The historian William H. Prescott, for example, says that some have justified the expulsion of the Jews from Renaissance Spain (a subject which, incidentally, Machiavelli himself discusses in *The Prince* 21) in terms of the 'vicious humours' of the Spanish body politic. 'But, to judge the matter rightly, we must take into view the actual position of the Jews at that time. Far from forming an integral part of the commonwealth, they were regarded as alien to it, as a mere excrescence, which, so far from contributing to the healthful action of the body politic, was nourished by its vicious humours, and might be lopped off at any time when the health of the system demanded it. Far from being protected by the laws, the only aim of the laws in reference to them was to define more precisely their civil incapacities, and to draw the line of division more broadly between them and the Christians.'[39]

There is a tendency among some modern interpreters of Machiavelli to interpret Machiavelli's notion of conflict in dialectical, rather than in humoral terms. In effect, what they are doing is actually to read Machiavelli's notion of conflict out of its proper intellectual context. Claude Lefort, for example, treats Machiavelli's notion of humoral conflicts in the modern sense of class conflict. According to him, the foundation of Machiavellian politics lies in the division of society into classes. These divisions are necessary, and their accommodation impossible. 'Car entre le désir du peuple de ne pas être commandé, opprimé, et celui de commander, opprimer, il n'y a pas de négociation concevable . . .'[40] Likewise, Agnes Heller sees Machiavelli as a precursor to Karl Marx. In speaking of the

struggle between the *popolo* and the *grandi* of Italy, and in urging the prince
to rely more on the people than on the *grandi*, 'he was replacing the
traditional early Renaissance notion of the people with a novel and modern
concept of it.'[41] According to Josef Macek, also, Machiavelli has a 'modern
conception of class struggle'.[42] Antonio Gramsci sees the prince as a Sorelian
political myth, representing the 'collective will'. According to Gramsci,
Machiavelli understood that the 'formation of a national-popular collective
will' would be impossible unless the great mass of peasant cultivators was
brought into political life. This is the significance of Machiavelli's reform of
the militia. In modern conditions, the communist party would be the 'new
prince' which, through its leadership, can create a collective will. But when
Gramsci touches the nerve of Machiavelli's position on divisions in society,
it is not difficult to see that the meaning of social humours escapes him.
Gramsci claims that the divisions in society are unnatural, and that they are
a transient, historical fact, 'answering to certain conditions' equally unnatural, such as the division of labour. Presumably, when the need for the
division of labour disappears, divisions of society will also disappear.[43]
Machiavelli's insight, however, is that divisions in society have their basis in
desires and humours; these (desires and humours) being natural, society
cannot rid itself of divisions. As he wrote early in his career, 'I have heard it
said that history is the mistress of our actions, especially of princes, that the
world is inhabited by men who always have had the same passions, that
there have always been those who serve and those who command, those
who serve willingly and those who serve unwillingly, those who rebel and
those who are put down.'[44]

There are fundamental differences, then, between the Machiavellian
notion of humoral conflict and the dialectical notion of class conflict.
According to the dialectical notion of conflict, there are no natural divisions
in society, and the resolution of all the so-called artificial divisions should
lead to a classless society. Machiavelli's insight, derived from pre-modern
medicine, is different. For him, each social humour validly exists in a social
group; if one group determines to eliminate the other, as happened in
Florence, civic freedom will be lost to oppression and domination. The
humoral conflict, if it is to produce healthy results, must preserve the
identity of all the contestants, and must give due satisfaction to all. Otherwise, the body politic as a whole will suffer. To this extent, Machiavelli is a
pluralist. One group requires the active opposition of the other group as a
condition for its own existence and vitality. In the humoral theory,
normatively, classes do not oppose each other for the purpose of mutual
exploitation. Indeed, mutual opposition and mutual toleration can and
must coexist in a healthy political system.

An adequate understanding of Machiavelli's notion of humours requires
a close scrutiny of his major works. As mentioned already, *The Prince*, the
Discourses and *Florentine Histories*, together with the 'Discursus', give us

three different ways in which political humours find political expression. It is to a consideration of these three different expressions that the next three chapters are devoted.

CHAPTER 7

The Prince

The Prince, in the words of John Pocock, is 'an analytical study of innovation and its consequences'.[1] For Machiavelli, innovation involves both the exercise of *virtù* and confrontation with Fortune. Its consequences are power, prosperity, empire, and glory. Underlying this analysis is a firm understanding of the structure of the regime in question. And since in *The Prince* Machiavelli limits himself to the study of the innovation of principalities, an understanding of the specific structure of this type of regime is especially crucial. Indeed, the question of structure must have figured highly in Machiavelli's mind, as can be gathered from the famous letter he writes to his friend Vettori, in which, for the first time, he divulges the news about *The Prince* to the outside world. In the letter he says that he has written a booklet, an *opusculo*, entitled *De principatibus (On Principalities)*, in which he has gone as deeply as possible into the subject, discussing the nature of principalities: of what kinds they are, how they are gained, how they are kept, and why they are lost.[2] The answers to each of these questions require a knowledge of how the humours of the principalities are related to one another and to the prince.

It is not surprising, then, that the first eleven chapters of *The Prince* deeply involve questions of structure. The analysis begins with the classification of all principalities into four kinds: hereditary, mixed, new, and ecclesiastical.

Although the hereditary principalities do not form the focus of the book, Machiavelli nevertheless starts with them. If they do nothing else, they at least form a foil for the other types of principalities. Even the hereditary principalities have to satisfy their relevant political 'classes', a requirement which poses relatively few problems, for they are governed by 'natural princes', as distinct from 'new princes'. A natural prince enjoys the 'natural' affection of his subjects and he is 'more loved' than is the new prince. All he must do is to foster this natural love, observe the ancient customs, and show ordinary industry. This is how the dukes of Ferrara maintained themselves in power; even though they were severely threatened from outside, the support they received from their subjects was strong enough to keep them in power.

The mixed principalities pose more difficult problems to the innovator. It is harder to satisfy the diverse humours of a newly acquired territory. Machiavelli has identified two problems which arise. The first arises when the new subjects become disillusioned with the new prince. While they may have originally welcomed him in the belief that he would satisfy their needs better than their erstwhile ruler, they later find out that this belief was mistaken. As Machiavelli writes, 'men willingly change their masters believing that they will better themselves. This belief makes them take up arms against them, but in doing so they deceive themselves, for later they learn through experience that they have become worse off.'[3] The second difficulty is that the new prince is obliged to hurt his new subjects through the very act of conquest. The result is that he has as enemies all those whom he has hurt, and as friends those whom he cannot satisfy to the extent to which they hoped that he would satisfy them.[4] Only those new princes who know how to overcome these difficulties will know also how to win and maintain a mixed principality. To prove this thesis, Machiavelli makes three case studies, considering Louis XII of France, Alexander the Great, and the territories annexed by Sparta and Rome.

Louis XII did not understand very well the principle of satisfying the political humours and for this reason he failed to satisfy the Milanese. Hence, he lost Milan almost as quickly as he won it. There were, of course, other military and diplomatic errors that he committed in Italy, which are brilliantly analysed in *The Prince* 3. But these were not nearly as costly to him as was his inability to secure the loyalty and support of his new Milanese subjects. Satisfying them was far more crucial to his success than having even the strongest of armies. For, as Machiavelli points out, the efforts of even the best army come to nought if the conqueror does not have the support of the conquered. 'Always, even though a new prince may have the strongest of armies, he always needs the support (*favore*) of the inhabitants when moving into a new province.'[5]

Alexander the Great fared much better than did Louis XII. He was able to conquer and keep the Persian Empire because he understood its humoral structure and could adapt his policies accordingly. He was therefore able both to conquer and to satisfy the relevant humours of the conquered territory. Machiavelli reaches this conclusion not by any direct analysis of the structure of Darius's empire but, indirectly, by means of a strikingly original analysis of the humoral structure of the Turkish Empire and the French monarchy.

Turkey was an absolute monarchy. 'The whole monarchy of the Turk is governed by one lord; the others are his servants.'[6] The most important humour of Turkey needing satisfaction, in Machiavelli's view, is neither the 'people', nor the 'viziers', but the army. The security of that country and its ruler depended on a satisfied and a loyal army. It was therefore necessary for the sultan 'to put off every other consideration and keep them his friends'.[7]

As for the vizirs, they were only his 'servants', whom he could make or unmake at will. Besides, they had 'no credit with the people',[8] nor did they, unlike the French barons, have any hereditary rights. Since they were all 'slaves and bound by obligation' to the sultan, it was not easy to corrupt them; and even if they could be corrupted, it was of little use to the conqueror since they (the vizirs) could not bring the 'people' with them. And the 'people' in an absolute monarchy like Turkey, being not free, are like a sullen, amorphous mass, and have no affection for those who directly govern them.

The key to innovating a country like Turkey lies, then, in the defeat of the army; once this is accomplished and the blood line of the sultan physically eliminated, the innovator will find no further resistance. And while it will of course be difficult to defeat such a country, once defeated, it will be easy to keep.

The humoral structure of France, on the other hand, was quite different. It was not an absolute monarchy: it had its barons, the 'people' who hated the barons, and the *parlement*, a judicial body which acted as buffer between the two classes. The barons derived their status not from the will of the king but from their hereditary rights. They had their own vassals who were bound to them by 'natural affection' – so much so that in times of trouble they preferred to follow the barons rather than the king. Moreover, the barons were potential rivals to the throne; an invader could easily shake their loyalty to the monarchy. Finally, the 'people' were emerging as a political force to be contended with, so that, in Machiavelli's judgement, the king had to tilt the balance in their favour rather than that of the barons. This he was able to do thanks to the institution of the *parlement*, which acted as a 'third force' between the two humours. Thus, the king,

> knowing the ambition of the powerful and their insolence, and judging it necessary for them to have a bit in their mouths to keep them in check, and on the other hand, knowing the hatred of the people against the barons, which is founded in its fear, and wanting to secure them, intended this not to be the particular concern of the king, so as to take from him the blame he would have from the barons when he favoured the people, and from the people when he favoured the barons; and so he constituted a third judge to be the one who would beat down the barons and favour the people without blame for the king.[9]

Machiavelli's conclusion here is that because of its humoral structure France would be easy to conquer but difficult to keep.

Applying the foregoing analysis to the case of Darius's empire, Machiavelli is now in a position to explain why Alexander succeeded in keeping his mixed principality. It was because the Persian Empire, in its humoral structure, resembled Turkey rather than France. The humours of the Persian Empire were such that once the army and the blood line of the defeated royal family were wiped out, there would be no moral resistance on the part of the people to the new ruler. As long as the new prince had a strong army, and as long as he was able to provide a tolerable level of material satisfaction to the new subjects, his position would be quite secure.

The comparative study of France and Turkey, based on the notion of the humours, enables Machiavelli to draw an important conclusion, namely that the humoral structure of a given body politic imposes a limit on what the *virtù* of the prince can accomplish within that body politic. If a given body politic is like Turkey, a strong army and the *virtù* of the prince will be all that is necessary to conquer it. But if a given body politic is like France, it will be virtually impossible to conquer and keep it, no matter how strong the army might be and how extraordinary the prince's *virtù*. As he writes, 'this has come not from much or little *virtù* in the innovator but from the diversity of the subject matter (with which he has to deal).'[10]

Machiavelli next discusses the problems connected with annexing erstwhile republics to a new mixed monarchy. It is infinitely more difficult to satisfy the humours of a republic than it is to satisfy those of a monarchy. The reason is that the constitutive humours of a republic are accustomed to self-government, whereas those of a monarchy are not. It is virtually impossible to subdue a free people, for they will be satisfied with nothing less than self-rule. The Romans found this out very quickly in their dealings with free cities: they found that of all the ways of subduing a free people, wiping them out completely was the only effective way. No other way was thought to be sufficiently secure. For 'in republics there is greater life, greater hatred, more desire for revenge; the memory of their ancient liberty does not and cannot let them rest, so that the most secure path is to wipe them out or live in them.'[11]

Turning now to the new principality – the third type analysed in *The Prince* – here too the theory of humours finds its application. There is no doubt that Machiavelli's immediate attention is focused on the *virtù* and the independence of the innovator, the need he has for the use of force, and the importance of making the sceptical and the unbelieving believe in his 'new modes and orders'. Taking for granted that the innovator of an entirely new principality should have extraordinary ability, the structural difficulties of ruling must nevertheless be faced. As Machiavelli points out, 'nothing is more difficult to handle, more doubtful of success, nor more dangerous to manage, than to put oneself as leader of an innovating process.'[12] The reason for this is basically structural, for the innovator must face a set of enemies and a set of friends. The enemies are those who benefit from the status quo, while the friends are those who give only lukewarm support to his innovative programmes. He has both to destroy his enemies and to convert his lukewarm supporters into enthusiastic ones. These tasks require a knowledge of the humoral structure of the people within the principality. In *The Prince* 6, Machiavelli makes only brief mention of the condition of the Israelites, the Persians, and the Athenians. Moses, Cyrus, and Theseus had to solve the specific problems which their respective communities were facing. In the final analysis, however, the test of their *virtù* and their innovative enterprise is whether they are able to satisfy the humours of their people.

It is unfortunate that Machiavelli does not give a detailed analysis of the humoral structure of Israel, Persia and Athens. This, however, is not the case when he discusses the activities of Hiero of Syracuse, Cesare Borgia, Agathocles, Liverotto, and Ferdinand of Aragon. In these cases, he does mention specific humoral issues. Hiero of Syracuse, for example, had to reorganize the entire humoral structure of Syracuse. We are told that he eliminated the old army and established a new one, and only when he had 'friendships and soldiers of his own', i.e. when he had satisfied the relevant groups, could his innovation succeed.[13]

From the perspective of the theory of humours, nothing can be more instructive than Machiavelli's analysis of the policies of Cesare Borgia. Though ultimately Borgia remains a failed prince, he is nevertheless presented as an exemplar for all innovators. And in no other instance is his example more worthy of imitation than in that of pacifying the humours of Romagna. The 'people' of that region were ravaged by their petty, predatory barons. Borgia's basic strategy in winning over that region was to weaken and destroy the barons and gain the loyalty of the 'people'. With this end in view, he weakened the influence of the Colonna and the Orsini's factions and converted their partisans into his own followers. Then, in order to give the 'people' a taste of good government, he put the region in the charge of Remirro de Orco, with instructions that he deal severely with all law-breakers. But Remirro's severity began to alienate the 'people' instead of winning them over and Borgia was afraid that the hatred the 'people' felt towards Remirro might be extended to himself. So, in order to purge the inflamed spirits of the 'people', to regain their affection for himself, and to convey to them that Remirro's severity did not have his sanction, he had Remirro assassinated, or, as the notorious passage in *The Prince* states, 'he had him placed one morning in the piazza at Cesena in two pieces, with a piece of wood and a bloody knife beside him. The ferocity of this spectacle both satisfied and stupefied the people.'[14] Indeed, this was one way of satisfying the humours of the people of Romagna. The instances of Agathocles the Sicilian and Liverotto da Fermo also reveal that they too were aware of the importance of satisfying the relevant social class in order to establish their own power. Thus, Agathocles killed 'all the senators and the richest' of the Sicilians, thanks to which he was able to hold on to power 'without any civil discord'.[15] Similarly, Liverotto had all the 'malcontents' and 'the leading men' (*primi uomini*) of Fermo killed. It was only after this was accomplished that he succeeded in establishing his 'new civil and military innovations'.[16]

The analysis of the policies of Ferdinand of Aragon, a 'quasi new prince',[17] is also relevant here. The key to his success as the innovator of Spain was the way he handled the barons and the people, i.e. the humours of Spain. He prevented the troublesome barons of Castile from becoming a threat to his power by keeping them busy in a war in Granada. On the other hand, he won the support of the people by expelling the Jews from Spain. In this way, he kept the spirits of his subjects always 'in suspense and admiration', so that neither the barons nor the people had any inclination to plot against him.[18]

It is in the analysis of the civil principality that the theory of humours finds its fullest application. In principalities of this kind, the prince comes to power with the favour of either the *grandi* or the *popolo*, and accordingly they have either an aristocratic or a popular monarchy. Machiavelli weighs the advantages and the disadvantages of each of these governments. On the whole, he prefers a popular monarchy to an aristocratic one, because it is easier to satisfy the humours of the *popolo* than to satisfy those of the *grandi*.

The *grandi* pose two major problems for the innovator. The first is that its individual members are potential rivals to the new prince; the position of the new prince is never secure in this respect. And so, while it is useful to have the support of the *grandi* to snatch power, it is never a secure source of support as far as maintaining one's power is concerned. The second problem is that even if one acquires power with the favour of the *grandi*, one still needs the support of the people to maintain it. Because of their numbers alone, the people make it difficult for the prince to hold on to his power without their favour. On the other hand, the *grandi* are more experienced in government, more astute, and more foreseeing. Therefore, a new prince cannot afford to alienate them either.

But again, it is easier to satisfy the humours of the people. First of all, they pose no threat to the prince; ordinarily, members of the populace do not aspire to the throne. Secondly, the needs of the people are normally decent and easy to meet: they expect only protection for their property and their honour. As long as the prince does not confiscate their property or violate their women, they are easily satisfied. Above all, Machiavelli warns, a prince should refrain from taking the property of others 'because men forget more quickly the death of a father than the loss of a father's patrimony'.[19] A popular innovator, therefore, would be a patron of all arts and sciences, patronizing accomplished individuals and honouring those who excel in any profession. He would encourage his subjects to think that they can carry on their business peacefully, both in commerce and agriculture, so that no one would be afraid of increasing his/her wealth for fear that it might be confiscated or unduly taxed. Moreover, he rewards those who through trade and commerce increase the wealth of the principality, and thereby furnish the prince with greater resources.[20]

Machiavelli's preference for popular monarchies is not based upon any ethical notion such as an assumed moral superiority of the people over the *grandi*; rather, it is based on his perception of the humoral shift of power from the feudal *grandi* to the new commercial *popolo*. In reference to his own time, he says that 'Now it is necessary for all princes except the sultans of Turkey and Egypt to satisfy the people rather than the army, because the people can do more than the army.'[21] In the final analysis, the Machiavellian innovator endeavours to satisfy the humour of whoever happens to be the strongest group of society at a given time. It does not matter who this may be – whether the *grandi*, the 'people', or the army. For as long as he has the most powerful group on his side, his innovation will be successful. Thus, the theory of humours, as used by Machiavelli, lays to rest once and for all the classical theory that a good prince is morally obliged to satisfy the needs of the community as a whole, or the common good.

This point is made explicit in Machiavelli's analysis of the Roman Principate. In most principalities, he notes, the prince has to contend with only two humours, those of the *grandi* and the *popolo*. The Roman emperors, however, had to contend with a third humour, viz. the army, which, with its 'cruelty and avarice', had become as bad as the *grandi*.[22] During the period under question, the Roman Army, especially the praetorian guard, became deeply involved in the government and administration of the provinces. The army had become a political force with a distinct humour of its own. Machiavelli points out that of the eleven emperors whose administration he examines – Marcus Aurelius, Pertinax, Alexander Severus, Commodus, Septimius Severus, Antoninus Caracalla, Maximinus, Heliogabalus, Macrinus and Julianus – only two – Marcus Aurelius and Septimius Severus – knew how to satisfy the 'right' humour without harming themselves. The others failed, and so came to sad ends at the hands of the army. For it was impossible to satisfy both the people and the army. The people loved quiet, and therefore preferred modest emperors, while the army loved emperors with a military mentality: those who were cruel and rapacious. Unfortunately, writes Machiavelli, 'most of them, especially those who came to the principate as new princes, once they recognized the difficulty of these two diverse humours, turned to satisfying the army, caring little about injuring the people.'[23] But even such a policy did not guarantee success: the demands of the army were beyond the ability of all of these except the two mentioned.

What is remarkable in this analysis is that, as far as Turkey and the Roman Principate were concerned, Machiavelli approves of the policy of satisfying the army and injuring the people. He maintains that while the principle that the 'people' should be satisfied is generally a good one, in actual fact it is always the stronger social humour that must be satisfied: 'for since princes cannot fail to be hated by someone, they first of all are forced not to be hated by the people; but when they cannot have this, they should do everything in their power to avoid being hated by that group which is most powerful.'[24] Thus, he observes that while in Italy it is necessary for princes to satisfy the people, in the Ottoman Empire and in Egypt it is necessary for princes to satisfy the army. The reason for the difference here is not difficult to see. There is no need for the princes of Italy and of Europe generally, he says, to show support for the army by 'extraordinary means', because the army is not entrenched in the administrative structure of the European monarchies, and the people have emerged as the key political group. Apart from the wealth they create through agriculture and commerce, the 'people' also provide the nurseries for recruiting a citizen army. Thus, for both economic and military reasons, the European monarchies need a satisfied people. But the situation in the Muslim states is quite different. In Turkey, 'the security and the strength' of the state depends on the cavalry and the infantry. It is necessary for the prince of that state 'to put off every other consideration and keep them his friends'. The same applies to Egypt, 'since the kingdom of the sultan is in the hands of the army'.[25]

The notion of humours even enters into Machiavelli's analysis of ecclesiastical principalities. Although such principalities are maintained by 'superior causes', and although their subjects can be easily satisfied because of the spiritual character of these states, nevertheless, insofar as they are political entities, their power structure is subject to the humours of the papal territory. Machiavelli singles out the barons of the papal states – the Colonna and the Orsini – as holding the key to the political power of the papacy. They control papal politics through their control of the College of Cardinals. In this way, at least until the time of Alexander VI and Julius II, these barons kept the papacy politically weak. Alexander VI, with Cesare Borgia as his instrument, dealt the first blow to the barons. Julius II followed this example by eliminating the barons of Rome and annihilating the factions of Romagna. Both saw to it that the Colonna and Orsini did not get cardinals, as the cardinals were the origin of the tumults among the barons, and the cause of party strife both within and without Rome.[26]

According to *The Prince*, it appears that the notion of *umori* has an ethical dimension of its own. It is because of this that the innovator ought to adapt himself to the humour of the political class whose support is most crucial for him, and he should do so even if the humour in question is a corrupting one. 'For when that community of which you judge you have need to maintain yourself is corrupt, whether it be the "people" or the army or the *grandi*, you must follow its humour to satisfy it, and then good deeds are your enemy.'[27] This injunction is in perfect harmony with the much more notorious injunction of chapter 15: 'it is necessary to a prince, if he wants to maintain himself, to learn to be able not to be good, and to use this or not use it according to necessity.'[28] Thus, adapting oneself to the humour of one's social base emerges as the Machiavellian version of prudence. Likewise, the ethical qualities discussed in chapters 15–19 of *The Prince* acquire a new meaning when seen in the light of the principle of adapting oneself to the dominant humours of society. The injunction that the innovator in Italy must do everything to please the 'people' can now be seen as a requirement of the theory of humours. The notions of cruelty well used and cruelty ill used also centre around the question of benefiting or alienating the 'people'. Under Italian conditions, not to be hated by the 'people' is the indispensable qualification of an Italian innovator. And a 'people' may well be less depraved than an 'army'. For, as we have mentioned already, Italy's military renewal depended primarily on the satisfaction of the 'people'.

This point is made explicit in chapter 24 of *The Prince*. The title of this chapter asks 'Why the Princes of Italy have lost their States'. Two answers are proffered. The first points to the defect of the Italian armies, and the second to the observation that 'some of them had a hostile people or if they had a friendly people, did not know how to secure themselves against the *grandi*'.[29] These two answers sum up the fruits of the analytical parts of the entire book. And they are closely related, since pleasing the 'people' is a condition for correcting the defects of the Italian army.

The famous exhortation in chapter 26 presupposes the previous analysis along the lines we have indicated. Rather than blame Fortune, Italians must do what is required of them at the level of human causality. The new Italian prince must be an able general and a competent 'doctor' who can 'heal the wounds' and 'cure the sores' of the Italian body politic. That is to say, he should be able to satisfy the relevant humours of Italy. In fact, this entails creating conditions that will satisfy the 'people'. In concrete terms, this means putting 'an end to the sacking of Lombardy, to the taxes on the kingdom [of Naples] and on Tuscany'.[30]

In conclusion, it is beyond reasonable doubt that the theory of political humours underlying *The Prince* enables one to understand the importance for innovating monarchies of satisfying the appetites of the crucial class. It also explains why the new ethic proposed by Machiavelli is highly natural-istic in character. The Machiavellian monarchy does not set the 'good life', the virtuous life, and the common good in the classical sense, as its end. The end of the new state is the procurement of material satisfaction, political security, and historical greatness as if they were the organic, naturalistic, needs of the state. There is no need to bring right reason and *phronesis* into this picture. Finally, the theory of humours gives us one way of distinguishing between *The Prince* and the *Discourses*. In the former, we find arguments for satisfying the dominant political humour through the agency of the prince. Monarchies cannot satisfy both humours of the body politic; the dominant humour is or ought to be given preference. In the *Discourses* on the other hand, as we shall see, arguments are developed to establish that only in good republics can both humours find a reasonable chance of being satisfied, and this not through the agency of a prince but through the virtue of the community as a whole, and through its *ordini*, constitution and laws.

CHAPTER 8

The Discourses

The notion of *umori* lies at the very heart of the argument of the *Discourses*. For it explains two issues most fundamental to that work, viz. the internal development of the Roman Republic and its external expansion as an imperial power. John Pocock has said more or less the same thing, though in slightly different language. He says that in the *Discourses*, Machiavelli offers two 'daring and arresting hypotheses' which form the 'foundation' of that work.[1] The first of these is that the disunion and strife among the patricians and the plebeians was the cause of the liberty, stability, and power of the Roman Republic; the second is that making the plebeians the guardians of liberty had the unexpected effect of making Rome a strong military power. These two hypotheses concerning the two fundamental issues of the work presuppose, as we shall see, the theory of humours. For it is this Hippocratic/Galenic medical theory which explains how unity can arise from the interaction of opposites, and how the satisfaction of the humours can have a beneficial effect on the organism as a whole. In what follows in this chapter, I shall first consider Machiavelli's analysis of Rome's internal development. This will be followed by a consideration of his analysis of her imperial expansion. Finally, the question will be raised as to why if Rome was such a perfect republic it succumbed to corruption and 'died'.

Umori *and Rome's Internal Development*

The first casualty of the application of the theory of humours to an analysis of the Roman constitution is the classical theory of the forms of government. According to this theory, governments are classified on the basis of numbers and the ethical theory of the common good. Thus, monarchy, aristocracy, and popular government are the good forms of government, while tyranny, oligarchy, and *licenzia* are the bad. Machiavelli mentions this theory early in the *Discourses*, though only for the record. He does not seem to have any analytical use for it at all. Instead what he proposes is an alternative theory based neither on numbers nor on ethics, but on the naturalistic theory of humours. A government is good if it satisfies the humours of all the constituent elements of society. It is utterly bad if it satisfies the humours of only a faction, and it is tolerably good if it attempts to satisfy the humours of the preponderant group in society through the instrumentality of a prince. Accordingly, as far as Machiavelli is concerned, there are only three 'forms' of government: the republic, the *licenzia*, and the monarchy. Republics are the only 'form' of government that can satisfy the humours of each of its constituents. The Roman Republic attempted to satisfy the humours of the patricians and the plebeians, and that is why, for Machiavelli, it remains the best of all republics, and why a careful analysis of its structure and function is the starting point of his political speculations.

The second casualty of the application of the theory of humours to the analysis of the Roman constitution is the theory of classical republicanism, so dear to the Florentine civic humanists. According to this theory, the doctrine of mixed government solves the problems of stability as well as those of political ethics. The institutions of the consuls, the senate and the tribunes of the plebeians are thought sufficient to check the natural tendency of all simple regimes towards instability and corruption. In Machiavelli's view, however, such an understanding of the Roman Republic does not tell us anything about what makes it 'perfect'. For a constitution must reveal not only its formal structures but also its internal dynamics, and only then does a perfect understanding of it become possible. According to him, what makes the Roman constitution perfect is the manner in which the discord between the people and the senate is resolved.[2] In his view, the distinction between the consuls and the senate, by itself, is insignificant, if not misleading. For they both represent the humours of the patricians. Instead, he argues that the key to the correct interpretation of the Roman Republic is the relationship between its two humours – the patricians and the plebeians – and not that of its three formal institutions – the consuls, the senate and the tribunes of the plebs.

Machiavelli is aware that his interpretation is both new and controversial. It is new because no one before him – neither Livy nor Plutarch – had applied it to Rome. It is controversial because past interpreters had believed union and concord (or *homonoia*) to be the primary cause of the greatness and the republicanism of Rome. No one ever thought of postulating internal conflict as a key to the study of the unity and power of Rome. But Machiavelli is prepared to argue against them. He goes 'against the opinion of many' who hold that the conflict between the two 'orders' made Rome such 'a disorderly republic', and that, had it not been for good fortune and military *virtù*, she would have turned out to be inferior to all other republics. For what the critics do not understand, he notes, is that where there is a good army there will also be good government. They do not understand that a good army is a precondition for good government, and Rome met this precondition precisely because it settled its humoral conflicts in the way it did. The Roman way of settling her internal conflict, then, turns out to be 'the first cause' of her greatness. Those who have criticized these conflicts are therefore criticizing what is in fact the very foundation of Roman republicanism.[3]

Such criticisms disregard two basic Machiavellian principles. The first is that the goodness of a thing must be judged by its effects, and the second, that in every republic there are two diverse humours, 'that of the people and that of the *grandi* and that the laws made in favour of liberty result from their discord'.[4] Moreover, they fail to realize that 'all the many good effects the [Roman] Republic produced resulted from only the best causes'. In short, there is a causal link between Roman republicanism, Roman virtue, Roman education, Roman jurisprudence, and the Roman conflict of humours: 'those examples of virtue have their origin in good education; good education in good laws; good laws in those tumults that many thoughtlessly condemn.'[5]

One of Machiavelli's toughest critics on this point was his friend Guicciardini. Even though Guicciardini, as we saw in chapter 6, approved of the humoral analysis of politics, he could not approve of the lengths to which Machiavelli had gone to argue this point. Conflict between the two orders, he thought, was one of Rome's greatest weaknesses, and one not to be imitated by anyone wishing to establish a republic. Rome would have been better off, he felt, had there been no humoral conflicts at all. What saved Rome from the disasters arising from such conflicts, and what in fact kept her free, was her military power. It was incomprehensible to him how anyone could praise the conflict of 'orders' as Machiavelli did: 'To praise the disunion was like praising an illness in a sick man simply because the medicine applied against it happened to be good.'[6]

The theory of humours explains why it made sense for Rome to become a popular rather than an aristocratic republic. For popular republics provide greater freedom and more satisfaction to the two humours than do aristocratic republics. The republican freedom as Machiavelli expounds it in the *Discourses*, is not the modern liberal notion of freedom, viz. the freedom of individuals based on the individual right to pursue unimpeded whatever ends one may choose for oneself. The republican freedom to which Machiavelli refers is instead the freedom, firstly, of one humour to pursue its ends without being obstructed by the ends of the other humour, and secondly, of individuals considered as members of a given group. This is the inescapable meaning of freedom that the theory of humours suggests. Machiavelli does not say that republics and political societies are composed of free individuals; rather, he says that they are composed of the two humours. In Machiavelli's analysis, the individuals become significant in the Roman Republic only as members of either the patrician or the plebeian humour. The freedom that these humours enjoy may well be called negative freedom, as Quentin Skinner calls it, provided it is understood that the freedom in question belongs primarily to the humours, and secondarily to individuals as members of these humours.[7] The patricians are free, not because they get everything they desire, but because they are generally satisfied with what they can get through compromise with the plebeians who assert their quite diverse desires. Similarly, the plebeians are free not because they get all they want, but because they are able to stand up to the patricians, and in doing so are able to secure for themselves a tolerable degree of power and material well-being. The story of Roman liberty as Machiavelli narrates it in the *Discourses*, is the story of the members of these humours restraining each other and, in doing so, of making gains for the whole. It is for this reason that he states axiomatically that all laws 'favourable to liberty' arise from these humoral conflicts.[8]

Umori, *Law, and Freedom*

The way laws are made and executed distinguishes a republic from a principality or a *licenzia*. It is the humours that shape the making and the functioning of laws in a republic. Machiavelli selects for analysis several of these laws, and in each case he focuses on how each 'class' accommodated its humours to those of its rivals. For only as long as such an attitude of accommodation prevailed could Rome retain its political health and liberty; as soon as such accommodation failed to materialize, the republic began to disintegrate.

Of all the laws of Rome, that which created the office of the tribunes of the plebs was by far the most important: it laid the foundation for all future accommodation between the humours of the patricians and the plebeians. In instituting this office, the Romans discovered two principles favourable to liberty: the first was that power should be shared by both humours, and the second, that the guardianship of republican liberty should rest in the hands of the plebeians rather than in those of the patricians.

The merit of the second principle is subjected to a penetrating psychological analysis. The issues involved are acquisitiveness, ambition, fear of loss, hope of gain, the natural rivalry between the rich and poor, the powerful and the marginalized. Civic freedom, if it meant anything, had to address these and related issues. Who has greater reason to make humoral tumults, Machiavelli asks: those who wish to acquire (the plebeians) or those who wish to maintain what they already possess (the patricians)? In theory there is nothing much to choose between the two. For both humours are capable of acting according to ambition, and the humour of either class could cause 'very great disturbances'. Machiavelli agrees with his humanist critics of the popular republicanism of Rome that in the end, i.e. in the later republic, the plebeians did behave ambitiously, i.e. in a politically pathological manner. And once they acquired a taste for power, they wanted, first, more of it, and later, all of it. They were not satisfied with the office of the tribunes; they successively demanded and obtained the offices of the consul, the censor, the praetor, and 'all other offices'. Nor was this enough for them; they wanted complete victory over the patricians and for this end began to 'idolize' leaders such as Marius and Caesar. Finally, 'this madness' (*furore*) led to the ruin of the republic. To this extent, he places the blame for the disintegration of the republic at the door of the plebeians.

However this might be, the story was quite different in the years of the early republic. Then the plebeians had 'greater desire' to live in liberty, and 'less appetite' for power and wealth than did the patricians. And as he notes later, in *Florentine Histories*, compared to the humours of the *popolo* of Florence, the humours of the Roman plebeians in the early republic were 'more reasonable'.[9] Moreover, Rome's determination to be an expanding and conquering republic also indicated that sharing power with the plebeians, and satisfying their humours, were the necessary prerequisites for her imperial success.

Machiavelli identifies three reasons why 'most of the time' the internal threat to liberty comes more from the wealthy and powerful than from their opposites. First, the desires produced by the fear of loss are similar to those produced by the hope of gain: 'the fear of loss produces in them the same desires as exist in those who wish to gain, because it is generally held that a man is not in secure possession of what he has if he does not gain something new in addition.'[10] The powerful are never satisfied with their power and they always seek to master others.[11] Whenever they stop fighting out of necessity, they begin to fight from ambition: 'whatever rank men climb to, never does ambition abandon them.'[12] Thus the privileged patricians consider themselves as insecure as the less privileged plebeians. Present advantage means little to them unless they can protect it by acquiring more. Secondly, it is the 'class' which has more power and wealth which indulges in the worst abuses of civic liberty, whereas the weaker 'class' is more disposed to protect it: since they cannot seize it themselves, they will not allow others to seize it. And thirdly, the ambitious behaviour of the wealthy and the powerful kindles in the hearts of their opponents envy and the desire for revenge, which in turn undermines internal liberty. It is for these very practical reasons that Machiavelli is prepared to endorse the Roman decision to place the guardianship of internal liberty in the hands of the plebeians.

The 'law of accusation'[13] is the first law that Machiavelli singles out to illustrate his thesis on the relationship between humours, internal liberty, and the rule of law. His point is that though the humours are the natural property of a body politic, they can nevertheless be made compatible with republican freedom, provided laws can be devised, not to counteract them, but rather to channel them. This was exactly what the Romans accomplished. Rather than suppress the opposing humours of the two classes, they allowed for their ordered expression. Thus if anyone acted 'in any way against free government' the law of accusation enabled citizens to bring charges against the culprit. This was the 'public', or 'legal', or 'ordinary' way of satisfying the humours as opposed to the 'private', or illegal, or 'extraordinary' way of doing it. 'Nothing makes a republic so stable and solid as to give her such an organization that the laws provide a way for the venting of the humours that agitate her.'[14]

One of the merits of such laws was that it made factionalism unnecessary. The case of Coriolanus is used to illustrate this point. Coriolanus, a patrician, never reconciled himself to the fact that the plebeians were given the office of the tribunes, and therefore waited for an opportunity to wreak vengeance on them. The opportunity presented itself when Rome was threatened by grain shortage and famine; Coriolanus then saw his chance to hurt the plebeians. He advised the senate to delay grain importation, while really intending to starve his enemies for a while. His behaviour was clearly antithetical to the spirit of internal liberty, and when the plebeians heard of his devious intentions, they threatened to mob him and kill him. The tribunes, however, intervened and stopped the plebeians from carrying out their partisan threat. In doing so, the tribunes did not act in a factional spirit, that is, they did not act in the interest of the 'class' to which they belonged; instead they acted in the interest of liberty, and of the republic as a whole. In other words, the tribunes dealt with Coriolanus according to the law and not according to their partisan interests.

For Machiavelli this incident has a deep significance for republican liberty; it shows how humours can be satisfied without damaging the proper interests of any one party. It also reminds everyone of the dangers inherent in the alternative course of action, i.e. had the plebeians taken the matter into their own hands, and dealt with Coriolanus 'privately' (*privati a privati*). Had the plebeians given vent to their 'malignant humours' in that way, they would have provoked the patricians to react accordingly, to the detriment of freedom. Machiavelli draws a causal link between such 'private' behaviour and the destruction of freedom: 'private injury produces fear; fear seeks for defence; for defence partisans are obtained; from partisans rise parties of citizens; from parties the ruin of states.'[15]

The second case that Machiavelli considers concerns calumny. If citizens and groups are to enjoy internal freedom, they should not act in a malicious, slanderous manner. If they do, their behaviour could unleash malignant humours and thereby destroy freedom. The example of Manlius Capitolinus is used to illustrate the point. He was moved by his jealousy against Furius Camillus, the general who led Rome to victory in the Gallic War of 390 BC. For his victory, Camillus was given a triumphal parade and the title 'the second founder of Rome'. This provoked jealousy in Manlius; he himself had done signally in the war by saving the Capitol from the enemies but in the eyes of the republic Camillus was the greater leader.

Manlius's jealousy against a fellow patrician was unfruitful from the start. First, he tried to turn the patricians against Camillus. And having failed in this attempt, he turned his attention to the plebeians, and began to spread calumnies against Camillus among them, accusing him of acting against their interests. Reports of the accusations greatly agitated the more gullible plebeians, and the republic was faced with a major crisis. The senate, however, did not act in a partisan way in this instance. Indeed, its judgement was not unduly influenced by the fact that Manlius himself was a senator. The senate acted according to the law, and appointed a Dictator to handle the matter. Manlius was found guilty and punished according to the law, for he could not substantiate his calumnies.

Machiavelli finds this instance instructive on two counts. The first is that unsubstantiated calumnies are incompatible with the flourishing of internal civic liberty. Freedom of action does not include the freedom to spread false rumours. It can be learned from this incident, he writes, 'how detestable calumnies are in free cities', and how important it is to repress them through laws.[16] As the law of accusations promotes republican freedom, the practice of slander damages it. For while calumnies depend on neither witnesses nor proofs, accusations need both. Accusations are made before 'magistrates, the people, the councils', whereas calumnies are spread in piazzas and corridors. In other words, freedom can flourish and can be enjoyed only if the citizens are virtuous and law-abiding. Once again, Machiavelli sees a causal connection between calumnies, malignant humours, hatred, divisions, partisanship, and the ruin of liberty.[17]

The second instructive point that Machiavelli sees here is that the Roman legal system functioned well in the early republic. Manlius's greater guilt is that he tried, though unsuccessfully, to stir up the malignant humours of both the patricians and the plebeians. He failed, in both instances, only because the senate was able and willing to act not in the interest of any particular party but rather according to the rule of the law regarding the matter.

A third case-study that Machiavelli uses to illustrate the problems related to humoral struggles, law-making and civic liberty concerns the Decemvirate (451–450 BC). He devotes considerable space to the discussion of this very troublesome, temporary 'institution' of the entire republican period.[18] How the Decemvirate, a freely appointed law commission, came to pose the most serious internal threat to civic liberty, and nearly turned Rome into a tyranny, fascinated him. As the humoral conflict between the patricians and the plebeians became acute, and an increasing number of 'disputes and dissentions' arose between them over the question of establishing 'new laws through which the city's liberty might be made more firm', both sides agreed to establish a ten-man commission with absolute powers. The entire constitution was suspended so that the ten could have a free hand in the work they were commissioned to do. This move, according to Machiavelli, was the pivotal error that the Romans committed. Without ascertaining the 'goodness or the badnesses' of the members of the commission, they imprudently gave them more than dictatorial powers. Absolute authority, even in a very short time – a year or two – will corrupt the matter of the body politic and create conditions conducive to both factionalism and ultimately the loss of liberty. Whether such a commission would produce good or bad results, states Machiavelli, will depend on whether its members are good or bad.[19] And as it happened, the members of this 'commission', all patricians, were bad, or corrupted by power, and its 'chairman', Appius Claudius, proved to be particularly wicked. His real interest in the Decemvirate was to use it as a means of realizing his own ambition of becoming the absolute ruler of Rome. With this end in mind, he tried to exploit the natural humoral conflicts between the two classes, first siding with the plebeians, and later with the patricians. In the midst of these internal squabbles, Rome was threatened from the outside, and so the Decemvirate was forced to abandon its nefarious plans. In the end, it was forced to resign. Appius was discovered and punished, a new set of laws, the Valerio-Horatian laws, was instituted, and the constitution restored.

How could such a dangerous constitutional experiment ever be undertaken by so virtuous a republic? This was Machiavelli's puzzle. It was undertaken, he notes, because of 'the same causes' that produce tyrannies everywhere: 'the too great desire of the plebeians to be free and the too great desire of the nobles to command. And when they do not agree to make a law in freedom's favour, but one of the parties rushes to support a single person, then tyranny quickly appears.'[20] In Machiavelli's analysis both the patricians and the plebeians acted imprudently, they were not behaving with the good of the body politic in mind, but rather with a concern only for the good of their own respective factions. Through the Decemvirate, the plebeians hoped to abolish the office of the consuls (the patrician base of power), while the patricians hoped to abolish the newly established office of the tribunes (the plebeian base of power).[21] For this end, both were willing to support the possibility of the one-man rule for which Appius Claudius was so desirous.

In the end, Appius Claudius failed because he was not as prudent as he was ambitious. Apart from his failure to calm the rebellion in the army, he was also involved in an illicit love affair with Virginia, whom 'he wished to take by force'.[22] She was an innocent victim; Appius was shown up and nearly lynched. All this made him unpopular with the plebeians. As for the patricians, Appius did not understand that he could never satisfy their ambitions with any promises he was able to make. For although the privileged 'class' wishes to tyrannize, there always remains a part of that 'class' which is outside the tyranny, and therefore hostile to the tyrant. As such, he could never win their full class support. Thus Appius, after losing the plebeian support, in taking the side of the patricians made a grave tactical error.

The conclusion that Machiavelli draws from the analysis of this institution is that constitutional government is an indispensable condition for the
enjoyment of liberty for both classes and individuals. No one person or
'class' should be placed above the constitution. There should always be
available in a republic the legal means whereby erring rulers, however
highly placed, can be brought to justice. Thus, in the period immediately
following the Decemvirate, Rome reverted to its old constitution.

In this context Machiavelli's defence of the constitutional provision for
the office of the Dictator is very significant.[23] The office was established to
enable the expanding republic to deal effectively with any 'urgent
perils' (*urgenti pericoli*) threatening its security; power was given to one man
to take decisions 'without consultation, and without appeal'.[24] The office
served as a guarantee of both internal liberty and external security. But the
problem that concerns Machiavelli is whether the creation of this apparently
illiberal office led to the final demise of republicanism in Rome.

Machiavelli recognizes that the office of the Dictator could fall into the
hands of the wrong person. This could happen especially if a young person
of extraordinary ability should arise in a state, for it is natural for human
beings to approve of such rare individuals in the beginning of things,
especially when they do not recognize their potential for future evil. This
may well have been the case when the Romans were so impressed by Julius
Caesar. What made Julius Caesar a menace to republicanism, however, was
not the office of the Dictator but the corruption of the military orders, and
the permission granted to generals to be away from Rome on prolonged
military commands. Such long absences enabled them to acquire a following among both the soldiers and their partisans. And it was this condition
which led to the emergence of dictators like Caesar. These dictators would
have arisen even if the office of the Dictator had not existed.[25] Yet, such
individuals get a partisan following only if corruption has already set in
within the body politic – and it can set in wherever wealth and power are
concentrated in a few hands. Thus, where this concentration of wealth is
present, civic liberty is always threatened.

The foregoing reflections bring Machiavelli to the analysis of the Agrarian Laws whose failure, in his view, was the fundamental cause of the
ultimate disintegration of the republic. The Agrarian Laws were not a single
law, but a series of laws frequently revised and updated during the period
485–121 BC. They sought to regulate the distribution of land conquered by
the Romans between the patrician magnates and the plebeian soldiers.
Their application gave rise to a spectacle of partisan humours on both sides
going out of control. On the one hand the patricians were never fully
willing to abide by the provisions of this law, which put a ceiling on how
much a single patrician family could hold. This provision was more
frequently violated than observed. The reason, as Machiavelli points out, is
that the desire for property was the strongest desire – stronger than the

desire for honour and office – driving the patricians. They were willing to share offices and honours with the plebeians, but when it came to sharing wealth they were altogether uncooperative. This uncontrolled desire of the patricians for property always posed a threat to the republican principle of keeping the individuals poor and the treasury rich.[26] It proved to be decisive and in fact fatal in the last decades of the republic.

This is not to say that there were not individual patricians who were models of virtuous conduct with regard to wealth. Machiavelli seems to glorify the spirit of 'poverty' of the citizens of the early Roman Republic. The spirit and the practice of poverty are said to be necessary for the flourishing of republican freedom. Whatever the record of the Agrarian Laws might be, he observes that, 400 years after Rome was founded, 'her people were still in the utmost poverty'.[27] Poverty did not close the door to public offices: 'such a state of society gave less desirability to riches.' Poverty was 'honoured' in the early republic, notes Machiavelli, up to about 186 BC; men such as Cincinnatus thought four *iugera* of land enough for them. Of the two fruits of war – land and honour – these virtuous Romans prized honour more than the land: 'to get honour from war was enough for them, and all the gain they left to the public.'[28] After achieving great victories on the battlefield, they, unlike Caesar, gladly returned to private life; they became 'economical, humble, careful of their little properties, obedient to the magistrates, respectful of their elders.'[29] Machiavelli's point is that poor men made good soldiers, and humble men good citizens. 'I could show with a long speech,' he writes, 'that poverty produces much better fruits than riches, and that one has honoured the cities, the provinces, the religions, and the other has overthrown them, if the writings of other men had not many times made the subject splendid.'[30]

At this point it is necessary to take a balanced view of Machiavelli's position on riches and poverty and their bearings on republican liberty. While he considers the opportunity to increase wealth and prosperity to be one of the good results of republican liberty,[31] at the same time he is aware of the dangers inherent in the uncontrolled desire for wealth. In the case of Rome, greed was the special vice of its ruling class – though, as we have seen, there were certainly many individual exceptions to this rule. It was against the evil of greed that Rome had to fight, even more determinedly than against her foreign enemies, if she was to remain free and prosperous. Ultimately, this was a war that Rome would lose. 'Rich state, poor citizens' (*publico ricco, privato povero*) was to be the secret of Roman republicanism; but it was a secret that could not be kept for too long. The force of malignant humours eventually overcame the habit of civic virtues. And the patricians were more guilty here than were the plebeians.

The plebeians, however, were equally culpable, though in another respect; they began to fight out of ambition. Either they wanted to imitate the rich and powerful patricians, or they felt jealous of them. Securing the office of the tribunes was in itself harmless; and they were led to this by necessity. But wanting to revive the Agrarian Laws retroactively was not a matter of necessity; in Machiavelli's view, it was a matter of pure ambition.[32] Indeed, the plebeians took recourse to 'extraordinary' methods to further their ambitious desires. Unlike the virtuous tribunes of the early republic, the tribunes of the later republic, the Gracchi brothers in particular, led the plebeians along an unvirtuous path. Their ambition and greed 'totally ruined Roman liberty'.[33] When they found that legal methods did not assist them in their agitation over the Agrarian Laws, they sought the support first of the Marian faction, and later of the Caesarean faction. Ultimately the 'malignant humours' produced by these laws led to civil war in which 'the victor was Caesar, the first tyrant of Rome; as a result, that city was never again free.'[34]

As much as Machiavelli stresses the importance of law and its virtuous observance by individuals and the two humours, he also stresses the need for its impartial and effective execution by public officials. In the examples given above we saw how, in the early republic, such impartial execution of laws was carried out by the tribunes and the senate. But there is another side to the story of the execution of republican laws, namely the elements of fear and terror. This is chillingly captured in the Machiavellian formula that 'in order to maintain newly gained liberty, Brutus's sons should be killed'.[35] There is no 'more powerful' remedy against corruption, 'none more effective or more certain nor more necessary than to kill the sons of Brutus'.[36] Junius Brutus, the father of Roman republicanism, not only passed judgment on his guilty sons, but was also present at their executions. In him, the love of republican liberty was stronger than even the love for his own children. Brutus's love of the fatherland and his terrible display of it, Machiavelli feels, has an exemplary quality for all lovers of liberty. The point is that (a) there always *will* be sons of Brutus, (b) there always *must* be, so that the exemplary act can be performed. Severity, fear, and display of terror are necessary if the law is to be an instrument of republican liberty. For not being naturally disposed to virtue and the good, humans would predictably yield only to force, fear, and terror. Only if their memories are regularly refreshed by such terrible spectacles as the killing of the sons of Brutus, can there be any assurance that a republic would continue to remain virtuous. Indeed, he recommends that every virtuous republic – if it wants to remain virtuous – should repeat such executions every ten years. Had Rome resorted to 'such enforcements' every ten years, he observes, she would never have become corrupt.[37]

Umori *and Rome's External Expansion*

It was the conflict between her humours, Machiavelli maintains, that made Rome free and powerful. In the foregoing pages we saw how this conflict

made Rome free: how it explained 'the perfection' of her constitution and
her laws, how it was 'the first cause' of her internal liberty and prosperity,
and how, unfortunately, good humours turned into malignant ones, and
how the immoderate pursuit of wealth led to the gradual disintegration of
the free institutions of Rome. It remains now to see how the very same
theory of humours can explain the imperial power of the republic, as well.

Machiavelli's central insight here is that the cooperation between the
patricians and the plebeians was the keystone of Roman power and of her
successes in both war and peace. The bulk of her army was recruited from
the plebeians; without them there could be neither successful wars nor
empire. The plebeians knew this, as did the patricians. The former used this
knowledge to their advantage, to wrest concessions from the latter. They
refused 'to give their names for going to war, so that to placate them it was
necessary in some way to satisfy them'.[38] At the heart of Roman republicanism, then, lies the darker idea of imperialism, something we do not see
in Aristotle's analysis of the mixed regime. It was because Rome wanted to
be powerful externally that she developed free institutions internally. The
Roman love of freedom was not based on an ethical principle applicable to
all states. It was never more than a convenient tool for conquest and empire.
So when Machiavelli says that it is easy to learn why this love of free
government springs up in people,[39] the saying has to be taken with a grain of
salt. For as he himself admits, republics that preach freedom at home
practise tyranny abroad. Of all the slaveries, he notes, 'the hardest' is that of
subjecting oneself to a republic: first, because it is more lasting and there is
little hope of escaping it, and second, because the goal of republics is 'to
enfeeble and weaken, in order to increase its own body, all other bodies'.[40]
The big republican fish lives on the small fish living around it.

The purpose of Machiavelli's celebrated comparative analysis of the
republics of Rome, Sparta and Venice[41] is to show why imperial republicanism is the best mode of republicanism. And the key to his argument is
once again the 'humoral tumults': his gaze is fixed on the issue of how these
republics managed such tumults between their plebeians and their patricians.

Sparta was an aristocratic republic; the guardianship of liberty was left in
the hands of the nobility. Lycurgus provided for 'more equality of property
and less equality of rank', such that there was 'equal poverty' among the
nobility and the plebeians.[42] Wealth and rank, in other words, did not go
together. Because of 'equal poverty' the plebeians had no reason to emulate
the nobility nor for the nobility to treat the plebeians injuriously. 'As a
result, the plebeians had no fear nor did they desire authority. And not
having imperium and not being afraid of oppression, the conflict they might
have had with the nobility and the reason for tumults were taken away.'[43]
Furthermore, foreigners were not allowed the privilege of citizenship, and
foreign trade was discouraged. In fact, to make Sparta less attractive to
outsiders and outsiders to Sparta, 'leather' money was made the legal

currency. Lycurgus sought to control the possibility of acquisitive humours becoming malignant humours by means of strict legislative and constitutional techniques. In other words, constitutionally Sparta was designed to be small and stationary, and its laws removed all reasons for humoral tumults.[44]

The case of Venice is not far different. It too was an aristocratic republic, and the guardianship of liberty stayed with the 'gentlemen' class. By constitutional arrangement and by voluntary agreement the *popolani* were kept out of government. Besides, the gentlemen of Venice were not like the feudal gentlemen elsewhere; they had no castles nor 'subjects whom they oppressed', their wealth was based not on land but on commerce and mobile property. In other words, the Venetian gentlemen were disposed to treat the *popolani* according to legal conventions. The final outcome of this situation was that Venice was able to govern itself 'without tumult'.[45] At the same time, its humoral balance prevented it from becoming a great imperial power.

Rome, by contrast, as we have already seen, wanted to be an expanding republic. For this reason, she made use of the plebeians in war and granted citizenship to conquered peoples. She deliberately allowed the plebeians the opportunity to increase their power and so also plenty of occasions for tumults. Machiavelli clearly establishes the link between Rome's humoral tumults and imperial expansion: 'if Rome had taken away the causes of tumults, she would have taken away the causes of expansion as well.'[46]

But the story does not end here. Machiavelli's clinching argument is that Rome made the wiser decision, because she understood not only the advantages of humoral tumults, but also those of natural necessity. Natural necessity dictates that all states be exposed to the need to expand. The wiser states prepare for expansion, while the foolish states neglect such preparations, yet still get forced down the expansionist path. 'Truly it is very natural and normal to desire to conquer, and always, when men do it who can, they will be praised or at least not blamed; but when they cannot, and want to do it all the same, there lie the error and the blame.'[47] The error and the blame of Sparta and Venice lie here: not being constitutionally prepared for empire, they nevertheless embarked upon it. Their humoral tumults, which they attempted to suppress, ultimately got the better of them, with very disastrous results.[48] 'Because all our actions imitate nature,' Machiavelli reasons, 'it is not possible or natural for a slender stem to hold large branches.'[49] Therefore it is very foolish for small states to attempt to conquer large states, which was what both Sparta and Venice did. At the very least, they should have involved their respective plebeians in the legislative process and the war. Because they did not meet this minimum requirement, and because they did not take into account necessity, they haplessly succumbed to their own desire for power.

Machiavelli's rejection of the Spartan and Venetian models of the republic is uncompromising. By contrast, his attitude towards the Swiss republics –

also small and free – is less critical, and certainly more respectful. They enjoyed, he reports, a truly 'free freedom' (*libera libertà*).[50] The Swiss were concerned only with defending their autonomous government from external threat (*mantenere libertà*) and not in extending their power over their neighbours (*acquistare imperio*).[51] This disposition, though admirable, is not worthy of imitation; the Swiss were able to follow such a policy because of their unique geography and the special conditions prevailing in that part of Europe. Machiavelli calls these conditions the 'many contrary humours' (*molti umori contrari*) of that region.[52] These were the humours of the Swiss republics themselves, of princes such as the Duke of Austria who maintained their little principalities, and of the Emperor. The Emperor enjoyed a great reputation among the Swiss as well as among the princes; he acted as a mediator and conciliator between them.[53] It is because of these conditions that the Swiss could be small and free and not be threatened by outside powers. In Machiavelli's view, however, the Swiss were the exceptions that proved the rule. And the rule is that only the Roman model could satisfy the humour for freedom and power. According to the Roman model, however, a good republic had to adopt an aggressive, rather than a defensive, foreign policy. Rome followed a policy of 'hegemony' over her neighbours, according to which she first sought to maintain a dominant position over them. When that position was fully consolidated, she simply annexed them and granted the people Roman citizenship.[54] In this manner, she gained full control over the entire Italian peninsula and regions beyond.

What is clear is that Machiavelli does not recommend republicanism for the sake of liberty alone. Self-government is not enough to satisfy the humours for wealth and power. Indeed, self-government without expansion, he feels, is a foolish policy. Only a policy of self-government with expansion is consistent with his theory of humours. The *virtù militare* that he greatly admired was an aggressive, not a defensive, capacity.

The superiority of republics over principalities lies precisely in that they are better able to satisfy the different humours of both individuals and 'classes'. A good republic allows its classes to express their humours, and permits its citizens to act according to theirs. This is what made Rome so great. Thus, she had a person of Fabius Maximus Cunctator's humour – of caution and delay – when faced with Hannibal; and she had a person of Scipio Africanus's humour – of daring – when the war had to be taken to the African shores. The free scope given to the expression of the humours makes republics more flexible than principalities: 'Thence it comes that a republic, being able to adapt herself by means of the diversity of her body of citizens to a diversity of the conditions of times better than a prince can, is of greater duration than a princedom and has good fortune longer.'[55]

Machiavelli believes that there is in the collective humours of the body politic a natural tendency to be aggressive towards other bodies politic. And even if for perfectly sensible reasons certain lawgivers and constitutions attempt to resist this tendency, in the end bodies politic would succumb to the temptation. This, according to him, was what happened to Sparta and Venice. For very laudable reasons they preferred to stay small and beautiful, peace-loving and stationary. But their good resolve did not and could not last for ever. In the end they were irresistibly attracted to the goal of empire. They attempted to build their respective empire only to discover that their internal institutions were not fitted for it. They embarked upon imperialism anyhow, and ended in inglorious defeat.

Machiavelli's conclusion is that it is difficult for republics to stand still or to overcome their natural procilivity for expansion. It is therefore better, he thinks, to plan for expansion and to design domestic institutions accordingly. An expanding republic cannot afford to be an aristocratic one; it must be a popular one, for it is from among the people that an expanding republic can recruit its army. This is what Rome discovered early in its republican history. As a result, it gave the plebeians a share in domestic power and foreign conquests. It satisfied the humours of the plebeians and at the same time built an army which no one could resist.

Machiavelli's explanation of how Rome became powerful is now complete. She took into account both the force of natural humours and the law of motion to which all states are subject. The result was that she chose to be free and imperialistic. As long as her military policies were carried out strictly within the bounds of law and prudence, Rome was able to satisfy the demands of both freedom and power.

The Decline of the Roman Republic

The theory of humours explains not only Rome's perfection but also how she came to lose that perfection. As a naturalistic theory it gives us an insight not only into the health, but also into the illness and mortality of bodies politic. Rome was no exception.

It is true that Machiavelli occasionally mentioned the idea of a perpetual republic. I do not think that he seriously believed that any sublunar entity, including a republic, even with the aid of periodic renewal, could overcome the limitations of existence in cyclic time. All sublunar entities in the long run must die. It is in this context that we see him speculating on the possibility of a perpetual republic. If the decennial executions could be carried out perpetually, he thought, Rome would never have become corrupt.[56] Similarly, if she was lucky enough to find a succession of virtuous leaders such as Camillus and Cincinnatus, she could have gone on for ever as a virtuous republic.[57] At the same time, on a more realistic note he believed that collective human passions were too unstable for them to guarantee perpetual stability. There is no way that the humours by themselves can provide for permanent wisdom. 'And because no certain remedy can be given for such disorders as arise in republics, it follows that a perpetual republic cannot be established; in a thousand unexpected ways her ruin is caused.'[58]

The question still remains: If Rome's constitution was so perfect, why did it finally self-destruct? This is a question which every student of Machiavelli is forced to ask, all the more so since so much is made of Rome's perfection. Piecing together the various comments which he makes on this question, the following picture emerges. At the most abstract level, the tumults connected with the Agrarian Laws and the prolongation of the military commands affected both internal liberty and the constitutional process.[59] The impasse to which the Agrarian Laws took Rome exposed the insatiable greed of the patricians and the vaulting ambitions of the plebeians. Individual patricians and the plebeians began to seek personal wealth and ambition at the expense of the liberty of others. They resorted to private ways, as opposed to the public, legal ways, of acquiring partisan following.[60] Citizens who should have been rewarded were injured in the later republic, and those who should have been trusted began to be viewed with fear and suspicion.[61] Instead of being given on the basis of merit and *virtù*, offices began to be given on the basis of patronage (*grazia*) and power. Honours were distributed 'outside the honourable and established causes'.[62] Legislation became the instrument of factions, so that the freedom of speech intended for debates turned into partisan harangues. Thus, ordinary citizens were either deceived or forced into decreeing their own ruin.[63]

Deterioration of the standards of Rome's foreign policy paralleled the deterioration of the standards of her internal policies. The practice of extending military commands abroad arose as a reaction to the practice of extending the tenure of civil magistrates at home. First, the plebeians wanted the one-year tenure of the tribunes to be extended. The patricians reacted to this by demanding a similar extension for the proconsuls in foreign lands.[64] Such prolongation of military commands created the conditions for the emergence and success of someone like Julius Caesar. In this way, notes Machiavelli bitterly, 'Caesar was able to conquer his own fatherland'.[65] Then there was the question of the foreign customs of the conquered peoples corrupting the virtuous customs of the Romans.[66] Furthermore, as Roman *virtù* failed and as her armies lost their 'ancient valour', the empire was being destroyed by the Goths, the Vandals, and others.[67] Finally, the republic conquered too many territories too fast, and overextended itself. It was as if there was some kind of inevitability working against the continued vitality of republicanism. 'If the Romans had never prolonged the magistracies and the commands, they might not have come so quickly to great power, for their conquests might have been later, but they would have come later still to slavery.'[68]

But the question still arises: If Rome had discovered the best way to satisfy her humours, why did the civil war occur and Rome lose her liberty to Caesar? Here Machiavelli links his theory of humours to his other companion theory of natural (celestial) motions operating in the universe: viz. natural motions that affect the fortunes of corporate bodies such as republics, churches, and kingdoms. The idea that the 'matter' or the 'subject' of a body politic passes through periods of virtue and corruption frequently recurs in Machiavelli's thought. When the 'matter' is virtuous, the corrupt behaviour of particular individuals will not cause general social disintegration. Likewise when the 'matter' is corrupt, the virtuous behaviour of ordinary citizens will not do anything to reverse the trend.[69] In the time of the Tarquins and the first Brutus, for example, the Roman people were not yet corrupt; later, in the time of the second Brutus, they had become completely corrupt. Because of this, Caesar was able to blind his followers and subvert the republic.[70] For when there is universal corruption, existing laws, however good they might be, become totally out of place. The laws suited to a good people are utterly unsuitable when this same people becomes corrupt: the same 'form' cannot inform two different kinds of 'matter'.[71] We note here clear evidence of Machiavelli's indebtedness to pre-modern physics and cosmology; as L.J. Walker has pointed out, according to pre-modern natural philosophy, matter must be suitably disposed before it can receive an appropriate form. Contrary forms, e.g. the hot and the cold, the dry and the moist, cannot subsist in the same matter. Nor can matter which has been disposed in some specific way receive a form contrary to the matter so disposed. So too with the body politic.[72] We note also that Machiavelli attaches the notion of the quality of time to this theory of pre-modern physics, thus introducing the elements of astrological thought. The 'matter' or the 'subject' of the body politic accordingly can undergo a qualitative change of being 'good' or 'bad', depending on the particular phase of the astral cycle in which it finds itself. This is made evident in his application of the notion of the quality of time to the life of countries. Thus political agents – those who apply form to matter – must consider the quality of the times in which they undertake their political actions.[73] For an action to be efficacious, there should be harmony between the times of the country, the times of the agent, and the action in question. Thus the massacre of the Ephors by Cleomenes and the assassinations perpetrated by Romulus were politically effective because at that time their respective 'subjects' – Sparta and Rome – were not yet 'spotted with corruption'.[74] Going one step further, he now explains the 'cosmic' reason for the failure of Manlius Capitolinus, and the success of Marius, in corrupting Rome:

> If Manlius had been born in the times of Marius and Sulla, when the material was already corrupt and he could have imprinted on it the form of his ambition, he would have had the same end as Marius and Sulla and the others who after them strove to gain tyrannical power. So likewise, if Sulla and Marius had lived in Manlius's times, in their first undertakings they would have been crushed . . . Of necessity, therefore, a man wishing

to get authority in a republic and to imprint a bad form on it, must come to it when its matter is already injured by time, having been little by little, from generation to generation, brought to evil.[75]

In conclusion, it may be noted that the theory of humours explains both the conditions under which a republic may flourish, satisfying the humours of its 'classes' and its citizens, and the conditions under which it may decline. That Machiavelli's theory of humours can explain both the *virtù* and the corruption of republics is certainly part of its originality. How the theory of humours can explain the corruption of republics is discussed at great length in *Florentine Histories*.

CHAPTER 9

Humours and Licenzia

Compared to the princedom and the republic, the *licenzia* provides the least desirable way of satisfying the political humours. As we have seen, the humoral need for security, freedom and expansion is best satisfied in well-ordered republics. And in a princedom, if the need for freedom is not fully satisfied, at least the need for security, and even expansion, is satisfied. In a *licenzia*, however, there is no true satisfaction of the need for either liberty, security, or expansion. Unfortunately for Machiavelli, his own much-loved Florence could never be either a true republic or a true princedom; it always remained, in his judgement, something in between. According to the 'Discursus', 'she has never been either a republic or princedom having the qualities each requires, because we cannot call that republic well-established in which things are done according to the will of one man yet are decided with the approval of many'.[1] In Machiavelli's judgement, Florence did not enjoy true republican freedom: her government, he says, did not change from liberty to slavery, but from slavery to licence.[2] As for expansion, there was none: her wars, often unnecessary, expensive and unsuccessful, impoverished rather than enriched her treasury.

Machiavelli is both critical and understanding of Florence's plight. As a secretary of its government for 14 years, he had of course acquired a most intimate understanding of what was wrong with the Republic. His numerous diplomatic papers and his comments both in *The Prince* and the *Discourses* bear witness to this. But it is in the 'Discursus' and the *Florentine Histories* that he finds the time and the leisure to write reflectively on the subject, in terms of causes and solutions. The fact that these works were commissioned by the Medici, whom he did not admire but whose patronage he badly needed for survival, need not put in doubt the soundness of his analyses and the integrity of his conclusions.[3]

The question of why Florence turned out to be a *licenzia*, however, is a much larger question than that of Machiavelli's interpretation of the Medici regime. Typically, the broader question of Florence's constitution and politics is analysed within the context of the theory of humours. Thus, in answer to the fundamental question, 'Why did the humoral struggles in Florence produce a *licenzia* there?', he finds that it is because these struggles always resulted in the creation of factions (*sette*). Ultimately, Florence did not know how to satisfy all her relevant humours. 'The reason why Florence has always changed her governments,' the 'Discursus' begins, 'is that she has never been either a republic or a principality having the qualities each requires, because we cannot call that republic well-established in which things are done according to the will of one man yet are decided with the approval of many; nor can we believe a republic fitted to last, in which there is no satisfaction of those humours that must be satisfied if republics are not to be ruined.'[4] The ruling idea of the *Florentine Histories*, as he states in the Preface, concerns the civil strife and internal hostilities in Florence and the effects these have produced there. Whereas in other cities such as Rome and Athens there was only one sort of conflict, which either increased or ruined the power of those cities, in Florence there were three: first, there were the conflicts within the nobility itself, secondly, those between the nobility and the *popolo*, and thirdly, between the *popolo* and the *plebe*. Not only did Florence have this puzzling three-tiered conflict, it also had a situation in which the victorious party, having conquered the others, also divided itself into two.[5] Whereas in Rome 'the diversity of humours', or 'the grave and natural' enmities between the patricians and the plebeians produced a constitutional unity between them, in Florence the same phenomena kept them disunited. Indeed, the same phenomenon produced different or even opposite effects in the two cities. The enmities in Rome were settled in debates (*disputando*), while those in Florence erupted into armed conflicts (*combattendo*); those in Rome resulted in laws, while those in Florence resulted in the exile and death of citizens; those in Rome increased military power, while those in Florence decreased it; those in Rome ultimately led to Caesarean tyranny, while those in Florence led to striking equality.[6] Whereas the plebeians of Rome were willing to share political power with the patricians, the *popolo* of Florence wanted 'to be alone in power' (*essere solo nel governo*). Their desires were always 'harmful and injurious' to the welfare of Florence. They drove the nobility to desperation, and ultimately to extinction. In Rome, the plebeians were gradually admitted into public offices, the magistracies and the army. This policy enabled a large number of them to bring themselves up to the level of the patricians in virtue and competence, so that Rome, thus united, was able to increase her freedom and power. Florence, on the other hand, did exactly the opposite. Its *popolo* contrived to deprive the nobility of its specific civil competence, namely skill and expertise in arms and warfare. The nobility were forced to 'de-naturalize' themselves; if they wished to have any share in power, they had not only to become but also to appear to be like the *popolo* 'in their conduct, their spirit, and their way of life'. Thus, they were forced to change their class ensigns and their family titles. In short, the *popolo* behaved like a new prince, and forced radical changes upon the power structure of Florence.

Machiavelli does not approve of the *popolo's* actions. He holds them especially responsible for Florence's unfree institutions and for the loss of the military tradition. The nobility possessed, he notes, virtue in arms and generosity of spirit. By destroying the nobility as a class, the *popolo* also destroyed all chances of Florence becoming a military power. And while they extinguished the military tradition in the nobility, a tradition so necessary for the political evolution of Florence, they were quite unable to rekindle it in themselves, where it did not exist in the first place. The result was that Florence, instead of growing into a great power, always grew 'humble and despicable'. Whereas in Rome, the political, military and diplomatic skills of the patricians were fruitfully transmitted to the plebeians, in Florence the comparable skills of the nobility were entirely lost because of the political stupidity and the intransigence of the *popolo*.[7]

Given the frequency of humoral conflicts, Florence had only two real options before it: it could satisfy the humours of its social groups either publicly or privately.[8] But the conflicts in question became means of achieving 'private', or personal and partisan ends, rather than 'public', or common and truly republican ends. The key factor in attaining power by private means was the availability of vast amounts of private wealth. Between such wealth and private ways of acquiring public power, Machiavelli believed, there was always a dangerous link. For he favoured a policy of the acquisition of only a moderate amount of private wealth, and of keeping the treasury, not the individual, rich. If vast amounts of private wealth were allowed to buy public power, the result would be the loss of freedom and the corruption of political institutions. Thus, as he remarks, in Florence private money was used to ensure a partisan following, to protect one's partisan friends from the law, to aid them, even when utterly undeserved, to secure public offices, and to organize public festivals and games to distract the attention of the dissatisfied. By contrast, public ways of solving humoral conflicts placed the stress on merit and virtue. According to this policy, one could distinguish oneself by serving in the army and in wars, by capturing cities and carrying out successful diplomatic offensives, and by effectively advising the state of its best interests. In Florence, however, the humoral conflicts never produced publicly beneficial results. 'The enmities in Florence were always those of factions and therefore always dangerous.'[9] Nothing was established there 'to cause fear in the optimates, so that they would not set up factions which are the ruin of government'.[10]

The bulk of the *Florentine Histories* and the 'Discursus' is taken up with the validation of these ideas, with reference to the different phases of the history of Florence.[11] Of special interest here are Machiavelli's analyses of the significance of the colonial origin of Florence, of the beginning of the humoral conflict in the early thirteenth century, of the struggle between the nobility and the *popolo*, between the *popolo* and the *plebe*, and of the Medici regime from 1434 to 1494.

The fact of Florence's unfree origin affects Machiavelli's analysis of Florence in a general way. For according to him, only states with a free origin can have a free constitution and a tradition of proper government. This is a key factor in the case of Rome; clearly, its founder did not depend on others. Florence, on the other hand, started as a 'market town' convenient for commerce and trade. These markets, he notes, were 'the cause' of the first building erected there. Florence later became a colony of the Roman Republic of the civil war period.[12] Thus, we are reminded of how, already from the beginning, the market, commerce, colonial status and civil strife came to be associated with Florence. With the decline of the Roman Empire, she came under the power of the Barbarians, until Charlemagne refounded her in the ninth century. After this, she existed successively under the Berengers and the German Emperors. But this millennial experience of being unfree and 'under the power of others' cast its shadow on Florence. Indeed, even after she had 'freed herself from the Empire'[13] and found 'a chance for taking a breath'[14] her attempts to make her own laws and act as a free community were not quite successful. Her new *ordini*, 'being mingled with the old', were not good. For even as an independent entity, she did not make laws for the common good, but only for the advantage of factions. Her chief failure here was not so much a lack of independence in the making of the laws, as an inability to execute them impartially. This was particularly true of laws regarding capital punishment: those who had power and the influence of money always managed to protect the guilty.[15]

The Guelf–Ghibelline humours, whose 'seeds' arose from the struggle between Henry IV and Gregory VII,[16] came to Florence only in 1215, more than a century after they had arrived in Italy. As a principle of division, they further exacerbated the already existing natural enmities between the nobility and the newly emerging *popolo*. As a result, the nobility and the *popolo* came to be divided along new lines, to which further impetus was given by a typically Florentine phenomenon: the feuds among her leading families.[17] The city was constantly in turmoil, not only because of the natural humoral conflicts common to all cities, but also because of several others: those between the *popolo* and the *grandi*, the Guelfs and the Ghibellines, the Blacks and the Whites, and the Uberti and the Buondelmonti.[18] The humoral character of these conflicts is highlighted by Machiavelli's use of the metaphors of the body and its illnesses: the late appearance of the Guelf–Ghibelline humours only made the Florentine body politic less able to withstand them. 'Just as in our bodies, where the later the illnesses come, the more dangerous and deadly they are, so with Florence: the later it was in joining the factions of Italy, by so much more was it afflicted by them.'[19]

Although the Guelf faction in Florence ultimately won over the Ghibellines, the natural conflict between the nobility and the *popolo* continued to move on its relentless course. By the end of the thirteenth century, the *popolo* had won a complete victory over the nobility, and the famous Ordinances of Justice (*Ordinamenti della iustizia*) of 1293 were promulgated. Though later critics see this legislation as a step forward in Florentine republicanism, Machiavelli sees it quite differently. It was a far cry from the fundamental legislation of the Roman Republic, which brought forth the institution of the Tribunate and made Rome a 'perfect' republic. Far from reconciling the two humours (in this case the Florentine nobility and the *popolo*), the Ordinances of Justice sought not only to eliminate the nobility altogether from a share in power but also to 'de-class' them. Machiavelli is highly critical of this. For one thing, it goes against the principles of his theory of humours, which require that each humour accord legitimacy to the other: 'It was not prudent always to strive for complete victory (*ultima victoria*),' he comments, and 'never wise to make men despair, because he who does not hope for good, does not fear ill.'[20] Yet complete victory was exactly what the *popolo* strove for; they sought to eliminate the nobility as a class. In doing so, they neglected to remember that in the wars of the past, it was the nobility that had stood by them with honour, and that if Florence were ever to become a respectable military power, she could do so only with the full cooperation of the nobility. Hence, 'it was neither good nor just to persecute them with so much hatred.'[21]

It is quite remarkable that although Machiavelli is often identified as a popular republican, as far as the Florentine Republic is concerned, he is very sympathetic to the nobility. This is so, not because he approves of their arrogance, but because, as he sees it, they were the repository of military virtue. To eliminate them from political and social life was tantamount to eliminating military virtue from the body politic. Just as in ancient Rome, the cooperation of the plebeians was indispensable for war, so in modern Florence the cooperation of the nobility was indispensable. For this reason, it was suicidal of Florence to destroy its nobility. 'This ruin of the nobility was so great and so humbled them that they never afterwards had the courage to take arms against the *popolo*; on the contrary they steadily became more courteous and abject. This was the cause by which Florence was stripped not merely of arms but of all generosity.'[22] As Machiavelli sees it, the destruction of the nobility had far-reaching consequences for Florence. First of all, it placed the government of Florence in the hands of 'men nurtured in trade' (*uomini nutricati nella mercanzia*), not a highly flattering description of the Florentine *popolo*. Secondly, it made Florence depend on the fortune of others, namely other states stronger than themselves, and on mercenaries. Thirdly, it resulted in an attitudinal change towards war. War was no longer considered an indispensable means of politics. Military virtue came to be separated from the virtues of citizenship. It came to be concentrated in or identified with men who were not citizens fighting for their fatherland, but those who looked upon war as a profession like trade and commerce, law and medicine. As he puts it, arms came into the hands of either the lesser princes or 'men without a state'. The former did not look upon war as a means of attaining political glory but rather as a means of increasing their private wealth. The 'men without a state' were no different; nurtured in arms from infancy, and this being their only skill, they sought to obtain through the military profession private possessions and power for themselves. Thanks to these two groups, war in Italy became a means of amassing private wealth, when it did not appear as a cruel joke. For, as Machiavelli notes, there was a tacit understanding among these lesser princes and mercenaries that when two states fought, both would generally lose.[23]

What Machiavelli criticizes here is, of course, the influence of the spirit of trade on the institution of war. Just as the spirit of trade contributes to political factionalism – to corrupting the potentially healthy political humours and turning them into politically malignant humours – so also it turns war into an abject 'profession' aligned to private profit-making. He would have liked to see the emergence in Florence of a constitution that would have permitted the nobility to transmit its military virtues and traditions to the *popolo*, so that the latter could be brought fully into the proper republican tradition: in this case a tradition of combining the commercial and the martial spirit. Such a constitution would have made Florence both free and powerful. The Ordinances of Justice, however, did not achieve this end. For all practical purposes, it was a partisan legislation, not worthy of a true republic. And the culprit responsible for this, in his view, was the *popolo*.

If the *popolo* had destroyed the nobility, they were not better disposed towards the Florentine plebs.[24] The conflict between the *popolo* and the plebs forms the central issue of Book Three of the *Florentine Histories*. The imaginary speeches found in this book are among the best, if not the best, in the entire work. They have a common theme: factional struggle has become so characteristic of Florentine republicanism that whoever is in power wants to be alone in it, and to destroy the opposition. This is of course true of the *popolo*; but it is equally true of the plebs, who came to power for a very brief period after the famous Ciompi Revolution of 1378. *Popolo* or plebs, Florentine factions had lost all sense of the common good. Their 'humanism' and their 'love of the fatherland' were totally inadequate to overcome their avarice and ambition.[25] The world of Florentine factionalism was one in which 'men devoured one another'.[26] They made laws and statutes not for the common good but for their own; wars, treaties and alliances were decided not for common glory but for the pleasure of the few.[27] The result was that when one party was defeated another appeared, because Florentine republicanism did not appreciate the importance of the principle of opposition to those who actually hold power in government. And without opposition to government no free government, let alone republican government, can function. It would be like a body without the opposition of its humours: without such opposition, the body cannot maintain its health, which consists in the balance of its humours. That is why, ruling without opposition, the victorious class either divided itself into new factions, or sought to destroy any other social class which challenged its abuse of freedom and power. This is exactly what happened to the plebs. They were ill-treated, underpaid, and kept completely under the control of the guildmasters. If they wanted to seek redress, as indeed they did, they had nowhere to turn except to the magistrates of the very same guilds that oppressed them. Machiavelli uses 'one of the most fiery and greatest experience' to deliver his own critique of the *popolo* in their relation to the plebs.

Living in a nasty world as they do, where humans devour one another, the plebs had to take advantage of the dissensions among the *popolo* themselves, and were forced to take up arms, plunder churches, and loot the property of their oppressors. For dangerous gain is to be preferred to quiet poverty. They were forced to take this course of action not by choice but by necessity – the necessity which a corrupt republic imposed on them. The *popolo* intimidate them by their birth ('the antiquity of blood') and their wealth; but distinctions based on these factors have no sanction in nature. For all men have 'one and the same beginning' (*uno medesimo principio*) and therefore are 'equally ancient and by nature are all made in one way. Strip us all naked; you will see us all alike; dress us then in their clothes and they in ours; without doubt we shall seem noble and they ignoble, for only poverty and riches make us unequal.'[28] Though by nature everything belongs in common, the fraudulent and the violent appropriate everything for themselves. The good and the prudent are always smothered by poverty and lack of power, 'for faithful servants are always servants, and good men always poor'. In a *licenzia*, no one can come out of servitude and poverty, except the rapacious. In such a society wealth is open more to rapine than to work (*più alle rapine che alla industria*), more to the evil than to the good arts. Given this condition of necessity, rules of good conscience have no role to play in political conflicts. For in such a society, those who win are always praised, no matter what means they employ. When hunger and prison threaten one, one cannot and should not be afraid of hell. Natural justice means nothing in a world given over to avarice and ambition. Necessity, not conscience, is the proper guide of action in such a world. 'When nothing teaches, necessity teaches ... when necessity pushes, rashness is judged prudence.'[29]

In fact, the speaker goes one step further: the plebs should not only seek to free themselves from the *popolo*; they should be satisfied with nothing less than becoming their masters. The *occasione* for them to achieve this end is now present, and it must be seized; they must attack before being attacked. 'Thus many of us will gain honour and all will gain security.'[30] In other words, the intentions of the plebs are not any nobler than those of the *popolo*. They are as intent on being alone in power as were the *popolo*, and before them, the nobles. Thus, the lesson of the Ciompi Revolution is that it did not fundamentally change anything in Florence. It was a failed attempt on the part of the plebs to overthrow and replace the *popolo*. It was not a republican revolution. The only good thing to emerge from the revolt of the plebs was the character of Michele Lando, a barefoot wool worker who became the leader of the Ciompi government. In Machiavelli's eyes, he managed to rise above partisan interests, and to govern the country in the true republican spirit. Machiavelli gives him high marks for this: 'in courage, in prudence and goodness he surpassed every citizen of his time. He deserves to be numbered among the few who have benefited their fatherland.'[31] For this very reason, however, he was hated by the faction-ridden country, which banished him for life from Florence. This is Machiavelli's criticism of Florentine republicanism: it could not find a place of honour for a person of Lando's republican spirit and achievements.

It is in the treatment of the Medici regime (1434–1494), however, that Machiavelli's analysis of Florence as a *licenzia* reaches its highest point of excellence. A short version of it can be found in the 'Discursus', while an extended version can be found in the *Florentine Histories* IV–VIII. What the Medici regime demonstrates, in his view, is that factionalism can take different forms, and that it need not be, as in the pre-Medici regimes, riddled with constant violence and instability. The Medicis showed how a corrupt republic can use factionalism to its advantage, to achieve a reasonable degree of stability. The key to their success in achieving this end was the power of their immense private wealth, prudently used. The Medici ascent to power was spread over several generations. Beginning with Salvestro, and continuing with Veri, Giovanni, Cosimo, Piero I, Lorenzo, Piero II, and Leo X, its golden age was of course the period of Cosimo and Lorenzo the Magnificent. The peculiar feature of the Medici regime is that it was able to maintain the facade of a republic while in fact it conducted its affairs as if it was a monarchy. And this was achieved without any formal change of the constitution of Florence, which remained, in name at least, republican. As Machiavelli puts it rather delicately, it 'tended to move more towards a princedom than towards a republic'.[32] The stability that the Medici were able to produce does not mean that factionalism was overcome; on the contrary, it only means that the Medici were able to manipulate it for their own benefit.

The key to their success in this was the liberal use of their private wealth. It was in this way that they gained indirect control over the government, and especially over the electoral machinery. No one could rise to power, nor obtain any significant position in government, who was not a protégé of the Medici. In other words, the Medici regime was a factional regime *par excellence*, and in Machiavelli's view it did irreparable damage to the prospects of Florence ever becoming free and powerful. And it did this damage in three principal ways.

In the first place, the Medici regime failed to satisfy all the humours of Florence, that is, the people of the first rank (the *primi*), those of the middle rank (the *mezzani*), and the rest of the citizens (the *ultimi*). The reason for its ultimate failure and for Florence's misfortunes was precisely this. The stability that the Medici were able to introduce was therefore not true humoral stability, which, as we have seen, can only result from the due satisfaction of all relevant humours. The stability produced by the Medici resembled instead the stability of a monarchy, which satisfies only those humours whose support it needs for its maintenance. Seen in this light, the Medici regime is a case-study in how the skilful use of private wealth can interfere with the functioning of free institutions, without anything effectively being able to put a stop to it. The love of freedom is no match for love of money. And the Medici, particularly Cosimo, understood this aspect of human appetites very well. As Machiavelli points out, with money Cosimo influenced not merely private citizens, but also the public government: not merely his friends, but also the *condottieri*. Florence became so corrupt under his influence that the citizens were ready 'to sell' their republic, and they found a 'buyer' (*comperatore*) in Cosimo.[33] In money, he found a novel means of satisfying the political humours of his followers. The contrast between Rome and Florence could not have been sharper; whereas Rome satisfied the humours of its groups through law and *ordini*, Florence, under the Medici, did so through patronage and the corruption of laws. Cosimo perfected the strategy of taking advantage of the humoral conflicts of Florence by controlling the electoral bags – he made sure that these bags contained the names of only his partisans.[34] With this type of indirect control, he had no need to intervene in every public dispute. By the same token, his enemies had no way of outwitting him either. As Machiavelli cryptically puts it, 'whoever opposed him lost either time and money or his position . . . civil strife always increased his influence in Florence.'[35] There was not one important citizen in Florence who was not financially in Cosimo's debt. Indeed, his power of credit was great even among foreign states. Through credit he so emptied Naples and Venice of money, Machiavelli observes, that he could dictate to them any terms he pleased.[36]

The second point of Machiavelli's criticism of the Medici concerns their failure to administer laws impartially, and therefore to maintain even a semblance of republican liberty. The most reprehensible aspect of the regime was that it protected the guilty from the magistrates purely on the basis of factional friendships.[37] The persons and properties of Cosimo's enemies, such as the Albizzi, were never safe. In Florence, as one of Cosimo's critics pointed out, 'the laws were less powerful than men'.[38] And 'because of the liberality of the Medici the people had been made deaf and liberty was not known in Florence . . .'[39] 'Every case that came before the magistrates, no matter how small, became part of a wider struggle between parties; secrets were made public, both good and bad men were favoured and opposed; good men as much as bad were in the same way torn to shreds; no magistrate did his duty.'[40] Perhaps nothing describes the story of their abuse of power and their violations of the law better than the imaginary speech which Machiavelli puts into Piero Medici's mouth. Addressing his supporters from his deathbed, he remarks:

> It does not suffice you to be leaders in so large a city, and for you who are
> so few to have those offices, dignities, and advantages with which earlier
> many citizens were wont to be honoured; it does not suffice you to
> divide among yourselves the goods of your enemies; it does not suffice
> you to distress all others with taxes, while you, free from them, have all
> the public profit, and distress everybody with every sort of injury. You
> plunder your neighbour of his goods, you sell justice, you escape civil
> lawsuits, you oppress peaceful men, and the arrogant you make powerful.
> I do not believe that in all Italy there are so many instances of violence
> and avarice as in this city.[41]

The third criticism of the Medici is that they further destroyed the military virtues of the Florentines.[42] The Medici were the models *par excellence* of those who were 'nurtured' in commerce, for whom wars were interesting only if they advanced their personal wealth. Machiavelli pointedly remarks that Cosimo was 'an unarmed man',[43] one 'who loved himself more than his fatherland, and this world more than the other'.[44] What a strange combination of loves here: and how different from the 'Eight Saints' who 'loved their fatherland more than their souls'.[45] What is the implication of Cosimo's loving himself more than his fatherland? Loving the fatherland would have meant loving it enough to defend it, to die for it in war. For Cosimo, however, the power of money became a substitute for the power of arms. As we have already seen, he sought to score victories in foreign affairs on the basis of his bank credit, rather than on the basis of the valour of the Florentine Army. And as Machiavelli points out, he did not expand the 'Florentine Empire' with any honourable conquests.[46] The same is true of Lorenzo; Italian arms were inactivated by his 'wisdom and authority', Machiavelli remarks with irony.[47] 'Lorenzo disarmed the people, in order to hold Florence,' the 'Ghiribizzi' notes bitterly.[48]

In this context, it is necessary to evaluate the significance of Machiavelli's recognition of the Medici's patronage of arts and letters. Cosimo, he notes, had caused the founding of the Platonic Academy of Florence and the introduction of Greek learning generally. He had also patronized Marsilio Ficino, 'the second father of the Platonic philosophy'.[49] Lorenzo continued this tradition even more extensively: apart from founding the University of Pisa, and the future University of Florence (under whose auspices Machiavelli himself wrote the *Florentine Histories*), he also patronized such luminaries as Angelo Poliziano, Cristoforo Landino, and Pico della Mirandola, 'a man almost divine'.[50] In the context of their neglect of military *virtù*, however, the patronage of arts and letters was a clear sign of Florence's decline as a political and military power. For, according to Machiavelli, intellectual virtues are related only negatively to political and military *virtù*. In the natural order of appearance, military *virtù* has to come before intellectual virtue, and generals before philosophers. This, he says, is the opinion of 'the prudent'. For nothing destroys the military spirit, so necessary for a healthy society, more than the cultivation of philosophy and letters or what he calls 'honourable leisure'. Indeed, nothing is more dangerous to a city than the devious influence exerted by philosophy. The Roman Republic understood this very well from its experiences with Diogenes and Carneades, whom Athens had sent as ambassadors. These two Greek philosophers began to acquire a following among the Roman youth, and so Cato, 'knowing the evil that such honourable leisure might bring upon Rome', forbade by law the presence of philosophers in Rome. For 'by such means countries come to ruin'.[51]

Briefly, for Machiavelli, the Medici patronage of arts and letters is better understood as a sign of decadence than as one of political and military vigour. The impact of the discouragement of arms and the encouragement of leisure was that the Florentine youth, like their counterparts in decadent Rome, became unwarlike and were given over to self-indulgence. The love of oneself, the love of money, and the love of luxuries are a deadly combination as far as political *virtù* is concerned. Being idle and 'without a profession', the youth of Florence were interested only in fashions, banquets, gambling and whores. The city was full of silly customs befitting idle courtiers, harmful to any well-ordered society. 'Their ambition was to appear magnificent in their clothing, and to use speech that was pithy and clever; he who most deftly nipped the others was the smartest and most highly regarded.'[52]

What is most valuable in Machiavelli's treatment of Florence as a *licenzia* is that his analysis is followed by proposed solutions to the problems raised. And both the analysis and the solutions are embedded in the theory of humours: Florence has three humours – the *primi*, the *mezzani*, and the *ultimi*: all three must be satisfied, each in its own way. Leo X and Cardinal Giuliano Medici will be 'the official directors', or constitutional heads, in the new republic being devised, as opposed to the unofficial or unconstitutional heads, as Cosimo and Lorenzo were, of their defective republics. The pope and the cardinal must become the true lawgivers of a new Florence, in the manner of Solon and Lycurgus; and he (Machiavelli) will be their constitutional draftsman. It goes without saying that a monarchy is quite unsuited to Florence, given her love of freedom and equality. Moreover, to make Florence into a monarchy would be 'inhuman' and 'unworthy' of those who are 'merciful and good'. Neither would reviving the previous Medici regimes, whether that of Cosimo or that of Lorenzo, be useful, since they were never able to satisfy all the humours of Florence. In short, Florence needs a genuinely new republican constitution, and Machiavelli claims that he has 'discovered' a plan for it. If only, he writes, Leo and Giuliano will accept 'this republic of mine',[53] he would also show them how to make it 'perfect'. Thus, twice in his writings, first in *Discourses* I. 2 and now in the 'Discursus', Machiavelli insists that perfection can come to a republic only if it gives adequate satisfaction to all its constituent humours.[54]

The first group to be satisfied is the *primi*. Machiavelli finds no contradiction between his claim that equality is characteristic of Florence and the fact that it has a three-tiered social structure. 'And although in Florence the citizens possess the equality mentioned above,' he writes to clarify this point, 'nonetheless some of her citizens have a higher spirit (*animo elevato*) and think they deserve precedence over others; it is necessary to satisfy them in organizing the republic.'[55] This is a most interesting point, since, as he notes, this is the very reason why the previous Florentine regime fell: 'the last government fell for no other reason than that it did not satisfy this humour.'[56] Thus, to satisfy this group (i.e. the *primi*) he recommends the creation of a College of Sixty-five: fifty-three from the major guilds, and twelve from the minor guilds. The chief magistrate or the *gonfaloniere* will be chosen from this College. To satisfy the *mezzani*, he proposes a Council of Two Hundred: forty from the minor guilds and one hundred and sixty from the major guilds. There remains the third group, the *ultimi*, made up of the generality of citizens (*tutta la universalità dei cittadini*). To satisfy this group, he recommends the reopening of the Council of One Thousand, or at least that of the Six Hundred. Without satisfying this group, there can be no 'perfect' republic. Hence, he recommends the creation of an additional body of sixteen *gonfalonieri*, either appointed by Leo X or chosen by the Council of One Thousand. Out of these sixteen, four will be chosen as Provosts, and will sit with the highest administrative bodies.

In addition to these three 'assemblies', Machiavelli recommends a Court of Appeal, consisting of thirty citizens. Such an institution will remove the worst feature of all Florentine regimes: the inability to dispense justice without fear or favour. Such an institution will also guarantee the independence of the judiciary and the security of the life, liberty and property of all citizens.

Even though the three 'assemblies', plus an independent judiciary, would safeguard republican liberty, Machiavelli is afraid that without adequate position for a leader or head, Florence would not be able to manage as a genuine republic. Florence requires a head (*capo*), he repeats twice.[57] And this head must be a 'public' or constitutional one. The bane of the previous

Medici regimes is that they had 'private' heads – the very hallmark of a *licenzia*.[58]

His insistence upon a genuine need for a constitutional head, and the fact that Leo and Giuliano were actually the unconstitutional heads of Florence, places Machiavelli in a quandary. And he does not come out of it very well. Although the retention of Leo and Giuliano as unconstitutional heads is inconsistent with the main insights of his draft for what he claims to be the 'perfect' republican constitution, he has no practical choice but to leave the two where they are. Thus, although he proposes a 'perfect' constitution for Florence, he concedes that during the lifetime of Leo and Giuliano, it will have to function as a monarchy,[59] with the two Medici prelates holding ultimate responsibility for armed forces, criminal justice and legislation.

Despite this embarrassing concession to hard realities, Machiavelli feels satisfied that he has found the best solution for the corruptions of a commercial republic. Such republics need to provide the opportunity for liberty, power and property, and the only consistent way of doing so is to give every relevant group a share in power and participation. A commercial republic can be free and powerful only if it has a sense of community, i.e. only if it recognizes its basically plural, humoral, character. According to the theory of humours, the interests of its constitutive groups, though in themselves antagonistic, are not antagonistic enough to weaken or kill the communal organism. On the contrary – and here we see the penetration of the theory of humours – controlled antagonism of the humoral sort keeps such organisms healthy and dynamic. Florence's ills arose from the fact that while it knew how to produce wealth, it did not know how to produce free institutions, nor how to secure itself from external threats. For these, at last, Machiavelli has found the cure: let each humour be satisfied the way it needs to be satisfied; let no rank of citizen feel that it is either threatened or deprived of its legitimate needs; let every rank be given a share in power. 'There is no other way of escaping these ills than to give the city the laws that can by themselves stand firm. And they always will stand firm when everybody has a hand in them, and when everybody knows what he needs to do, and in whom he can trust, and no citizen, whatever his rank, either through fear for itself or through ambition, will need to desire further innovation.'[60] This is the peroration of the 'Discursus', Machiavelli's truly magnificent draft constitution for Florence. This may be considered as reflecting the substance of what is uplifting in Machiavelli's vision of politics. But what needs to be noted is that the framework within which it is presented is none other than the pre-modern theory of humours.

CONCLUSION

If the foregoing analysis leads us anywhere, it is, I think, to the realization that a pre-modern cosmology and a pre-modern anthropology underlie Machiavelli's political theory. What possible effect can this realization have on the received understanding of his political theory? If nothing else, it forces us to reconsider at least two issues: the issue of Machiavelli's modernity and that of Machiavellism itself.

Machiavelli's Modernity

Machiavelli is considered by many to be the founder of modern political philosophy. Indeed modernity is the pivotal concept of Leo Strauss's influential interpretation of Machiavelli. According to Strauss, evidence of Machiavelli's modernity consists of the open break which he makes with the political philosophy of Plato and Aristotle, his attack on Christianity, the lowering of the standards of politics from what ought to be to what is, and his inauguration of a project to control chance. 'It is in trying to understand modern philosophy that we come across Machiavelli,' Strauss has written.[1] 'Present-day political science often traces its origin to Machiavelli . . . To understand the basic premise of present-day political science, one would have to understand the meaning of the epoch-making changes effected by Machiavelli; for that change consisted in the discovery of the continent on which all specifically modern political thought, and hence especially present-day political science, is at home.'[2] According to Strauss, the major difference between classical political science and Machiavelli's political science involves the notion of chance. The former holds that the realization of the best regime depends upon chance. 'Machiavelli attacks this view,' says Strauss, 'both by demanding that one should take one's bearings, not by how men ought to live but by how they actually live, and by suggesting that chance could or should be controlled. It is this attack which laid the foundation for all specifically modern political thought.'[3] Furthermore, according to Strauss, Bacon and Spinoza, Harrington and Algernon Sydney, Montesquieu and

Rousseau, Hegel and Nietzsche, built their political philosophies on the foundations laid by Machiavelli.[4]

Harvey C. Mansfield, Jr. concurs with Strauss on this point. To understand modernity, says Mansfield, we must go back to its beginnings, that is, back to Machiavelli. Though a civic humanist, says Mansfield, Machiavelli declares himself 'for progress in terms we recognize'. Indeed, Mansfield is unhappy with those who are reluctant 'to admit, or even consider, that Machiavelli might be chiefly responsible for the spirit of modernity and thus is himself the origin of the modern world'.[5] Going even further, Mansfield claims that Machiavelli exhibits a 'new understanding of nature, one that overturns natural law and natural right in the Aristotelian tradition'.[6]

There is no question that Machiavelli wants to innovate traditional political theory. As he states in *The Prince* 15, he seeks to depart from the orders of his predecessors. Or, as he declares in the famous Preface to *Discourses* I, he seeks to introduce new modes and orders into political theory, to open up new routes not taken by others. He certainly has a new project: one which is partly destructive and partly constructive. It is destructive insofar as political Platonism, Aristotelianism, Augustinianism, and Thomism are concerned. It is constructive insofar as it proposes a new end for politics: namely the satisfaction of the appetites for riches and glory. This satisfaction must take place according to the requirements of our individual and collective humours. Political regimes must reflect the humours of those who constitute them. Their task is to satisfy the humours of their constitutive elements, and religion and morality are to be used as part of the means of accomplishing this task. Politics alone emerges as the highest human calling, to which everything else should be subordinated. This is what is new and innovative in Machiavelli's project.

The question, however, now arises: is being 'new' the same as being a 'modern'? Does Machiavelli's innovation necessarily imply modernity? In trying to answer these questions, it is important not to overlook Machiavelli's own uses of the notions of 'ancients' and 'moderns'. For, significantly enough, he does not call his new teaching either 'ancient' or 'modern'; he simply calls it 'new'. At the same time, he claims that his 'new' teaching is based both on a careful study of 'ancient' things, and his own experience of 'modern' things. Thus, in the Dedicatory Letter to *The Prince*, he maintains that the lessons of this work are founded on knowledge of the actions of great men 'learned by me from long experience with modern things and a continuous reading of ancient ones'.[7] Similarly, according to the Preface to *Discourses* I, he says that the teachings of this work too are based on the 'experience of present things' and 'knowledge of ancient ones'.[8] While he does not consider his project to be either 'ancient' or 'modern', there is no doubt that he thinks very highly of the ancients. He praises modern jurists and modern physicians (i.e. the jurists and physicians of his day) precisely because their knowledge is based on the teachings of ancient jurists and ancient physicians. And one of his major complaints against modern (i.e. his contemporary) rulers, lawgivers, and generals is that their actions bear no resemblance whatsoever to the virtuous actions of ancient rulers, lawgivers, and generals. It is to correct this 'error', this lack of appreciation for ancient political virtue, that Machiavelli writes the *Discourses*.[9] In the same vein, ancient *virtù* is contrasted with modern corruption: likewise, ancient religion with modern or 'present' religion. Ancient *virtù*, of course, is not the virtue of the Platonic and Aristotelian traditions. Rather, it is the political virtue exhibited, for example, by Hannibal and Scipio, Alexander and Cyrus: virtue dedicated to the building of strong and conquering states, whether monarchical or republican. It is part of Machiavelli's project to undermine the ancient tradition of moral virtue in favour of the ancient tradition of political virtue of conquerors and lawgivers. And by 'present' religion, he means Christianity; its reinterpretation, or rather its adaption for political purposes, is also part of his new project.[10]

Elsewhere in his writings, Machiavelli makes a habit of illustrating his arguments with examples taken from both 'ancient' and 'modern' sources. In *Discourses* I. 56, cases from ancient and modern sources are cited to prove that before great changes occur in states, there are signs that prognosticate them and men who predict them. Similarly, in *Discourses* II. 29, where he discusses the fundamental issue of the intervention of heaven in human affairs, he uses several examples from ancient sources to support his argument. He is prepared to furnish modern examples as well, but thinks it unnecessary. 'We could bring in support of what we have said some modern examples, but because we do not consider them necessary, since this is enough to satisfy anybody, we omit them.'[11]

Briefly, a careful scrutiny of Machiavelli's own uses of the terms 'ancient' and 'modern' indicates that by 'ancient' he means things, events, ideas or persons belonging to pre-Christian classical culture, and by 'modern' he means things, events, ideas, or persons belonging to the Christian culture. The overall purpose of his new teaching is to persuade his readers to reject the present, i.e. modern, i.e. Christian understanding of things, and to imitate the ancients – but only those among the ancients who stress *vita activa*, and this only insofar as such imitation will enable them to reject the 'present' and bring out something 'new'.[12]

While his opposition to the moderns is undisguised, his attitude towards the ancients is nuanced. He admires those ancients who value practice more than theory, action more than contemplation. These include Moses and Romulus, Theseus and Cyrus, Solon and Lycurgus. He thinks Cato was right to ban the philosophers Diogenes and Carneades from Rome, and with them the teaching of philosophy itself.[13] He considers the cultivation of philosophy and the theoretical life to be a sign of decadence, or what he calls 'honourable leisure' (*onesto ozio*). He certainly wants to reverse the classical order of action and contemplation in favour of an order which values only action. For him, action and its results constitute the real; theory, or the life of the mind as such, has no place in his cosmos, except as mere imaginings, without any ontological status whatsoever. The only glory worth striving for is that which comes from realizing actual political goals. Solon and Lycurgus attained the highest glory precisely because they were able to found actual republics. Plato and Aristotle did not and could not attain the highest glory precisely because they were just philosophers, who produced only 'paper republics'. 'And so much has this glory been esteemed by men seeking for nothing other than glory that when unable to form a republic in actual fact (*una republica in atto*), they have done it in writing (*in iscritto*), as Aristotle, Plato, and many others, who have wished to show the world that if they have not founded a free government, as did Solon and Lycurgus, they have failed not through their ignorance but through their impotence for putting it into practice.'[14] Briefly, then, what Machiavelli wants to remove from his new political philosophy is any trace of natural justice and natural law, any link to *orthos logos* or *recta ratio* (right reason), and any recognition of dependence on Providence.

But the crucial question is: does such rejection make Machiavelli a modern in the contemporary sense of that term? In answering this question, we must pay close attention to the intellectual underpinnings of Machiavelli's own position. We must examine the nature of the arguments he uses to justify his innovation. And here we necessarily uncover his dependence upon a pre-modern cosmology and a pre-modern anthropology. First of all, the assertion that effective truth is the only truth worth pursuing is a consequence of adopting the view that the universe is basically a system of motion emanating from the heavenly bodies, and that the only worthwhile good that human beings can achieve is the good of satisfying the desire for riches, power and glory. The case for effective truth is built in opposition to the view that the universe is governed by Reason or Mind. That the theoretical or philosophic life is seen as a sign of decadence follows from Machiavelli's conception of the structure of reality as basically a system of physical motion, operating both naturally and occultly.

Secondly, Machiavelli's new political science presupposes a definite view of history. This presupposed view of history is not a modern one. It is cyclic, and very much dependent upon the three-fold causality operating in human affairs: the human, the elemental or natural, and the celestial. The 'things of the world' and 'human things' (two of Machiavelli's favourite phrases) are subject to the necessary pattern of rise and fall. There is a causal connection between the 'heaven, the sun, the elements, and men', in motion, order, and power. This means that the pattern of the rise and fall of civilizations must be explained not only in psychological and moral terms, but also in natural and cosmic terms. The idea that history is an entirely human creation is absent in Machiavelli, and insofar as this is true, his idea of history cannot be called modern.

Thirdly, as we have seen, Machiavelli's new political philosophy rejects the relevance of the traditional notion of moral virtue and *phronesis*. But the arguments in favour of his new moral philosophy are derived from his cosmology and anthropology. The latter has room only for what he calls 'natural talent' (*ingegno*), imagination (*fantasia*), temperament, and the humours. And as anyone can see, there is nothing modern in this view of human nature. The Machiavellian self is very much subject to the influence of the quality of the times, and therefore, indirectly, to the regime of the heavenly bodies. The ethic that Machiavelli's anthropology permits is an ethic of effective truth, but an effective truth achievable only when the 'quality' of the times is right – hardly a modern notion of action. For him, ethics have no basis in what is called natural justice.[15] This state of affairs frees the human agent to act in any way he or she is able to act (i.e. in a way compatible with his or her temperament), and in so doing, to treat virtue and vice as equally useful means of attaining the desired end. Machiavelli's amoralism is built on a dated philosophical anthropology.

His attack on Christianity is also based on a pre-modern cosmology. For Machiavelli, religion has its ultimate basis in the 'judgement' of the heavens. Here he follows the 'scientific' teachings of the conjunctionist astrology of his day. He believes in the astrological theories concerning the origin, renewal, and demise of religions.[16] Machiavelli's fundamental criticism of Christianity is that it claims that its origin and purpose are supra-cosmic. It claims to have its origin in God's design for humanity, God who is lord and master of heaven and earth. It is precisely because of its supra-cosmic origin and destiny that Christianity can claim a transcendental *summum bonum*, and can despise, within certain limits, a view of life dedicated entirely to 'worldly glory'. For Machiavelli, however, 'worldly glory' is the *summum bonum* of human beings, and there is no better way of attaining it than through politics. Religion, therefore, has necessarily to be an instrument of politics, and any notion of 'paradise' or eternal life must be dismissed as imaginary and lacking ontological foundation.

Much has been made of Machiavelli's attitude towards Fortune. Many have concluded that his political theory contains a plan for overcoming chance, and that here, more than anywhere else, we have a glimpse of his modernity. But we must wonder whether his stand on Fortune amounts to anything more than an appeal to an activist approach towards politics, and whether it goes beyond rejecting *ozio* and an attitude of resignation to fate. Leo Strauss has used his formidable exegetical skills to reduce Machiavelli's notion of Fortune to 'chance understood as the cause simply of unforeseen accidents'.[17] But for Machiavelli, as we have seen, unforeseen accidents have their general cause in the motions of the planets. Besides, every unforeseen accident comes within the context of a particular 'quality of time', which makes it either good or bad for human beings. Strauss completely ignores the question of the 'quality of time' (an astrological notion) in his assessment of Machiavelli's position on Fortune. Insofar as Machiavelli is committed to the notion of the 'quality of time', his project of conquering chance can hardly be called modern. For, as long as human beings are thought to be subject to the 'quality' of the times, there is no way they can overcome chance, since it is Fortune that is supposed to give time its 'quality'. In opposition to the fatalists, Machiavelli argues that even if we are subject to the rule of the 'quality of the times', we must act according to our temperament. We must 'sweat' over things, and not leave them completely to chance (*sorte*).[18]

Finally, it is argued that the lowering of the standards of political action from what ought to be to what actually is, makes Machiavelli a modern. No more does one have to concern oneself with 'what ought to be done'. The focus of the 'new' philosophy is instead on 'what is done' and 'how men live'. But how indeed does the Machiavellian actor live and act? As fully autonomous and unencumbered by the influences of the planets and the elements? Has the lowering of the standards by itself made the actualization of the lowered goals any easier? Let us look at the empirical evidence that Machiavelli himself supplies. Borgia and Castruccio, Soderini and Savonarola, failed not because their goals were too high, but because they were unlucky and/or unarmed. Hannibal and Scipio, Julius II and Fabius Maximus, succeeded not because their goals were low, but because their respective humours and the 'quality' of their times harmonized with their behaviour. Bentivoglio failed to assassinate Julius II not because his norms of behaviour were too high, but because he lacked the right temperament. The list could be lengthened, but it is not necessary. Machiavelli's 'new' idea of success and failure has nothing to do with high or low standards; it has everything to do with the theories of the 'quality of the times', humours, and temperament. And arguments based on such notions can scarcely be called modern. The conclusion is inescapable: while Machiavelli is certainly an innovator, he is not a modern, either in his or in our sense of modernity.

Machiavelli and Machiavellism

If Machiavelli is not a modern, how do we account for the continuous operations of Machiavellism in modern history? To answer this question, it is necessary first of all to clarify the relationship between Machiavelli and Machiavellism. By a quirk of history, Machiavelli's name has come to be associated with a certain kind of political behaviour, according to which rulers and politicians de facto act out of expediency, disregarding moral rules and conscience, or with a devilish and manipulative cunning, which is something else again.[19] This type of political behaviour existed before Machiavelli and continues to exist independently of him. Historically, however, this kind of political behaviour has come to be called 'popular' or 'vulgar' Machiavellism. But 'vulgar' Machiavellism is not one of Machiavelli's inventions; it is part of the nature of political behaviour, as Kautilya's *Arthasastra* also attests.

When we raise the question of why 'vulgar' Machiavellism exists, we get different answers from different philosophers. Political philosophers before Machiavelli always recognized the *fact* of 'vulgar' Machiavellism. They tried to explain it from within their own philosophic frameworks, whatever these might have been – whether in consideration of the composite nature of human beings, or of the role of the passions, ignorance, original sin, moral weakness and so on. To take an unexceptional example, even St Thomas Aquinas recognizes that 'vulgar' Machiavellism is unavoidable in ordinary politics. He argues that human law or politics 'does not forbid all the vices, from which upright men can keep away, but only those grosser ones (*graviora*) which the average man can avoid, and chiefly those which do harm to others and have to be stopped if human society is to be maintained, such as murder, theft and so forth.'[20] Politics does not require that all acts of virtue be carried out, nor that 'all acts of vice' be forbidden.[21] Aquinas recognizes that very often the good that is sought in politics is not 'good simply' (*bonum simpliciter*), but 'good with reservations' (*bonum secundum quid*).[22]

Political philosophers before Machiavelli also recognized that individual morality is not the same as public morality. Aristotle, for example, teaches that 'Political wisdom and practical wisdom are the same state of mind, but their essence is not the same.'[23] The reason for the difference, Aristotle explains, is that public morality is based on law or legislative wisdom, while individual morality is based on the practical judgement of each individual.

Similarly, philosophers before Machiavelli knew very well that the justice of the city was imperfect, often mixed with the self-interest of a given group, and therefore in opposition to the natural justice of humanity. They also knew that perfect retribution was not to be expected from political justice. As Maritain rightly points out, 'The concept of perfect and infallible retribution for human deeds, with its absolute adamantine strength, is a *religious* conception relating to the eternal destiny of human persons; it is not the ethico-philosophical concept which has to be shaped relating to the destiny of human communities in time and history.'[24] In other words, political justice cannot ensure that the guilty might not sometimes escape punishment, nor that injustice might not sometimes be more profitable than justice.

All this and more were known and accepted as facts of political life, at least since the time of Plato's *Republic*. But the pre-Machiavellian political philosophers do not go beyond *explaining* why evil and injustice exist in political communities. They never go so far as to *justify* culpable evil and injustice. What Machiavelli does, however, is to give philosophical justification for resorting to culpable evil and injustice as legitimate means of achieving and defending certain political ends. In other words, with

Machiavelli we pass from the so-called 'vulgar' Machiavellism to philosophic Machiavellism. Thus, in Machiavelli's Machiavellism we can find
not only an explanation of but also a justification for culpable evil and
injustice.

Now, can philosophic Machiavellism account for the influence of modern Machiavellism, i.e. the post-Machiavellian Machiavellism, the
Machiavellism, for example, of Bacon and Spinoza, Hobbes and Locke,
Montesquieu and Rousseau, Hegel and Nietzsche?[25] Here we come across
a general problem we have examined throughout this book, namely that
Machiavelli's philosophical arguments, as founded on an antiquated cosmology and anthropology, are no longer acceptable to moderns. As we
have seen, his critiques of morality, religion, history, Fortune, and forms of
government, are all based on premises we no longer accept as tenable.
Insofar as this is true, it is not fair to hold Machiavelli accountable for what
Bacon and others mentioned above have done, or are alleged to have done,
in his name. Simply on the basis of *en passant* encomiums these later philosophers shower on Machiavelli, one may not necessarily conclude that
they argue from Machiavelli's actual premises. As philosophers in their own
right, they argue instead from their own premises, which are quite different
from those of Machiavelli, especially in consideration of his cosmology and
anthropology. And yet, while these others begin from premises that are
different from Machiavelli's, they seem to arrive at conclusions similar to
his. How is this possible? Can we start from non-Machiavellian premises
and still arrive at Machiavelli's Machiavellism? This could be so only if we
accept the view that there is an uninterrupted line of progression from
Machiavelli to modernity. Those who defend such a view of course would
argue that Machiavelli does not anticipate everything that later Machiavellians
will discover. But they would also insist that there is a core common to
Machiavelli and modern Machiavellians. This is the view, it seems, that is
conveyed by Strauss's metaphor of the three waves of modernity – the
modernity that allegedly originates in Machiavelli and culminates in
Nietzsche.[26]

Such a view clearly implies that the foundations of Machiavelli's philosophic Machiavellism are modern. But such a view, as we have argued in
the present study, is no longer tenable. The fact of the matter is that later
Machiavellians have built their brand of Machiavellism on foundations
quite different from Machiavelli's. No modern Machiavellian has ever
argued from the discredited theory of the heavens nor on the basis of the
doctrine of conjunction. And philosophic anthropology is no longer based
on *fantasia*, humours, and temperament. There are today many varieties of
philosophic Machiavellism. In fairness both to Machiavelli and to modern
Machiavellians, each of these should be studied in terms of its own specific
premises. Machiavelli's historic responsibility is limited to having made
philosophic Machiavellism justifiable and even respectable in some quarters.

Perhaps later Machiavellians have arrived at some of Machiavelli's general conclusions from their own quite different premises. But Machiavelli cannot be held responsible for what they have done.

With the introduction of modern science and modern notions of nature and the self, the philosophical foundations on which Machiavelli erected his Machiavellism have collapsed. One would expect that with the collapse of these foundations the conclusions would also collapse. But posterity often seems to think otherwise: it appears to want to hold on to Machiavelli's conclusions, even it if is willing to abandon his premises. This is the unenviable position in which posterity finds itself.

If posterity wants to be coherent in its attitude towards Machiavelli, the first thing it must do is not to confuse Machiavelli's Machiavellism with the Machiavellism of later Machiavellians. Post-Machiavellian Machiavellism should be understood in terms of the premises which Machiavelli himself never held. In this respect, Allan Bloom's recent attempt to link Machiavelli to modernity and the Enlightenment seems unconvincing. He writes: 'Danton's "*de l'audace, encore de l'audace, toujours de l'audace*", is but a pale, merely political duplicate of Machiavelli's original call to battle.'[27] He continues: 'Bacon's assertion that science will make man "master and possessor of nature", and the commonplace that science is the conquest of nature, are offsprings of Machiavelli's revolution and constitute the political face adopted by modern philosophy.'[28] But if the arguments of the present study have demonstrated anything, it is that Machiavelli did not have a modern notion of science. In astrological natural philosophy he may well have found a substitute for modern science, but this is quite different from saying that he supports modern science or that modern science is compatible with Machiavellism. Bacon, Galileo, Descartes and others who followed Machiavelli had a new vision of nature and the self which cannot be found in him.

What is permanent in politics is 'vulgar' Machiavellism, for which, as everyone agrees, Machiavelli cannot be held responsible. For the first time, Machiavelli, as we have argued, gives vulgar Machiavellism its philosophic justification, based, alas, on pre-modern premises. But the philosophic justification which he gives is quite different from the philosophic justification which later Machiavellians give to theirs. This is the crucial distinction which all those who discuss various kinds of Machiavellism should keep in mind.

If modern Machiavellism is objectionable, no amount of attack directed against Machiavelli is going to remove the basis of the objection. If modern Machiavellism should be questioned, as indeed it should be, the questioning must begin with modernity itself. For one thing should be clear by now: by attacking Machiavelli one cannot save the world from the Machiavellism of modernity.

NOTES

Introduction

1.   See Russell Price, 1973, pp. 315–45; 1977, pp. 588–631; 1982, pp. 383–445; Victor A. Santi, 1979; John Plamenatz, 1972, pp. 157–78; Thomas E. Flanagan, 1972, pp. 127–57; J. H. Whitfield, 1969, pp. 141–63; Marcia L. Colish, 1971, pp. 323–51; J. H. Hexter, 1956, pp. 113–38.

2.   Jacob Burckhardt, 1944, p. 315. For a criticism of Burckhardt's 'mentality' and for his 'gross' underestimation of the volume of astrological publication in early modern Italy, and for identifying astrology with superstition and separating it from 'any doctrines and philosophical system', see Brian P. Copenhaver, 1988, p. 267.

3.   Lynn Thorndike, 1955, p. 273.

4.   Ibid., p. 275.

5.   See Garin, 1983, 24–25, *passim.*

6.   *The Cambridge History of Renaissance Philosophy*, p. 3. The volume devotes three chapters to questions related to astrology.

7.   Kristeller, 1988, p. 136.

8.   See S.J. Tester, 1987, and Patrick Curry, 1987.

9.   'It is most certainly a great thing to consider how blind men are to the things in which they sin and what sharp persecutors they are of the vices they do not have. I could bring up as examples things Greek, Latin, Hebrew, and Chaldean, and go off even to the land of Sofi and Prester John and bring them before you, if instances right at home and recent were not enough.' Machiavelli to Vettori, 5 January 1514, Martelli, p. 1164.

10.   In a contemporary work, Paolo Cortesi's (1465–1510) *De Cardinalatu*, an entire chapter is devoted to the question of how 'Cardinals should abstain from the practice of Chaldaic divination' (Divinationem chaldaicam esse fugiendam a cardinalibus). See J. F. D'Amico, 1982, p. 43.

11.   See Bernardo Machiavelli, 1954, p. 14. As students of Machiavelli know, it was our Niccolò who at the age of 17 had to collect the bound copy of Livy from a local bookbinder.

12.   D. III. 6, p. 205.

13.   'Domiziano osservava i natali de' senatori, e quelli che vedeva felici e propizii al principato, ammazzava. Volle ammazzare Nerva, suo successore; se non che da uno matematico suo amico li fu detto che non vi era pericolo, perché doveva morire di corto, essendo vecchio; donde ne nacque poi che Nerva fu suo successore.' Machiavelli, 'Sentenze diverse', Martelli, p. 918.

14.   L. Arthur Burd, 1968, p. 355, n.9.

15.   Cassirer, 1961, p. 130.

16. Ibid., p. 156.
17. Ibid., pp. 158–59.
18. Hans Baron, 1943, p. 37.
19. Ibid., p. 29.
20. Ibid., p. 45.
21. Leo Strauss, 1959, p. 40.
22. Leo Strauss, 1951, pp. xix–xx.
23. Strauss, 1959, p. 47.
24. Strauss, 1969, p. 202, p. 222.
25. Ibid., p. 209.
26. Ibid., p. 221–2.
27. See Eugenio Garin, 1970, pp. 56–72.
28. Gennaro Sasso, 1987, p. 224. Sasso is speaking here only of D.II.5, not of Machiavelli's writings as a whole; even so he dismisses, too hastily I think, Paola Zambelli's excellent suggestion that there is in fact a connection between D.II. 5 and astrology. Ibid., pp. 390–93.
29. See Chabod, 1964, pp. 213–15.
30. See Sasso, 1967, pp. 232–33.
31. Sasso, 1987, p. 77.
32. Skinner, 1981, p. 65.
33. Harvey C. Mansfield Jr., 1975, p. 69, and 1989, p. 128, from what appears to be an excess of caution, warns readers against the practice of squeezing Machiavelli into his 'context', and of 'the methodological error of explaining Machiavelli's thought by that of his contemporaries'.
34. 'Fu Niccolò in tutte quante le sue composizioni assai licenzioso, sì nel tassare persone grandi, ecclesiastiche e secolari, come anche nel ridurre tutte le cose a cause naturali o fortuite.' From Ricci's letter, quoted by Pasquale Villari, 1877, I, p. 483. Villari adds that this intellectual orientation not only procured him many enemies but also embittered him later in his life. What is more, his penchant for 'reducing all facts to natural causes' led both to the interdiction of all his works by the Council of Trent, and 'to his well-merited immortality'. Ibid., pp. 483–84.
35. 'Tutte le cose che sentono, questi filosofi e astrologi le vogliono risolvere in cause naturali, o attribuirle al cielo più presto che a Dio.' Savonarola, 'Prediche sopra l'Esodo X', cited by Strauss, 1969, p. 335, n. 82.
36. 'Questi tali sono gente private della grazia di Dio e della sua speciale provvidenzia, e communemente sono uomini pessimi e privati d'intelletto e sanza fede; anzi reggano e governano ogni loro cosa per via di astrologia; il che non solamente è contrario alla Scrittura Sacra, ma *etiam* alla filosofia naturale, perchè non possono sapere le cose contingenti future, nè molti particulari che possono accadere.' Savonarola, 1952, vol. 1, p. 164.
37. See Chabod, 1980, p. 213.
38. Garin, 1965, p. 185.
39. Garin, 1969, p. 15.
40. Sasso, 1967, pp. 281 ff.
41. Noted by Felix Gilbert, 1965, p. 330.
42. Garin, 1969, p. 157.

Chapter 1   *The Astrological Debate*

1. Kuhn, 1957, p. 92.
2. Garin, 1983, pp. 19–20.
3. J. D. North, 1980, 205. On the importance of Abu Ma'shar, see Richard LeMay, 1987, pp. 57–75.

4. Ptolemy, 1980, pp. 117–19. 'Since, then, prognostication by astronomical means is divided into two great and principal parts, and since the first and more universal is that which relates to whole races, countries, and cities, which is called general, and the second and more specific is that which relates to individual men, which is called genethlialogical, we believe it fitting to treat first of the general division, because such matters are naturally swayed by greater and more powerful causes than are particular events.'
5. Ptolemy, 1980, p. 39.
6. Ptolemy, 1980, pp. 21–35; 221–29.
7. Ptolemy, 1980, pp. 165–69; 177–91; 241–51; 437–57.
8. 'Rather is it true that the movement of the heavenly bodies, to be sure, is eternally performed in accordance with divine, unchangeable destiny, while the change of earthly things is subject to a natural and mutable fate, and in drawing its first causes from above it is governed by chance and natural sequence. Moreover, some things happen to mankind through more general circumstances and not as a result of an individual's own natural propensities...other occurrences, however, accord with the individual's own natural temperament through minor and fortuitous antipathies of the ambient.' Ptolemy, 1980, pp. 23–25.
9. Ibid., p. 27.
10. Burckhardt, 1944, p. 316.
11. Thorndike, 1959a, p. 826.
12. Ibid., p. 839.
13. I. F. I. 24, p. 649.
14. Thorndike, 1959a, p. 877, p. 888.
15. Graziella Federici Vescovini, 1987, p. 33.
16. Ibid.
17. Garin, 1969, p. 161.
18. Thorndike, 1959a, p. 892.
19. See Savonarola, 1513, III. 4, p. 28.
20. See Bacon, 1928, p. 276. He believed, among other things, that the secret of the successes of Moses, Aaron and Solomon as political and religious leaders were due to their knowledge of astrological natural science. Ibid., pp. 408–09.
21. 'Without rash assertion but with humble reverence I say that, although the blessed incarnation and the nativity of Christ was miraculous and supernatural in many respects, nevertheless nature too could cooperate in many ways with divine omnipotence in this divine work of conception and nativity, as a servant assisting its Lord and Creator, and could in these matters through the virtue of the heavens and stars cooperate with the natural virtue of His Mother, the Virgin'. D'Ailly, *Vigintiloquium*, cited in Lynn Thorndike, 1959b, p. 105.
22. Ibid., p. 106.
23. 'Et in hoc concordant omnes astronomi quia numquam fuit aliqua istarum conjunctionum sine aliqua magna et notabili mutatione in hoc mundo.' Ibid., p. 107.
24. Ibid., p. 108.
25. Pomponazzi, cited in Garin, 1983, p. 100.
26. '. . . dicendo che mai non si fa cosa grande nel mondo ala quale non preceda qualche grande conjunctione, e tutte le gran cose passate le attribuiscono a certe conjunctione grande, lequali dicono che furono in quelli tempi.' Savonarola, 1513, III. 4, p. 28.
27. Ficino, 1980, p. 185.
28. *Mandragola*, Act II, Scene 6.
29. For the details on the practice of horoscope-casting in Medicean Florence, see Philip McNair, 1976, p. 272.
30. Ridolfi, 1967, pp. 58–60 and p. 290, n. 4.
31. Maimonides, 1986, pp. 227–37.
32. On Langenstein's critique of astrology, see Nicholas H. Steneck, 1976.

33. For further details on the political role that astrology played in the fourteenth century, see Coopland, 1952, pp. 63–65, *passim*; Garin, 1983, p. 24, points out that both Langenstein and Oresme were read in Florentine circles.
34. See Hilary Carey, 1987, pp. 41–57.
35. For more on Pelacani's thought, see G. Vescovini, 1979.
36. Vespucci to Machiavelli, 25 August 1501, p. 1030. The verses read: 'Praedixi tibi papa, bos, quod esses/ Praedico moriere, hinc abibis/ Succedet rota, consequens bubulcum.'
37. Thorndike, 1959b, p. 574.
38. Machiavelli to the Signoria, 18 November 1503, S. Bertelli, 1964a, *Legazioni e commissarie*, II, p. 649.
39. Machiavelli to the Signoria, 26 November 1503, Ibid., p. 683.
40. Thorndike, 1959b, pp. 544-58.
41. F. Cognasso, 1965, p. 349.
42. Ibid., p. 350.
43. Ibid., p. 358.
44. Burckhardt, 1944, p. 316.
45. 'Io vorrej che tu dicessi a' chommessarij che, havendo a pigliare govedi la possessione di Pisa, che i' nessuno modo essi entrino avanti le 12 ore et ½, ma se possible è, entrino a ore 13 passate di pocho pocho, che sarà hora filicissima per noj. Et se govedì non s'avessi a pigliare, ma sia venerdì, medesimamente a hore 13 et uno pocho pocho poj et non havanti le 12 ½: simile sabato mattina, quando non s'avessi el venerdì. Et quando non si possa osservare né tempo né ora, faccisi et piglisi quando si può in nomine Dominj. Et questo diraj per mia parte ad Antonio da Filichaia.' Lattanzio Tedaldi to Machiavelli, 5 June 1509, p. 1107.
46. Tedaldi to Machiavelli, 11 October 1506, p. 1090.
47. Guicciardini, 1972, pp. 43–45. Note that Machiavelli also in D. I. 56 mentions the tale of the apparition of men-at-arms above the air in Arezzo.
48. See Guicciardini, 1984, p. 81.
49. Ridolfi, 1963, p. 127.
50. Cassirer, 1963, p. 100.
51. Ibid., p. 101.
52. Gombrich, 1970, p. 295.
53. Ibid., p. 190.
54. Gombrich, p. 190; in the 'Melancholia' the globe over the man's head shows the important date of 1484, the date of the conjunction of Jupiter and Saturn in Scorpio. Ibid., p. 213.
55. Ibid., pp. 211–12.
56. Ibid., p. 199.
57. Pico, 1572.
58. Savonarola, 1513.
59. Pico, 1572, Preface, p. 413.
60. Burckhardt, 1944, p. 319.
61. Garin, 1969, p. 11.
62. Savonarola, 1513, II. 1, pp. 9–10.
63. Savonarola, 1513, Preface, p. 2; III. 6, p. 34.
64. 'Praeter communem motus et luminis influentiam nullam vim coelestibus peculiarem inesse.' Pico, 1572, III. 5, p. 461.
65. 'Occultas vires coelestibus non inesse, per quas occultas rerum proprietates producant, sed calorem tantum lumenque vivificum.' Ibid., III. 24, p. 510.
66. 'Neque specificas neque individuales rerum differentias a coeli motu pendere.' Ibid., III.9, p. 468.
67. 'Non posse coelum eius rei signum esse, cuius causa non sit.' Ibid., IV. 12, p. 542.
68. 'Periodos humorum ad siderum motus non esse referendos.' Ibid., III. 17, p. 500.

69. 'Ingeniorum et morum varietatem non omnino pendere a primis qualitatibus.' Ibid., III. 22, p. 508; 'Mores hominum a coelo non fieri'; Ibid., IV. 9, p. 537; 'Corporeas dispositiones non effici a coelo.' Ibid., IV. 11, p. 540.

70. Ibid., III. 23, pp. 508–9.

71. 'Malas leges sicuti nec bonas coelo non subijci.' Ibid., IV. 10, p. 539.

72. Ibid., III. 27, pp. 517–18.

73. Ibid., p. 519.

74. 'Nihil magnum in terra praeter hominem, nihil magnum in homine praeter mentem et animum, huc si ascendis, coelum transcendis, si ad corpus inclinas et coelum suspicis, muscam te vides et musca aliquid minus.' Ibid., p. 519.

75. 'Tempus rerum non ab astrologica . . . sed ab historia esse petendum.' V. 8, p. 564.

76. 'Petendum igitur tempus rerum a magistra rerum historia nemo ambigat, cuius in ea re discipula Astronomia arbitra esse non potest.' Ibid., p. 565.

77. Ibid.

78. Ibid., VII. 2, pp. 621–23.

79. Ibid., 'Initia urbium, regnorum, factionum, legum ignota esse, nullamque artem astrologos tradidisse qua possint investigari.' IX. 6, p. 666.

80. 'Fortunam vero cum dico, coelum non dico.' Ibid., III. 27, p. 519.

81. 'Fortuita a coelo non esse.' Ibid., IV. 2, p. 522.

82. Savonarola, 1513, II. 3, pp. 12–13; 1, 2 and 3, pp. 6–7; Pico, 1572, IV. 3, pp. 523–4.

83. Aristotle, 1970, II. 4, 195b31–197a35.

84. Cassirer, 1963, p. 110.

85. Garin, 1965, p. 110.

86. Bellanti, 1502, p. 134.

87. 'Jo (sic) Scot ac divo Thomas ducentibus navigavi.' Bellanti, 1502, p. ii.

88. 'Bona externa ad fortunam referenda, non ad virtutem.' Pontano, 1530, II. p. 164, *passim*.

89. Ibid., p. 187.

90. Garin, 1983, p. 93.

Chapter 2   *Heaven, History, and Politics*

1. See Carlo Pincin, 1966, pp. 72–83; and Cecil H. Clough, 1975, pp. xxiv–xxix.

2. '. . . perché le leggi civili non sono altro che sentenze date dagli antiqui iureconsulti, le quali, ridutte in ordine, a' presenti nostri iureconsulti judicare insegnano. Né ancora la medicina è altro che esperienze fatte dagli antiqui medici, sopra le quali fondano e' medici presenti e' loro judizii.' D. I. Preface, p. 76.

3. '. . . nello ordinare le republiche, nel mantenere li stati, nel governare e' regni, nello ordinare la milizia ed amministrare la guerra, nel judicare e' sudditi, nello accrescere l'imperio, non si truova principe né republica che agli esempli delli antiqui ricorra.' Ibid., p. 76.

4. 'Il che credo che nasca non tanto da la debolezza nella quale la presente religione ha condotto el mondo, o da quel male che ha fatto a molte provincie e città cristiane uno ambizioso ozio, quanto dal non avere vera cognizione delle storie, per non trarne, leggendole, quel senso né gustare di loro quel sapore che le hanno in sé.' (D.I. Preface, p. 76. The 1531 Roman edition of the *Discourses* reads 'educazione' instead of 'religione'. On Machiavelli's conception of the 'educational' or pedagogical function of religion, see ch. 3 *infra*.)

5. 'Volendo, pertanto, trarre li uomini di questo errore, ho giudicato necessario scrivere, sopra tutti quelli libri di Tito Livio che dalla malignità de 'tempi non ci sono stati intercetti, quello che io, secondo le cognizione delle antique e moderne cose, iudicherò essere necessario per maggiore intelligenzia di essi, a ciò che coloro che leggeranno queste mia

declarazioni, possino più facilmente trarne quella utilità per la quale si debbe cercare le cognizione delle istorie.' Preface, p. 76.

6. 'Donde nasce che infiniti che le leggono, pigliono piacere di udire quella varietà degli accidenti che in esse si contengono, sanza pensare altrimenti di imitarle, iudicando la imitazione non solo difficile ma impossibile; come si il cielo, il sole, li elementi, li uomini, fussino variati di moto, di ordine e di potenza, da quello che gli erono antiquamente.' Ibid.

7. Pincin, 1966, p. 74 (my italics).

8. Ibid., p. 74 and p. 79.

9. 'Di poco aveva Dio fatto le stelle,/ il ciel, la luce gli elementi e l'uomo/dominator di tante cose belle,/ e la superbia degli Angeli domo,/ di paradiso Adam fatto ribello/ con la sua donna pe 'l gustar del pomo;/ quando che, nati Cain ed Abello,/ col padre loro e de la lor fatica/ vivendo lieti nel povero ostello,/ potenzia occulta che 'n ciel si nutrica, tra le stelle che quel girando serra, a la natura umana poco amica,/ per privarci di pace e porne in guerra,/ per torci ogni quiete e ogni bene,/ mandò due furie ad abitare in terra.' ('Dell'Ambizione', p. 984.)

10. See D. I. 3, beginning.

11. '. . . essendo le cose umane sempre in moto, o le salgano, o le scendano . . .' D. II Preface, p. 145.

12. 'E vedesi una città o una provincia essere ordinata al vivere politico da qualche uomo eccellente; ed, un tempo, per la virtù di quello ordinatore, andare sempre in augmento verso il meglio. Chi nasce allora in tale stato, ed ei laudi più gli antichi tempi che i moderni, s'inganna . . . Ma coloro che nascano dipoi, in quella città o provincia, che gli è venuto il tempo che la scende verso la parte più ria, allora non s'ingannano.' Ibid.

13. Ibid.

14. 'E veramente, se la virtù che allora regnava, ed il vizio che ora regna, non fussino più chiari che il sole, andrei col parlare più rattenuto, dubitando non incorrere in questo inganno di che io accuso alcuni. Ma essendo la cosa sì manifesta che ciascuno la vede, sarò animoso in dire manifestamente quello che io intenderò di quelli e di questi tempi; acciochè gli animi de' giovani che questi mia scritti leggeranno, possino fuggire questi, e prepararsi ad imitar quegli, qualunque volta la fortuna ne dessi loro occasione.' Ibid., p. 146.

15. '. . . né e cieli vogliono o possono sostenere una cosa che voglia ruinare ad ogni modo.' 'Parole da dirle', p. 13.

16. 'Perché gli è offizio di uomo buono, quel bene che per la malignità de' tempi e della fortuna tu non hai potuto operare, insegnarlo ad altri, acciochè, sendone molti capaci, alcuno di quelli, più amato dal Cielo, possa operarlo.' D. II. Preface, p. 146.

17. 'Sogliono le provincie, il più delle volte, nel variare che le fanno, dall'ordine venire al disordine, e di nuovo di poi dal disordine all'ordine trapassare; perché, non essendo dalla natura conceduto alle mondane cose il fermarsi, come le arrivano alla loro ultima perfezione, non avendo più da salire, conviene che scendino; e similmente, scese che le sono, e per li disordini ad ultima bassezza pervenute, di necessità, non potendo più scendere, conviene che salghino; e così sempre da il bene scende al male, a da il male si sale al bene. Perché la virtù partorisce quiete, la quiete ozio, l'ozio disordine, il disordine rovina; e similmente dalla rovina nasce l'ordine, dall'ordine virtù, da questa gloria e buona fortuna.' I. F. V. 1. p. 738.

18. Ficino, 1978, pp. 6–8. What follows is a summary of this letter. It may be remembered that some of Machiavelli's colleagues in the Signoria, such as Marcello Virgilio Adriani, were friends or disciples of Ficino.

19. 'Vedi le stelle e 'l ciel, vedi la luna/vedi gli altri pianeti andare errando/or alto or basso, senza requie alcuna;/quando il ciel vedi tenebroso, e quando/lucido e chiaro; e così nulla in terra/ vien ne lo stato suo perseverando./ Di quivi nasce la pace e la guerra;/ di qui dipendon gli odi tra coloro/ ch'un muro insieme ed una fossa serra./ Da questo venne il tuo primo martoro;/ da questo nacque al tutto la cagione/ de le fatiche tue senza ristoro./ Non ha cangiato il cielo opinione/ ancor, né cangerà, mentre che i fati/ tengon ver te la lor dura

intenzione./ E quelli umori in quai ti sono stati/ cotanto avversi e cotanto nimici,/ non sono ancor, non sono ancor purgati;/ ma come secche fien le lor radici/ e che benigni i ciel si mostreranno,/ torneran tempi più che mai felici.' Martelli, pp. 961–62.

20. 'Quel regno che sospinto è da *virtù*/ ad operare, o da necessitate,/ si vedrà sempre mai gire a l'insù;/ e per contrario fia quella cittate/piena di sterpi silvestri e di dumi,/ cangiando seggio dal verno a la state,/tanto ch' al fin convien che si consumi/ e ponga sempre la sua mira in fallo,/ che ha buone leggi e cattivi costumi./ Chi le passate cose legge, sallo/ come gl' imperii comincian da Nino,/ e poi finiscono in Sardanapallo./ Quel primo fu tenuto un uom divino,/quell'altro fu trovato fra l'ancille/ com'una donna a dispensar il lino./ La virtù fa le region tranquille:/ e da tranquillità poi ne risolta/ l'ozio: e l'ozio arde i paesi e le ville./ Poi quando una provincia è stata involta/ ne' disordini un tempo, tornar suole/virtute ad abitarvi un'altra volta./ Quest'ordine così permette e vuole/ chi ci governa, acciò che nulla stia/ o possa star mai fermo sotto 'l sole./ Ed è, e sempre fu, e sempre fia/ che 'l mal succeda al bene, il bene al male,/ e l'un sempre cagion de l'altro sia.' Martelli, p. 967. Note the naturalistic, astrological use of the notions of 'good' and 'bad' here.

21. For the text of both versions see Martelli, p. 939.

22. 'Io canterò l'italiche fatiche/seguite già ne' duo passati lustri,/sotto le stelle al suo bene inimiche.' Martelli, p. 940. Note again the astrological use of the word *bene* ('good') here.

23. I. F. I. 25, pp. 649–50.

24. I. F. III. 5, p. 694.

25. Ibid., II. 33, p. 681.

26. 'Discursus', p. 31.

27. 'Egli è cosa verissima, come tutte le cose del mondo hanno il termine della vita loro; ma quelle vanno tutto il corso che è loro ordinato dal cielo, generalmente, che non disordinano il corpo loro, ma tengonlo in modo ordinato, o, che non altera, o, s'egli altera, è a salute, e non a danno suo.' D. III. 1, p. 195.

28. 'E questi dottori di medicina dicono, parlando de' corpi degli uomini, "quod quotidie aggregatur aliquid, quod quandoque indiget curtione."' Ibid.

29. Ibid., p. 196.

30. See Thorndike, 1959b, p. 197.

31. 'Ma sendo tutte le cose degli uomini in moto, e non potendo stare slade, conviene che le salghino o che le scendino; e a molte cose che la ragione non t'induce, t'induce la necessità: talmente che, avendo ordinata una republica atta a mantenersi, non ampliando, e la necessità la conducesse ad ampliare, si verebbe a tôr via i fondamenti suoi, ed a farla rovinare più tosto. Così, dall'altra parte, quando il Cielo le fusse sì benigno che la non avesse a fare guerra, ne nascerebbe che l'ozio la farebbe o effeminata o divisa ... Pertanto, non si potendo, come io credo, bilanciare questa cosa, né mantenere questa via del mezzo a punto; bisogna nello ordinare la republica, pensare alle parte più onorevole; ed, ordinarle in modo, che, quando pure la necessità le inducesse ad ampliare, elle potessono, quello che'elle avessono occupato, conservare.' D. I. 6, pp. 86–87.

32. D. II. 19.

33. 'Quanto alle cause che vengono dal cielo, sono quelle che spengono la umana generazione, e riducano a pochi gli abitatori di parte del mondo. E questo viene o per peste o per fame o per una inondazione d'acque.' D. II. 5, p. 154.

34. '... perche' la natura, come ne' corpi semplici, quando e' vi è ragunato assai materia superflua, muove per se medesima molte volte, e fa una purgazione, la quale è salute di quel corpo; così interviene in questo corpo misto della umana generazione, che, quando tutte le provincie sono ripiene di abitatori, in modo che non possono vivervi, né possono andare altrove, per essere occupati e ripieni tutti i luoghi; e quando la astuzia e la malignità umana è venuta dove la può venire, conviene di necessità che il mondo si purghi per uno de 'tre modi; acciocché gli uomini, sendo divenuti pochi e battuti, vivino più comodamente, e diventino migliori.' Ibid., p. 155.

35. Thorndike, 1959c, p. 180.
36. Ibid., p. 178.
37. D. I. 5, p. 155.
38. 'Innanzi che seguino i grandi accidenti in una città o in una provincia, vengono segni che gli pronosticono, o uomini che gli predicano.' 'Donde ei si nasca io non so, ma ei si vede per gli antichi e per gli moderni esempli, che mai non venne alcuno grave accidente in una città o in una provincia, che non sia stato, o da indovini o da rivelazioni o da prodigi o da altri segni celesti, predetto.' D. I. 56, p. 139.
39. 'La cagione di questo credo sia da essere discorsa e intepretata da uomo che abbi notizia delle cose naturali e soprannaturali: il che non abbiamo noi.' Ibid.
40. 'Pure, potrebbe essere che, sendo questo aere, come vuole alcuno filosofo, pieno di intelligenze, le quali per naturali virtù, preveggendo le cose future, ed avendo compassione agli uomini, acciò si possino preparare alle difese, gli avvertiscono con simili segni.' Ibid.
41. For these and points related to spirits and astrology, see Thorndike, 1959b, pp. 268–73. Machiavelli's mention of apparitions above Arezzo was of great interest to Henry More (1614–87), the Cambridge Platonist. However, he used the reference to argue for things quite different from what Machiavelli had argued for. In his *Antidotus adversus Atheismus* (1653), More used Machiavelli in defence of theism: '. . . huius modi armatorum congressus super certas civitates conspectos fuisee facile esset ex historia abunde confirmare . . . Machiavellus refert de Aretio, agnoscens istiusmodi prodigia crebro occurrere in historia, certosque esse praenuncios motuum ac conturbationum illius republicae ac regionis ubi apparent. Verba eius tam libera sunt et ingenua, iudiciumque tam egregium (quamvis philosophum se nolit profiteri) de causis horum adeo mirabilium spectaculorum, ut operae pretium duxerim huc trancribere . . .' In one of his other works, *Enchiridium Metaphysicum* (1671), More again referred to D. I. 56. 'Imo vero sponte earum veritatem agnoverunt, et inter primos Machiavellus admodum libere et ingenue, Disp. de Rep. lib. I. ca. 56, ubi de his aeris spectaculis agens, aliisque prodigiis consimilibus . . . Ubi non solum agnoscit Machiavellus, sed summa cum confidentia harum asserit historiarum veritatem, indeque iudicio solido planeque philosophico spirituum intelligentiarumque existentiam infert . . . Ex fortuitis vero nubium unius in alteram lapsibus et ordinariis corruscationibus haec non fieri, manifestum id indicium est quod paulo supra notat Machiavellus, nempe, quod motus civiles temporumque mutationes praenunciant, eventu ut plurimum omnis implente fidem.' Garin, 1970, pp. 59–60, n. 25.
42. 'Pure, comunque e' si sia, si vede così essere la verità; e che sempre dopo tali accidenti sopravvengono cose istraordinarie e nuove alle provincie.' D. I. 56, p. 139.
43. Machiavelli to Guicciardini, 5 November 1526, p. 1247.
44. 'Se e' si considererà bene come procedono le cose umane, si vedrà molte volte nascere cose e venire accidenti, a' quali i cieli al tutto non hanno voluto che si provvegga.' D. II. 29, p. 188.
45. 'Perchè il più delle volte si vedrà quelli a una rovina ed a una grandezza essere stati convinti da una commodità grande che gli hanno fatto i cieli, dandogli occasione, o togliendogli, di potere operare virtuosamente.' Ibid., p. 189.
46. Livy, 1976, p. 381.
47. See also D. II. 1.
48. 'E veramente i cieli non possono dare agli uomini maggiore occasione di gloria, né gli uomini la possono maggiore desiderare.' D. I. 10, p. 93.
49. Machiavelli takes this for granted in D. I. 39 and D. III. 43.
50. 'Non sia pertanto, nessuno che si sbigottisca di non potere conseguire quel che è stato conseguito da altri; perché gli uomini, come nella prefazione nostra si disse, nacquero, vissero e morirono, sempre, con uno medesimo ordine.' D. I. 11, p. 95.
51. Strauss, 1969, p. 209; Harvey C. Mansfield, Jr., 1979, p. 282.
52. For a brief account of the use of these two forms in the Renaissance, see Peter Burke, 1974, p. 211.

53. D. II. 2, p. 150.
54. Mansfield, 1988, p. ix.
55. Gilbert, 1972, pp. 97–8.
56. Mansfield, 1988, p. viii.
57. Ibid., pp. viii–ix. See also Michel-Pierre Edmond, 1989, pp. 247–52, and David R. Lachterman, 1991, pp. 226–8.
58. Strauss, 1969, p. 209.
59. Aristotle, 1970, II. 4, 196b 6–9.

Chapter 3   Heaven, Religion, and Politics

1. E. I. 12.
2. '. . . giudicando i cieli che gli ordini di Romolo non bastassero a tanto imperio, inspirarono nel petto del Senato romano di eleggere Numa Pompilio per successore a Romolo, accioché quelle cose che da lui fossero state lasciate indietro, fossero da Numa ordinate.' D. I. 11, p. 93.
3. '. . . cum interesse rebus humanis celeste numen videretur,' Livy, 1976, I. 21, p. 56.
4. Ibid., I. 16, p. 53.
5. 'La quale religione se ne' principi della republica cristiana si fusse mantenuta, secondo che dal datore d'essa ne fu ordinato, sarebbero gli stati e le republiche cristiane più unite, più felici assai, che le non sono.' D. I. 12, p. 95.
6. Machiavelli, 1950, p. 151.
7. Walker, 1975, II. p. 34.
8. 'Questo modo di vivere, adunque, pare che abbi renduto il mondo debole, e datolo in preda agli uomini scelerati; i quali sicuramente lo possono maneggiare, veggendo come l'università degli uomini, per andarne in Paradiso, pensa più a sopportare le sue battiture che a vendicarle. E benchè paia che si sia effeminato il mondo, e disarmato il Cielo, nasce più sanza dubbio dalla viltà degli uomini, che hanno interpretato la nostra religione secondo l'ozio, e non secondo la virtù.' D. II. 2., pp. 149–50. Note here the use that Machiavelli makes of '*Paradiso*' and '*Cielo*' to draw the important distinction between the theological notion of paradise and the astrological notion of heaven.
9. Critics have had their share of the difficulty with interpreting the meaning of 'disarmed heaven' and 'effeminate earth'. See for example Strauss, 1969, pp. 102, 179, and 314; and John M. Headley, 1988, p. 399.
10. 'Egli è cosa verissima, come tutte le cose del mondo hanno il termine della vita loro; ma quelle vanno tutto in corso che è loro ordinato dal cielo, generalmente, che non disordinano il corpo loro, ma tengonlo in modo ordinato, o che non altera, o, s'egli altera, è a salute, e non a danno suo. E perchè io parlo de' corpi misti, come sono le republiche le sètte, dico che quelle alterazioni sono a salute, che le riducano inverso i principii loro.' D. III. 1, p. 195.
11. D. III. 1, p. 195.
12. Ibid., pp. 196–7.
13. Strauss, 1959, p. 45.
14. Savonarola, 1513, p. 28.
15. See Plethon, 1966, p. xvi; see also Joseph Gill, 1964, p. 92. Plethon it may be remembered was instrumental in bringing about the revival of Platonism in Florence and in persuading Cosimo Medici to establish the Platonic Academy of Florence, whose first director was Ficino.
16. 'E debbono, tutte le cose che nascano in favore di quella, come che le giudicassono false, favorirle e accrescerle: e tanto più lo debbono fare, quanto più prudenti sono, e quanto più conoscitori delle cose naturali.' D. I. 12, p. 95.

17.   Machiavelli, 1950, p. 150.

18.   Prezzolini, 1967, p. 31.

19.   Walker, 1975, I., p. 244.

20.   Bondanella and Musa, 1979, p. 211.

21.   Claude Lefort, 1972, p. 492.

22.   D. I. 12, p. 95.

23.   D. I. 14, p. 97.

24.   D. II. 2, p. 149.

25.   D. I. 14.

26.   D. I. 11.

27.   I.F. I. 5.

28.   D. I. 12, p. 96.

29.   D. III. 1, pp. 196–7.

30.   D. II. 2, pp. 149–50.

31.   'The Golden Ass', V, lines 106–127.

32.   I have used 'Tractato della Humilità composto per frate Hieronymo da Ferrara', Incun. IV. 798, Vatican Library, Microfilm copy at the University of Calgary Library.

33.   Martelli, p. 933.

34.   Ibid.

35.   'Questa sola virtù è quella che in fra tutte l'altre piace a Dio.' Martelli, p. 36.

36.   For an English translation of the text and the analysis of the 'Allocution', see Parel, 1990a, pp. 525–7.

37.   'On Ambition', lines 16–24.

38.   See note 31 above. The same idea occurs in *The Prince* 26: 'God does not do everything, so as not to take from us free will and part of the glory that pertains to us.'

39.   See Martelli, pp. 30–1.

40.   P. 26, p. 297.

41.   Letter of Machiavelli to Bartolomeo Cavalcanti, 6 October 1526, Martelli, p. 1245.

42.   I. F. VI. 34.

43.   I. F. VII. 17.

44.   I. F. VIII. 11.

45.   I. F. VIII. 19.

46.   P. 26. For God's other partisan favours towards the Medici family, see I. F. VII. 21, VIII. 10 and 36.

47.   D. I. 11, p. 94.

48.   Letter of Machiavelli to Ricciardo Bechi, 9 March 1498, Martelli, p. 1011.

49.   D. I. 11, pp. 94–5.

50.   P. 6, p. 264.

51.   De Grazia, 1989, pp. 31–56.

52.   I. F. VIII. 36.

53.   P. 26, p. 297.

54.   I. F. VI. 21; see also P. 7.

55.   'Dio è amatore degli uomini forti, perché si vede che sempre gastiga gli impotenti con i potenti.' Martelli, p. 626.

56.   D. II. Preface, Martelli, p. 146.

57.   P. 25, p. 295.

58.   Ibid.

59.   D. II. 29.

60.   P. 6.

61.   P. 26.

62.   'Sono questi modi crudelissimi, e nimici d'ogni vivere, non solamente cristiano, ma umano; e debbegli qualunque uomo fuggire, e volere piuttosto vivere privato, che re con

tanta rovina degli uomini; nondimeno, colui che non vuole pigliare quella prima via del bene, quando si voglia mantenere conviene che entri in questo male.' D. I. 26, p. 109; see also D. III. 41, p. 249; P. 18, p. 284.
63.   See Strauss, 1969, pp. 142, 204, 205, 225.
64.   Ibid., pp. 225–6.
65.   Ibid., pp. 209, 214, 217, 223.
66.   Ibid., p. 145.
67.   Ibid., pp. 145–6.
68.   Ibid., p. 147.
69.   Ibid., p. 148; see also p. 197 and p. 334, n. 52.
70.   De Grazia, 1989, p. 31.
71.   Ibid.
72.   Ibid., p. 120.
73.   Ibid., p. 69.
74.   Ibid., p. 58.
75.   Ibid., p. 89.
76.   Ibid., p. 90.
77.   Ibid., p. 65.
78.   A.G. VI, Martelli, pp. 374–5. My italics. De Grazia leaves out the crucial passage in italics. See De Grazia, 1989, pp. 65 and 399; for evidence of the fact that Machiavelli believed in omens affecting the outcome of diplomatic activity, see *supra*, chapter 1, n. 49.

Chapter 4   Fortune

1.   For a useful categorization of the various meanings of Fortune in Machiavelli, see Price, Russell and Skinner, 1988, pp. 104–7; and, especially, Pitkin, 1984, pp. 138–69.
2.   Ptolemy, 1980, pp. 23–25.
3.   Boethius, 1962, p. 102.
4.   See Dante, 1970, pp. 75–77.
5.   For the evolution of such a secular attitude towards Fortune in the field of economic activities, see Bec, 1967, pp. 301–357.
6.   See Ptolemy, 1980, pp. 23–25.
7.   Ibid., pp. 221–459.
8.   '. . . e tempi e le cose universalmente et particularmente si mutano spesso . . .' Martelli, p. 1083.
9.   P. 25, Martelli, p. 295.
10.   'E assomiglio quella a uno di questi fiumi rovinosi, che, quando s'adirano, allagano e' piani, ruinano gli alberi e gli edifizii, lievono da questa parte terreno, pongono da quell'altra; ciascuno fugge loro dinanzi, ognuno cede allo impeto loro, senza potervi in alcuna parte obstare.' Ibid.
11.   Ibid.
12.   Sasso, 1981, p. 208, n. 9. Sasso, however, does not alert the reader to the astrological tone of this distinction.
13.   Machiavelli, 1968, pp. 359–60.
14.   Machiavelli, 1971, p. 295.
15.   Machiavelli, 1965a, p. 99; 1981a, pp. 121–2; 1970, pp. 138–9.
16.   Machiavelli, 1950, p. 92.
17.   Machiavelli, 1985, p. 99.
18.   Machiavelli, 1965b, p. 90.
19.   Machiavelli, 1986, p. 82.
20.   Machiavelli, 1988a, p. 85.

21.   'Questa da molti è detta onniopotente,
perché qualunche in questa vita viene,
o tardi o presto in sua forza sente.

Costei spesso gli buon sotto i piè tiene,
gl'improbi innalza; e se mai ti promette
cosa veruna, mai te la mantiene.

E sottosopra e regni e stati mette,
secondo ch'a lei pare, e' giusti priva
del bene che gli ingiusti larga dette.

Questa incostante dea e mobil diva
gl'indegni spesso sopra un seggio pone,
dove chi degno n'è, mai non arriva.

Costei il tempo a suo modo dispone;
questa ci esalta, questa ci disface,
senza pietà, senza legge o ragione.' Martelli, pp. 976–77.

22.   'Tutto quel regno suo, dentro e di fuora,
   istoriato si vede e dipinto
di que'trionfi de' qua' più s'onora.

Nel primo loco, colorato e tinto,
si vede come già sotto l'Egitto
il mondo stette subiugato e vinto:

e come lungamente il tenne vitto
con lunga pace, e come quivi fue
ciò ch'è di bel ne la natura scritto;

veggonsi poi gli Assirii ascender sue
ad alto scettro, quand'ella non volse
che quel d'Egitto dominassi piue;

poi, come a' Medi lieta si rivolse;
da' Medi a' Persi: e de' Greci la chioma
ornò di quello onor ch'a' Persi tolse.

Quivi si vede Menfi e Tebe doma,
Babilon, Troia e Cartagin con quelle,
Ierusalem, Atene, Sparta e Roma.

Quivi si mostran quanto furon belle
alte, ricche, potenti; e come, al fine,
fortuna a' lor nimici in preda dielle

Quivi si veggon l'opre alte e divine
de l' imperio roman; poi, come tutto
il mondo infranse con le sue rovine.

Come un torrente rapido, ch'al tutto
superbo è fatto, ogni cosa fracassa
dovunque aggiugne il suo corso per tutto;

e questa parte accresce e quella abassa,
varia le ripe, varia il letto e 'l fondo,
e fa tremar la terra donde passa;

cosi Fortuna, col suo furibondo
impeto, molte volte or qui or quivi
va tramutando le cose del mondo.' Ibid., pp. 978–79.

23.   'E tanto le fu favorevole la fortuna, che, benché si passasse dal governo de' Re e delli
Ottimati al Popolo . . . nondimeno non si tolse mai, per dare autorità agli Ottimati, tutta
l'authorità alle qualità regie, né si diminuì l'autorità in tutto agli Ottimati, per darla al
Popolo; ma rimanendo mista, fece una republica perfetta . . .' D. I. 2, p. 81.

24. D. II. 1, p. 147.
25. D. II. 30, p. 191.
26. D. II. 1, p. 147.
27. D. II. 30, p. 191.
28. Ibid.
29. D. II. 29, p. 189.
30. D. II. 29, p. 189.
31. 'Affermo, bene, di nuovo, questo essere verissimo, secondo che per tutte le istorie si vede, che gli uomini possono secondare la fortuna e non opporsegli; possono tessere gli orditi suoi, e non rompergli.' Ibid., pp. 189–90.
32. 'Ghiribizzi', Martelli, p. 1083.
33. Ibid.
34. D. III. 9, p. 212.
35. Ibid.
36. Potenzia, onor, ricchezza e sanitate
stanno per premio; per pena e dolore,
servitù, infamia, morbo e povertate.
Fortuna il rabbioso suo furore
dimostra con quest' ultima famiglia;
quell'altra porge a chi lei porta amore.
Colui con miglior sorte si consiglia,
tra tutti gli altri che in quel loco stanno,
che ruota al suo voler conforme piglia;
perche' gli umor ch'adoperar ti fanno,
secondo che convengon con costei,
son cagion del tuo bene e del tuo danno.
Non però che fidar ti possa in lei,
ne' creder d'evitar suo duro morso
suo' duri colpi impetuosi e rei;
perché, mentre girato sei dal dorso
di ruota per allor felice e buona,
la suol cangiar le volte a mezzo il corso;
e, non potendo tu cangiar persona,
né lasciar l'ordin di che 'l ciel ti dota,
nel mezzo del cammin la t'abbandona.
Però, se questo si comprende e nota,
sarebbe un sempre felice e beato,
che potessi saltar di rota in rota;
ma perché poter questo ci è negato
per occulta virtù che ci governa,
si muta col suo corso il nostro stato.
Non è nel mondo cosa alcuna eterna:
Fortuna vuol così, che se n'abbella,
acciò che 'l suo poter più si discerna.
Però si vuol lei prender per sua stella,
e quanto a noi è possibile, ogni ora,
accomodarsi al variar di quella.' Martelli, p. 978; my italics.
37. 'Se poi con gli occhi tuoi più oltre arrivi,
Cesare e Alexandro in una faccia
vedi fra que' che fur felici vivi.
Da questo esempio, quanto a costei piaccia,
quanto grato le sia, si vede scorto,

chi l' urta, chi la pigne o chi la caccia.
Pur nondimanco al desiato porto
l'un non pervenne, e l'altro, di ferite
pieno, fu a l'ombra del nimico morto.
Appresso questi son genti infinite,
che per cadere in terra maggior botto,
son con costei altissimo salite.
Con questi iace preso, morto e rotto,
Ciro e Pompeio, poi che ciascheduno
fu da Fortuna infin al ciel condotto.
Avresti tu mai visto in loco alcuno
come una aquila irata si trasporta,
cacciata da la fame e dal digiuno?
E come una testudine alto porta,
acciò che 'l colpo del cader la 'nfranga,
e pasca sé di quella carne morta?
Così Fortuna, non ch'ivi rimanga,
porta uno in alto, ma che, ruinando,
lei se ne goda e lui cadendo pianga.
Ancor si vien dopo costor mirando
come d'infimo stato alto si saglia,
e come ci si viva variando.
Dove si vede come la travaglia
e Tullio e Mario, e li splendidi corni
più vole di lor gloria or cresce, or taglia.
Vedesi alfin che tra' passati giorni
pochi sono e' felici; e que' son morti
prima che la lor ruota indrieto torni
o che voltando al basso ne li porti.' Ibid., p. 979. My italics.

38. 'Ghiribizzi', p. 1082.

39. '. . . laudes astronomie quamque humano generi utilitatem tribuat melius est sicco pede transire quam imo gurgite mergi. Sat est quod sententia tua verissima dicenda est, cum omnes antiqui uno ore clament sapientem ipsum astrorum influxus immutare posse, non illorum cum in eternis nulla possit cadere mutatio; sed hoc respectu sui intelligitur aliter et aliter passum ipsum immutando atque alterando.' Bartolomeo Vespucci to Machiavelli, from Padua, 4 June 1504, Martelli, p. 1064. Vespucci was a Florentine 'doctor of medicine' who lectured on astrology at the University of Padua. Obviously, Machiavelli sought his opinion on the subject of astrology. Thorndike gives us the title and a brief analysis of his inaugural lecture at Padua. See 'Bartholomaei Vespucci Florentini Oratio habita in celeberrimo gymnasio Pataviano pro sua prima lectione A.D. 1506 laudes prosequens quadrivii ac presertim astrologiae quae ibi publice profitetur.' Thorndike, 1959c, pp. 164–65.

40. 'Et veramente, chi fussi tanto savio che conoscessi e tempi et l'ordine delle cose et adcomodassisi ad quelle, harebbe sempre buona fortuna o e' si guarderebbe sempre da la trista, et verebbe ad essere vero che 'l savio comandassi alle stelle et a' fati.' 'Ghiribizzi', Martelli, p. 1083.

41. 'Né si truova uomo sì prudente che si sappi accomodare a questo; sì perché non si può deviare da quello a che la natura lo inclina; sì etiam perché, avendo sempre uno prosperato camminando per una via, non si può persuadere partirsi da quella.' P. 25, Martelli, p. 296.

42. Ibid., p. 1082.

43. Ibid., p. 1083.

44. P. 25, p. 296.

45. Cumont, 1960, p. 61.

46. Ibid.
47. Martelli, p. 81.
48. P. 3, p. 260.
49. Bertelli, 1964a, II, p. 912.
50. '. . . né mai arebbe deviato da quelli modi a' quali la natura lo inclinava.' P. 25, p. 296.
51. '. . . nella natura sua onorevole e collerica'. 20 November 1503, Bertelli, 1964a, II, p. 655.
52. 'umor collera maligna', 'Decennale I', Martelli, p. 948.
53. 'ira natural,' 'Decennale II', Martelli, p. 952.
54. Martelli, p. 615.
55. 'fu dal ciel ucciso', Martelli, p. 948.
56. P. 7, p. 266, p. 268.
57. Martelli, p. 625.
58. Ibid.
59. 'Ghiribizzi', p. 1083.
60. Machiavelli takes this opportunity to argue that republics are better off than monarchies, since they have various individuals with different humours attempting to meet the different requirements of different times. To depend on the same man for all seasons would be unwise, because 'a man accustomed to acting one way never changes'.
61. '. . . e sempre mai si procede, secondo ti sforza la natura . . . E che Fabio facessi questo per natura, e non per elezione, si vide . . . noi non ci possiano opporre a quello a che c'inclina la natura . . .' D. III. 9, p. 213.
62. Martelli, p. 616.
63. P. 7, p. 267.
64. '. . . la Fortuna ha fatto che, non sapendo ragionare né dell'arte della seta et dell'arte della lana, né de' guadagni né delle perdite, e' mi conviene ragionare dello stato . . .' Letter of Machiavelli to Francesco Vettori, 9 April 1513, Martelli, p. 1131.
65. Even so orthodox a thinker as Archbishop Antoninus of Florence, citing the authority of Albert the Great, connects a person's aptitude for a particular profession to that person's humour and temperament. Arguing that merchants and craftsmen should follow professions which suited their humour, etc., Antoninus wrote: 'Et sic etiam secundum Albertum Magnum homines a natura dociles inclinantur ad scientias varias secundum qualitatem complexionum. Nam melancolici ad poeticas, phlegmatici ad morales, sanguinei ad naturales, colerici ad mathematicas vel metaphysicas. Ita et cetera opera mecanica et artes unus inclinatur magis ad unam, alius ad aliam, et naturali instinctu et divina providentia etiam disponente ad pulchritudinem universi et ostentionem suae sapientiae, quae tantas et tam varias operationes artificium inspiravit mentibus hominum.' S. Antoninus, 1959, p. 294. Notice that though there is a reference to complexions and humours, there is no reference here to planets or Fortune; instead the reference is made to Divine Providence.
66. Pico, 1572, p. 454; for Ptolemy's theory on the connection between the various professions and astral influences, see Ptolemy, 1980, pp. 383–93.
67. '. . . perché il nostro libero arbitrio non sia spento, iudico potere essere vero che la fortuna sia arbitra della metà delle azioni nostre, ma che etiam lei ne lasci governare l'altra metà, o presso, a noi.' P. 25, p. 295.
68. It is instructive to note what Aquinas says about the principle of co–causality. In *Summa Contra Gentiles* III. 70, he explains 'How the same effect is from God and from a natural agent.' Although the specific discussion here is on the question of how God and natural agents act together, the principle involved here, *mutatis mutandis*, can be applied to the question of how God and human agents act together. The same effect is not to be attributed to God and a natural agent, says Aquinas, in such a way that 'it is partly done by God and partly by the natural agent; rather it is wholly done by both, according to a different mode, just as the same effect is wholly attributed to the tool and also wholly to the one who uses the tool.' 'Patet etiam quod non

sic idem effectus causae naturali et divinae virtuti attribuitur quasi partim a Deo, et partim a naturali agente fiat, sed totus ab utroque secundum alium modum: sicut idem effectus totus attribuitur instrumento, et principali agenti etiam totus.' Aquinas, 1961, p. 99.

69. 'Dio non vuole fare ogni cosa, per non ci torre el libero arbitrio e parte di quella gloria che tocca a noi.' P. 26, p. 297. His linking of freedom of choice, Providence, and glory, reminds one of Aquinas's fourth argument in *Summa Contra Gentiles* III. 73, linking Providence, freedom of choice, and the praise of virtue. In that argument Aquinas states that God's Providence tends to multiply goods among the things that are governed by Him. Providence does not wish to deprive things of their proper good. But if freedom of choice is taken away from man, many goods would be removed. One such good is the praise for virtue. Praise for virtue means nothing, if man does not act freely. 'Providentia est multiplacativa bonorum in rebus gubernatis. Illud ergo per quod multa bona subtraherentur a rebus, non pertinet ad providentiam. Si autem libertas voluntatis tolleretur, multa bona subtraherentur. Tolleretur enim laus virtutis humanae, quae nulla est si homo libere non agit.' Aquinas, 1961, p. 103.

70. For an opposite view see Colish, 1971, p. 326. She writes: 'Although he does not expound his doctrine of free will in detail, Machiavelli thus clearly places himself within the tradition of thinkers who see in man's free will the sign of human independence, the ground of ethically meaningful choices, and the guarantee that man will be reduced to the status of a plaything at the mercy of capricious and uncaring cosmic forces.'

71. 'Io iudico bene questo: che sia meglio essere impetuoso che respettivo; perche' la fortuna è donna, ed è necessario, volendola tenere sotto, batterla e urtarla. E si vede che la si lascia più vincere da questi, che da quelli che freddamente procedano; e però sempre, come donna, è amica de' giovani, perché sono meno respettivi, più feroci e con più audacia la comandano.' P. 25, p. 296.

72. Strauss, 1969, p. 216.

73. '. . . la natura ha creati gli uomini in modo, che possono desiderare ogni cosa, e non possono conseguire ogni cosa . . .' D. I. 37, p. 119.

74. '. . . gli appetiti umani insaziabili, perché, avendo, dalla natura, di potere e volere desiderare ogni cosa, e, dalla fortuna, di potere conseguitarne poche; ne risulta continuamente una mala contentezza nelle menti umane, ed uno fastidio delle cose che si posseggono . . .' D. II. Preface, p. 145. Leo Strauss, in my view, misunderstands the meaning of the term 'natura' here and in D. I. 37 cited above. He seems to think that nature in these passages refers to non-human nature. In my view, it refers to human nature, each human being's particular nature. This misunderstanding leads to another misunderstanding: Strauss says that Machiavelli identifies nature and chance or blurs the distinction between nature and chance. See Strauss, 1969, pp. 217–19.

75. D. I. 19, p. 105.

76. D. II. Preface, p. 146.

77. Strauss, 1969, pp. 22–3.

78. Pitkin, 1984, p. 165.

79. Ibid., p. 161.

80. See Ibid., p. 151.

81. Ibid., p. 151.

82. The river metaphor is used again in the poem 'On Fortune'. See note 22 above.

Chapter 5 Virtù

1. P. 6, p. 264.

2. D. II. 2, p. 148.

3. D. I. 56, p. 139; D. I. 58, p. 141.

4. Martelli, p. 978.

5. '. . . amo la patria mia più dell'anima'. Martelli, p. 1250.
6. I. F. III.7, p. 696.
7. Strauss, 1969, p. 31.
8. See D. P. Walker, 1975, pp. 12, 77–78.
9. 'malignità dello animo loro'. D. I. 3, p. 81.
10. P. 8, p. 269.
11. Ibid., 7, p. 267.
12. Ibid.
13. D. I. 27, p. 110.
14. D. I. 9, p. 90.
15. P. 19, p. 288.
16. Ibid., 21, p. 291.
17. Ibid., 18, p. 284.
18. D. III. 25, p. 232; 31, p. 239.
19. In this work, following the humanist tradition, Machiavelli makes various historical figures deliver imaginary speeches. There are some fifteen of these in the entire work. These speeches of course reveal Machiavelli's own views on the given issues.
20. I. F., Martelli, p. 631.
21. 'Memoriale of 23 October 1522, to Raffaello Girolami When He was Ambassador to the Emperor', Allan Gilbert, 1965, p. 118.
22. D. III. 41.
23. 'L'amore della patria è causato dalla natura.' A.G., IV, Martelli, p. 354. I interpret nature here to mean particular human nature defined by one's humours, and not inanimate nature.
24. Martelli, p. 1083.
25. 'Accutezza d'inventare, e ghiribizzare, che fia sansa maestro, o avvertitore.'
26. D. Dedicatory Letter and D. I. Preface, pp. 75, 76.
27. P. 7, p. 266.
28. Ibid., 26, p. 297.
29. A. G., Martelli, p. 302.
30. Ibid., *La vita . . .*, p. 616.
31. 'Homo non propter ingenium, sed propter virtutem est laudandus.' Ficino, 1978, p. 201.
32. Alberti, 1972, p. 113.
33. 'Nec ingenium ab astro, siquidem incorporale, sed a Deo.' Pico, 1572, p. 517.
34. 'Io credo che, come la Natura ha facto ad l'uomo diverso volto, così li habbi facto diverso ingegno et diversa fantasia. Da questo nascie che ciascuno secondo lo ingegno et fantasia sua si governa.' Martelli, p. 1083.
35. Oakeshott, 1975, p. 244.
36. Martelli, p. 1083. Note Machiavelli's use of the astrologically significant words *universalmente et particularmente* here: 'perché e tempi et le cose universalmente et particularmente si mutano spesso . . .', etc.
37. See Gianfrancesco Pico della Mirandola, 1930.
38. Ibid., p. 33.
39. Ibid., p. 37.
40. Ibid., p. 29.
41. Ibid., p. 51.
42. Ibid.
43. Ibid., p. 53.
44. Ibid.
45. Ibid., p. 53. Caplan very incorrectly translates 'caelum' as 'climate'. In a footnote, Gianfrancesco draws attention to his uncle's famous *Disputationes Adversus Astrologos* in support of his position on the relationship between astrology, humours, and imagination. See Ibid., p. 54.

46. Ibid., p. 59.
47. Ibid.
48. Ibid., p. 45.
49. D. III. 8, pp. 212–13.
50. 'conoscitori della occasione'. 'Del modo di trattare i popoli della Valdichiana ribellati', Martelli, p. 15.
51. D. I. 10, 93.
52. *Mandragola*, Act V. Scene 4; according to Act II. Scene 6, Machiavelli knows the most astrologically propitious time for Lucrezia to take the mandrake: 'This evening after supper, because the moon is right and the time can't be more suitable.'
53. Machiavelli to Vettori, 4 February 1513, Martelli, p. 1168.
54. Machiavelli to Vettori, 25 February 1513, Martelli, p. 1171.
55. Machiavelli to Vettori, 31 January 1515, Martelli, p. 1191.
56. 'Capitolo Pastorale', Martelli, pp. 994–97.
57. Maritain, 1956, p. 321.
58. Ibid., p. 320.
59. Croce, 1952, p. 655.
60. Ibid., p. 657.
61. Berlin, 1972, p. 169.
62. Ibid., p. 178.
63. Ibid., p. 185.
64. Ibid., p. 184.
65. Ibid., p. 205.
66. Ibid., p. 204.
67. Ibid., pp. 188, 192, 201.
68. Meinecke, 1957, p. 31.
69. Strauss, 1969, p. 233; see also p. 9.
70. Ibid., p. 294.
71. See 'Allocuzione fatta ad un magistrato', Martelli, p. 36.
72. D. III. 41, p. 249.
73. D. III. 47, p. 253.
74. D. III. 8, p. 212.
75. D. I. 3, p. 82.
76. P. 17, p. 282.
77. D. I. 29, p. 111; 37, p. 119; II. Preface, p. 145.
78. D. I. 6, p. 86.
79. D. III. 21, p. 227.
80. 'una excessiva *virtù*'. Ibid.
81. See I. F. III. 25, and IV. 14; and Whitfield, 1969, pp. 37–55.
82. P. 18, p. 284.
83. P. 18, p. 283.
84. Maritain, 1956, pp. 321–53.
85. Ibid.
86. Strauss, 1969, p. 299.
87. Ibid.

Chapter 6   Humours

1. Hippocrates, 1950, p. 204.
2. Throughout the rest of this study I use the term *class* to refer to the constitutive humours of the body politic. I do not attach a Marxist meaning to class. As used here, class simply stands for the basic group unit of the body politic.

3. Plato, 1968, p. 243.
4. Jaeger, 1968, p. 417.
5. Barker, 1979, p. xxx.
6. Plutarch, 1819a, pp. 117, 123. For Plutarch's other uses of the concept of humours, see 1819b, p. 210; and 1819c, pp. 74–75.
7. Wardman, 1974, p. 57.
8. Aquinas, 1961, p. 219.
9. '. . . it is the business of the ruler, like a wise doctor, duly to keep the body of the state healthy, so that the vital spirit, "per proportionabile medium", can be at one with it. He may observe that one of the four vital humours goes beyond or lags behind right proportion in the combination, and that the body is thereby estranged from its proper combination. This may occur through an excess of covetous melancholy, which gives rise to the most varied pestilences of the body – usury, fraud, deceit, theft, pillage, and all the arts by which great riches are won not by work but by certain deceitful craftiness, which can never exist without doing harm to the State; or again, it may occur through choleric dissensions, wars, factions, and schism; or through sanguine ostentation, excess, debauchery and such like; or through phlegmatic sloth in all good works, in the daily toil for existence, and in the defence of the fatherland. Then the body becomes paralysed, feverish, swollen up or bled dry; then must he seek a remedy, consult books, and give ear to the wisest State physicians; and when he has found a remedy he must bring it forth and test it by means of taste, sight and smell . . .' Cusa, 1964, pp. 119–20.
10. Savonarola, 1973, pp. 17–22. For the Ptolemaic source of this particular argument, see Ptolemy, 1980, pp. 121–23; 135–37.
11. Burd, 1968, pp. 282–83.
12. 'E però non abbiamo a cercare di uno governo immaginato e che sia più facile a apparire in su' libri che in pratica, come fu forse la republica di Platone; ma considerato la natura, le qualità, le condizioni, la inclinazione, e per stringere tutte queste in una parola, gli umori della città e de' cittadini, cercare di un governo, che non siamo sanza speranza che pure si potessi persuadere ed introducere, e che introdotto si potessi secondo el gusto nostro comportare e conservare, seguitando in questo lo exemplo de' medici che, se bene sono più liberi che non siamo noi, perché agli infermi possono dare tutte le medicine che pare loro, non gli danno però tutte quelle che in sé sono buone e lodate, ma quelle che lo infermo secondo la complessione sua ed altri accidenti è atto a sopportare.' Guicciardini, 1932, p. 99. For other significant uses of this notion see Ibid., pp. 211, 219, 260.
13. Skinner, 1984, p. 209.
14. '. . . così interviene nelle cose di stato.' P. 3, p. 260.
15. 'medicine forti'. P. 3, p. 258; for the parallel passage see D. III. 27, p. 233. Internal rebellions sometimes have no other 'medication' than that of killing their leaders.
16. 'E questi dottori di medicina dicono, parlando de' corpi degli uomini, "quod quotidie aggregatur aliquid, quod quandoque indiget curatione".' D. III. 1, p. 195; for the parallel passage see D. II. 5, p. 155: 'Just as in simple bodies when a great deal of superfluous matter is brought together, nature many times moves of herself and makes purgation for the health of those bodies, the same process appears in this mixed body of the human race.'
17. P. 26, p. 297.
18. 'E quelli umori in quai ti sono stati
    cotanto avversi e cotanto nimici
    non sono ancor, non sono ancor purgati;
    ma come secche fien le lor radici
    e che benigni i ciel si mostreranno,
    torneran tempi più che mai felici.' 'L'Asino', III, Martelli, p. 962.
19. 'perché gli umor ch'adoperar ti fanno,
    secondo che convengon con costei,
    son cagion del tuo bene e del tuo danno.' 'Di Fortuna', Martelli, p. 978.

20.   One is impressed by Machiavelli's familiarity with these Latin medical aphorisms. Earlier in D. III.1, we had seen him quoting medical texts in Latin.

21.   'Perché in ogni città si trovono questi due umori diversi; e nasce da questo, che il populo desidera non essere commandato né oppresso da' grandi, e li grandi desiderano comandare e opprimere il populo...' P. 9, p. 271.

22.   '. . . e' sono in ogni republica due umori diversi, quello del popolo, quello de' grandi; e come tutte le leggi che si fanno in favore della libertà, nascano dalla disunione loro . . .' D. I. 4, p. 82.

23.   'Le gravi e naturali nimicizie che sono intra gli uomini popolari e i nobili, causate da il volere questi comandare e quelli non ubbidire, sono cagione di tutti i mali che nascono nelle città; perché da questa diversità di umori tutte le altre cose che perturbano le republiche prendano il nutrimento loro.' I. F. III. 1, p. 690.

24.   '. . . né si può credere quella repubblica esser per durare, dove non si satisfa a quelli umori, a' quali non si satisfacendo, le repubbliche rovinano.' 'Discursus', p. 24.

25.   'E' si conosce facilmente, per chi considera le cose presenti e le antiche, come in tutte le città ed in tutti i popoli sono quegli medesimi desiderii e quelli medesimi omori . . .' D. I. 39, p. 122.

26.   '. . . perché tutte le cose del mondo, in ogni tempo, hanno il proprio riscontro con gli antichi tempi. Il che nasce, perché, essendo quelle operate dagli uomini, che hanno ed ebbono sempre le medesime passioni, conviene di necessità che le sortischino il medesimo effetto.' D. III. 43, p. 250.

27.   P. 9, p. 271.

28.   D. I. 4, p. 83.

29.   D. I. 5, p. 83.

30.   D. I. 5, p. 84.

31.   'È cosa veramente molto naturale e ordinaria desiderare di acquistare; e sempre, quando gli uomini lo fanno che possono, saranno laudati o non biasimati; ma quando non possono e vogliono farlo in ogni modo, qui è lo errore e il biasmo.' P. 3, p. 261.

32.   D. I. 37, p. 119.

33.   See, for example, I. F. IV.1, p. 715.

34.   See 'Rapporto delle cose della Magna Fatto questo di 17 giugno 1508', Martelli, p. 66, and 'Ritratto delle cose della Magna', Ibid., p. 69.

35.   '. . . e da questi due appetiti diversi nasce nelle città uno de' tre effetti, o principato o libertà o licenzia.' P. 9, p. 271.

36.   'Quinci nasce che una republica ha maggiore vita, ed ha più lungamente buona fortuna, che uno principato; perché la può meglio accomodarsi alla diversità de' temporali, per la diversità de' cittadini che sono in quella, che non può uno principe.' D. III. 9, p. 213.

37.   '. . . alla quale perfezione venne per la disunione della Plebe e del Senato . . .' D. I. 2, p. 81.

38.   Locke, 1960, p. 432. If Locke is in favour of a government based on 'people', then of course, in Machiavellian language, he would be asking for a factional government. For Machiavelli, a good government would have to satisfy all the relevant humours of the state.

39.   Prescott, 1837, p. 148.

40.   Lefort, 1972, p. 723, *passim.*

41.   Heller, 1981, pp. 332–33.

42.   Macek, 1980, p. 115.

43.   Gramsci, 1970, pp. 135–44.

44.   'Del modo di trattare i popoli della Valdichiana ribellati', Martelli, p. 14.

Chapter 7   *The Prince*

1.   Pocock, 1975, p. 156.

2.   '. . . io ho . . . composto uno opusculo *De principatibus*, dove io mi profondo quanto io

posso nelle cogitationi di questo subbietto, disputando che cosa è principato, di quale spetie sono, come e' si acquistono, come e' si mantengono, perché e' si perdono.' Machiavelli to Vettori, 10 December 1513, Martelli, p. 1160.

3. '. . . li uomini mutano volentieri signore, credendo migliorare; e questa credenza gli fa pigliare l'arme contro a quello; di che e' s'ingannono, perché veggono poi per esperienza avere peggiorato.' P. 3, p. 258.

4. '. . . tu hai inimici tutti quelli che hai offesi in occupare quello principato, e non ti puoi mantenere amici quelli che vi ti hanno messo, per non li potere satisfare in quel modo che si erano presupposto . . .' Ibid.

5. '. . . perché sempre, ancora che uno sia fortissimo in sugli eserciti, ha bisogno del favore de' provinciali a intrare in una provincia.' Ibid.

6. P. 4, p. 262.

7. P. 19, p. 288.

8. P. 4, p. 263.

9. '. . . perché quello che ordinò quel regno, conoscendo la ambizione de' potenti e la insolenzia loro, e iudicando essere loro necessario uno freno in bocca che li correggessi e, dall'altra parte, conoscendo l'odio dello universale contro a' grandi fondato in sulla paura, e volendo assicurarli, non volse che questa fussi particulare cura del re, per torli quel carico ch' e' potessi avere co' grandi favorendo e' populari, e con li populari favorendo e' grandi; e però constitui uno iudice terzo, che fussi quello che, sanza carico del re, battessi e' grandi e favorissi e' minori.' P. 19, pp. 285–86.

10. 'Il che non è nato dalla molta o poca *virtù* del vincitore, ma dalla disformità del subietto.' P. 4, p. 263.

11. 'Ma nelle republiche è maggiore vita, maggiore odio, più desiderio di vendetta; né li lascia, né può lasciare riposare la memoria della antiqua libertà: tale che la più sicura via è spegnere o abitarvi.' P. 5, p. 264.

12. P. 6, p. 265.

13. P. 6, p. 265.

14. P. 7, p. 267.

15. P. 8, p. 269.

16. P. 8, p. 270.

17. P. 21, p. 291.

18. P. 21, p. 291.

19. P. 17, p. 282; P. 19, p. 284.

20. P. 21, p. 292.

21. P. 19, p. 288.

22. P. 19, p. 286.

23. 'E li più di loro massime quelli che come uomini nuovi venivano al principato, conosciuta la difficultà di questi due diversi umori, si volgevano a satisfare a' soldati, stimando poco lo iniuriare il populo.' P. 19, p. 286.

24. '. . . perché, non potendo e' principi mancare di non esere odiati da qualcuno, si debbano prima forzare di non essere odiati dalle università; e, quando non possano conseguire questo, si debbano ingegnare con ogni industria fuggire l'odio di quelle università che sono più potenti.' Ibid.

25. Ibid., p. 288.

26. P. 11, p. 274.

27. '. . . quando quella università, o populi o soldati o grandi che sieno, della quale tu iudichi suo per mantenerti, avere bisogno, è corrotta, ti conviene seguire l'umore suo per satisfarle; e allora le buone opere ti sono nimiche.' P. 19, p. 287.

28. 'Onde è necessario a uno principe, volendosi mantenere, imparare a potere essere non buono, e usarlo e non l'usare secondo la necessità.' P. 15, p. 280.

29. 'E se si considerrà quelli signori che in Italia hanno perduto lo stato a' nostri tempi . . .

si troverrà in loro, prima, uno commune defetto quanto alle armi . . . di poi, si vedrà alcuno di loro o che arà avuto inimici e' populi, o, se arà avuto el populo amico, non si sarà saputo assicurare de' grandi . . .' P. 24, p. 294.
30.   P. 26, p. 297.

Chapter 8   *The* Discourses

1.   Pocock, 1975, pp. 194–96.
2.   'E tanto le fu favorevole la fortuna, che benché si passasse dal governo de' Re e delli Ottimati al Popolo, per quelli medesimi gradi e per quelle medesime cagioni che di sopra si sono discorse; nondimeno non si tolse mai, per dare autorità agli Ottimati, tutta l'autorità alle qualità regie; né si diminuì l'autorità in tutto agli Ottimati, per darla al Popolo; ma rimanendo mista, fece una republica perfetta; alle quale perfezione venne per la disunione della Plebe e del Senato . . .' D. I. 2, p. 81.
3.   'I say that those who condemn the tumults between the patricians and the plebeians seem to me to find fault with what was the first cause of freedom in Rome.' ('Io dico che coloro che dannano i tumulti intra i Nobili e la Plebe, mi pare che biasimino quelle cose che furono prima causa del tenere libera Roma . . .') D. I. 4, p. 82.
4.   '. . . e che e' non considerino come e' sono in ogni republica due umori diversi, quello del popolo, e quello de' grandi; e come tutte le leggi che si fanno in favore della libertà, nascano dalla disunione loro . . .' Ibid., p. 82.
5.   Ibid., p. 82.
6.   'Non fu adunche la disunione tra la plebe ed el senato che facessi Roma libera e potente, perché meglio sarebbe stato se non vi fussono state le cagione della disunione . . . ma laudare le disunione è come laudare in uno infermo la infermità, per la bontà del remedio che gli è stato applicato.' Guicciardini, 1984, p. 44.
7.   See Skinner, 1984, pp. 205–19.
8.   D. I. 4.
9.   I. F. III. 1.
10.   D. I. 5, p. 84.
11.   D. I. 1.
12.   D. I. 37, p. 119.
13.   D. I. 7.
14.   'E però non è cosa che faccia tanto stabile e ferma una republica, quanto ordinare quella in modo che l'alterazione di quegli omori che l'agitano, abbia, una via da sforgarsi ordinata dalle leggi.' D. I. 7, p. 87.
15.   Ibid.
16.   D. I. 8.
17.   D. I. 8.
18.   D. I. 35, 40–46.
19.   D. I. 35.
20.   D. I. 40, p. 124.
21.   Ibid.
22.   Ibid.
23.   D. I. 33–34; 49–50; III. 25, 28.
24.   D. I. 33.
25.   D. I. 34.
26.   D. I. 37.
27.   D. III. 25, p. 232.
28.   Ibid.
29.   Ibid.

30. Ibid.
31. D. II. 2.
32. D. I. 37.
33. D. I. 37.
34. Ibid.
35. D. III. 3, p. 198.
36. D. I. 16, p. 100.
37. D. III. 1.
38. D. I. 4, p. 83.
39. D. II. 2.
40. Ibid.
41. D. I. 6, 55; D. II. 3.
42. D. I. 6, p. 85.
43. Ibid.
44. '. . . levevano via tutte le cagioni de' tumulti.' Ibid., p. 85.
45. Ibid.
46. '. . . volendo Roma levare le cagioni de' tumulti, levava ancora le cagioni dello ampliare.' Ibid.
47. P. 3, p. 261.
48. D. I. 6; D. II. 3.
49. D. II. 3, p. 151.
50. For an account of his opinions of the Swiss see his 'Rapporto della cosa della Magna' of 1508, Martelli, pp. 63–68, and his 'Ritratto delle cose della Magna', Ibid., pp. 68–71.
51. See 'Rapporto', p. 67, and 'Ritratto', p. 70.
52. 'Rapporto', p. 66, 'Ritratto', p. 69.
53. D. II. 19.
54. D. II. 3 and 4.
55. D. III. 9, p. 213.
56. D. III. 1, p. 196.
57. D. III. 22, pp. 228–29; also D. I. 20, p. 105.
58. 'E perché a simili disordini che nascano nelle republiche non si può dare certo rimedio, ne seguita che gli è impossibile ordinare una republica perpetua, perché per mille inopinate vie si causa la sua rovina.' D. III. 17, p. 223. For a dissenting view that Machiavelli has a notion of progress, and that the idea of a perpetual republic is tied to that notion, see Harvey C. Mansfield, Jr., 1981, p. 305 and n. 55.
59. D. III. 24.
60. D. III. 28.
61. D. I. 29.
62. '. . . oneste e determinate cagioni'. D. I. 29, p. 200.
63. D. I. 18, p. 103.
64. D. III. 24, p. 231.
65. Ibid., p. 231.
66. D. II. 19.
67. D. II. 8, p. 157.
68. D. III. 24, p. 231.
69. D. I. 16, p. 99.
70. D. I. 17, pp. 101–2.
71. '. . . perché altri ordini e modi di vivere si debbe ordinare in uno suggetto cattivo, che in uno buono; né può essere la forma simile in una materia al tutto contraria.' Ibid., p. 103.
72. Walker, 1975, II. p. 45, n.7.
73. D. III. 8 and 9.
74. D. I. 18, p. 104.

75. D. III. 8, p. 212. The notion of 'right time' (*debiti tempi*) is critical to Machiavelli's analysis. In the *Art of War*, ch. VII, p. 388, for example, Fabrizio bemoans his fate that he is too old and nature has not served him well. But he hopes that his young listeners, 'in right time' will feel disposed to advise their rulers as to what needs to be done. In D. I. 35, p. 118, to take another example, he remarks that his view that a free vote in a republic never injures anyone is based on the presupposition that it is given at the 'right time': 'When I say that authority given by free vote never injures any republic, I presuppose a people never bringing itself to give it, except with proper limitations and at the proper times.'

Chapter 9   Humours *and* Licenzia

1.   'Discursus', p. 24.
2.   I. F. VII. 1.
3.   No doubt scruples concerning his objectivity towards the Medici crossed his mind, as is evident from his correspondence. To Vettori he writes of the difficulty he had in writing the sections on the Medici period. Gianotti also testifies to the same difficulty. But Machiavelli finds a solution to these problems; he puts his criticisms of the Medici into the mouths of their enemies, and in this way is able to maintain both his intellectual integrity and a client relationship with his patrons.
4.   Martelli, p. 24.
5.   I. F. Preface, pp. 632–33.
6.   According to Nicolai Rubinstein, the 'striking equality' in question refers to the establishment of the Great Council in 1494. See Rubinstein, 1972, p. 24.
7.   I. F. III. 1, 690–91.
8   '. . . o per vie publiche, o per modi privati.' I. F. VII. 1, p. 792. For the parallel analysis see D. III. 28, p. 235.
9.   Ibid.
10.   'Discursus', p. 24.
11.   It is interesting that in the 'Discursus', Machiavelli is concerned only with the history of Florence from 1393, whereas in the *Florentine Histories* he goes back to her pre-Christian beginnings as a colony of republican Rome, founded by Sulla.
12.   I. F. II. 2.
13.   I. F. Preface.
14.   D. I. 49.
15.   D. I. 49, p. 131.
16.   I. F. I. 15.
17.   I. F. II. 12.
18.   I. F. II. 21.
19.   I. F. II. 2, p. 660.
20.   I. F. II. 14, p. 667.
21.   Ibid.
22.   I. F. II. 42, p. 690.
23.   I. F. I. 39.
24.   The plebs formed the disenfranchised underclass (*sottoposti*) of the Florentine Republic. Machiavelli calls them by different names: *plebe, infima plebe, popolo minuto*, the *ultimi*, the *basso*.
25.   I. F. III. 11, p. 699.
26.   '. . . gli uomini mangiano l'uno l'altro.' Ibid., 13, p. 701.
27.   Ibid., 5, p. 693.
28.   Ibid., 13, p. 701.
29.   'Io credo certamente che, quando altri non ci insegnasse, che la necessità ci insegni . . . ma dove la necessità stringe è l'audacia giudicata prudenza . . .' Ibid., pp. 701–2.

30. Ibid.
31. Ibid., 17, p. 706.
32. 'Discursus', p. 25; see also I. F. IV. 27, VII. 5.
33. I. F. IV. 27, p. 733.
34. I. F. VII. 2.
35. Ibid., VII. 5, p. 796.
36. Ibid.
37. Ibid., IV. 27.
38. Ibid., IV. 33, p. 738.
39. Ibid., VIII. 8, p. 822.
40. Ibid., IV. 28, p. 733.
41. Ibid., VII. 23, p. 808.
42. A general description of their attitude towards war is found in I. F. VI. 1.
43. Ibid., VII. 5, p. 795.
44. Ibid., VII. 6, p. 797.
45. Ibid., III. 7, p. 696.
46. Ibid., VII. 6, p. 797.
47. Ibid., VIII. 36, p. 843.
48. 'Ghiribizzi', p. 1082.
49. I. F. VII. 6.
50. Ibid., VIII. 36.
51. I. F. V. 1, p. 738.
52. Ibid., VII. 28, p. 811.
53. 'questa mia republica,' 'Discursus', p. 27.
54. According to D. I. 2, p. 81, as we have seen, Rome attained its perfection because of the way the conflict between the patricians and the plebeians was managed. And in the 'Discursus' the word 'perfection' is used twice, pp. 29 and 30, to make the same point with regard to Florence.
55. 'Discursus', p. 27.
56. Ibid.
57. 'Dicursus', pp. 25–26.
58. Rubinstein correctly points out that Machiavelli recognizes the need for constitutional leadership in Florence, if it was to survive as a republic and at the same time maintain its freedom. See Rubinstein, 1972, pp. 26–27.
59. 'Discursus', p. 30.
60. 'Discursus', p. 31.

Conclusion

1. Strauss, 1987, p. 297.
2. Strauss, 1975, pp. 22–23.
3. Ibid., pp. 110–11. The same point regarding chance is made in Strauss, 1959, pp. 46–47.
4. Strauss, 1959, pp. 44–55; 1987, pp. 297–300.
5. Mansfield, 1981, pp. 294–95.
6. Mansfield, 1989, pp. 127, 121. My italics.
7. Martelli, p. 256.
8. Martelli, p. 76.
9. Ibid.
10. Ibid., p. 76; and D. II. 2, p. 149.
11. Martelli, p. 189.
12. D. I. Preface, p. 76; D. II. Preface, p. 146; I. F. V. 1, p. 739. On the general question

of the debate between 'ancients' and 'moderns', see Tilo Schabert, 1986, pp. 9–21; on the Renaissance debate on the meaning of 'ancient' and 'modern' from Salutati to the time of Machiavelli, see Charles Trinkaus, 1987, pp. 11–21; on a recent interpretation of the modernity of *The Prince*, see Robert Hariman, 1989, pp. 3–31.

13. I F. V. 1, p. 738.

14. 'Discursus', Martelli, p. 30.

15. D. I. 2, and the 'Allocuzione fatta ad un magistrato', Martelli, pp. 37–37, explain why this is so.

16. See, D. II. 2, p. 150 where Machiavelli talks about the world growing effeminate and Heaven becoming disarmed. Strauss's interpretation of this notion misses, I think, its astrological point. He writes: 'But the disarmament of the world and of heaven itself is ultimately due to the destruction of the Roman Empire, of all republican life.' Strauss, 1987, p. 309.

17. Strauss, 1969, p. 223.

18. P. 25, p. 295.

19. On Machiavellism, see Felix Gilbert, 1973, pp. 116–126; Strauss, 1987, pp. 297; Maritain, 1956, 319–53; F. Meinecke, 1957.

20. Aquinas, 1966, pp. 123–5.

21. Ibid., p. 127.

22. Ibid., p. 43.

23. Aristotle, 1966, p. 1141b.

24. Maritain, 1956, p. 346. My italics.

25. For a positive response to this question, see Strauss, 1959, pp. 40–55; 1987, pp. 297–300.

26. Strauss, 1959, pp. 40–55.

27. Bloom, 1987, p. 286.

28. Ibid.

BIBLIOGRAPHY

Alberti, Leon Battista. 1972. *I Libri della Famiglia*, eds. Ruggiero Romano and Alberto Tenenti, Turin.

Allen, Don Cameron. 1973. *The Star-Crossed Renaissance: The Quarrel About Astrology and Its Influence in England*, New York.

Anglo, Sydney. 1969. *Machiavelli: A Dissection*, London.

Antonio, St. 1959. *Santi Antonini Summa Theologica*, Tomus III, Graz.

Aquinas, Thomas, St. See Thomas, Aquinas, St.

Aristotle. 1966. *Nicomachean Ethics*, trans. David Ross, Oxford.
——1970. Physics, Books I and II, trans. W. Charlton, Oxford.
——1979. *The Politics of Aristotle*, ed. and trans. Ernest Barker, Oxford.

Bacon, Roger. 1928. *The Opus Majus of Roger Bacon*, trans. Robert B. Burke, vol. 1, Philadephia.

Barker, Ernest (ed.). 1979. *The Politics of Aristotle*, Oxford.

Baron, Hans. 1943. 'Towards a More Positive Evaluation of the Fifteenth-Century Renaissance', *Journal of the History of Ideas*, IV, pp. 21–49.
——1988. *In Search of Florentine Civic Humanism*, 2 vols., Princeton, NJ.

Bec, Christian. 1967. *Les Marchands ecrivains*, Paris.

Bellanti, Lucio. 1502. *Lucii Bellantii Senensis Mathematici ac Physici Liber de astrologica veritate. Et in Disputationes Joannes Fici adversus astrologos responsiones. Defensio Astrologiae Contra Joannem Picum Mirandulum*, Venice.

Berlin, Sir Isaiah. 1972. 'The Originality of Machiavelli', in *Studies in Machiavelli*, ed. Myron P. Gilmore, Florence.

Bertelli, Sergio. 1961. 'Noterelle Machiavelliane: un codice di Lucrezio e di Terenzio', *Rivista Storica Italiana*, LXXIII, pp. 544–58.
——1964a. *Niccolò Machiavelli: Legazioni e Commissarie*, I–III, Milan.
——1964b. 'Noterelle Machiavelliane: An-cora su Lucrezio e Machiavelli', *Rivista Storica Italiana*, LXXVI, pp. 774–93.

Bloom, Allan. 1987. *The Closing of the American Mind*, New York.

Boethius. 1962. *The Consolation of Philosophy*, trans. Richard Green, Indianapolis.

Bonadeo, Alfredo. 1969. 'The Role of the "Grandi" in the Political World of Machiavelli', *Studies in the Renaissance*, XVI, pp. 9–31.
——1970. 'The Role of the People in the Works and Times of Machiavelli', *Bibliotheque d'Humanisme et Renaissance*, XXXII, pp. 351–77.
——1973. *Corruption, Conflict, and Power in the Works and Times of Niccolò Machiavelli*, Berkeley.

Bondanella, Peter E. 1973. *Machiavelli and the Art of Renaissance History*, Detroit.

Bondanella, Peter and Musa, Mark. 1979. *The Portable Machiavelli*, Harmondsworth, Middlesex.
——1986. *Niccolò Machiavelli: The Prince*, Oxford.

Brown, Alison. 1986. 'Platonism in Fifteenth-Century Florence and Its Contribution to Early Modern Political Thought', *Journal of Modern History*, 58 (1986), pp. 383–413.

Brucker, Gene A. 1962. *Florentine Politics and Society 1343–1378*, Princeton, NJ.

Burckhardt, Jacob. 1944. *The Civilization of the Renaissance*, trans. S.G.C. Middlemore, London.

Burd, Arthur L. 1968. *Il Principe*, Oxford.

Burke, Peter. 1974. *Tradition and Innovation in Renaissance Italy*, London.

Calvanico, Raffaele. 1962. *Fonti per la storia della medicina e delle chirurgia per il regno di Napoli nel periodo Angiovino, 1273–1410*, Naples.

Carey, Hilary. 1987. 'Astrology at the English Court in the Later Middle Ages', in *Astrology, Science and Society: Historical Essays*, ed. Patrick Curry, London.

Cassirer, Ernst. 1942. 'Giovanni Pico della Mirandola', *Journal of the History of Ideas*, III, pp. 123–44, 319–46.
——1961. *The Myth of the State*, New Haven.
——1963. *The Individual and the Cosmos*, trans. Mario Domandi, Oxford.

Cavini, Walter. 1973. 'Un inedito di Giovan Francesco Pico della Mirandola. La Questio de falsitate astrologiae', *Rinascimento*, XIII, pp. 133–75.

Chabod, Federico. 1965. *Machiavelli and the Renaissance*, trans. David Moore, New York.
——1980. *Scritti su Machiavelli*, Turin.

Chiappelli, Fredi. 1952. *Studi sul linguaggio del Machiavelli*, Florence.

Clough, Cecil H. (ed.). 1970. 'Niccolò Machiavelli's Political Assumptions and Objectives', *Bulletin of the John Rylands Library*, 53, pp. 30–75.
——1975. 'Father Walker's Presentation and Translation of Machiavelli's *Discourses* in Perspective', in *The Discourses of Niccolò Machiavelli*, trans. Leslie J. Walker, 2 vols., vol. 1, pp. xv–xlviii.
——1976. *Cultural Aspects of the Italian Renaissance*, Manchester.

Cochrane, Eric W. 1961. 'Machiavelli: 1940–1960', *The Journal of Modern History*, XXXIII, pp. 113–37.

Cognasso, Francesco. 1965. *L'Italia nel Rinascimento*, vol. II, Turin.

Colish, Marcia L. 1971. 'The Idea of Liberty in Machiavelli', *Journal of the History of Ideas*, XXXII, pp. 323–51.

Coopland, G. W. 1952. *Nicole Oresme and the Astrologers: A Study of His Livres de divinations*, Cambridge, MA.

Copenhaver, Brian P. 1988. 'Astrology and Magic' in *The Cambridge History of Renaissance*, eds. Charles B. Schmitt and Quentin Skinner, Cambridge, pp. 264–301.

Croce, Benedetto. 1952. *Benedetto Croce, Man and Thinker*, ed. Cecil Sprigge, Cambridge.

Cumont, Franz. 1956. *Oriental Religions in Roman Paganism*, New York.
——1960. *Astrology and Religion Among the Greeks and the Romans*, New York.

Curry, Patrick (ed.). 1987. *Astrology, Science and Society: Historical Essays*, London.

Cusa, Nicholas (Lat. Nicolaus Cusanus). 1964. *De concordantia catholica*, cited in *Saturn and Melancholy*, eds. Raymond Klibansky, Erwin Panofsky, Fritz Saxl, London.

D'Amico, J. F. 1982. 'Cortesi's Rehabilitation of Pico della Mirandola', *Bibliotheque d'Humanisme et Renaissance*, 41, p. 43.

Dante, Alighieri. 1970. *Inferno*, ed. J. M. Dent, London.

De Grazia, Sebastian. 1989. *Machiavelli in Hell*, London.

Dulles, Avery. 1941. *Princeps Concordiae*, Cambridge, MA.

Durling, Richard J. 1961. 'A Chronological Census of Renaissance Editions and Translations of Galen', *Journal of the Warburg and Courtauld Institutes*, 24, pp. 230–306.

Edmond, Michel-Pierre. 1989. 'Machiavel et la question de la Nature, *Revue de Metaphysique et de Morale*, 94, pp. 347–52.

Eysenck, H. J. and Nias, D. K. B. 1982. *Astrology: Science or Superstition?*, Harmondworth, Middlesex.

Ficino, Marsilio. 1937. *Disputatio contra judicium astrologorum,* in *Supplementum Ficinianum*, 2 vols., ed. P. O. Kristeller, Florence.
———1963. *Teologia platonica*, 2 vols., ed. Michele Schiavone, Bologna.
———1978. *The Letters of Marsilio Ficino*, 2 vols., trans. Members of the Language Department of the School of Economic Science, London.
———1980. *The Book of Life*, trans. Charles Boer, Irving, Texas.

Flanagan, Thomas E. 1972. 'The Concept of Fortuna in Machiavelli', in *The Political Calculus*, ed. A. Parel, Toronto, pp. 127–57.

Garin, Eugenio. 1963. *Portraits From the Quattrocento*, trans. Victor A. and Elizabeth Velen, New York.
———1965. *Italian Humanism*, trans. Peter Munz, Oxford.
———1969. *Science and Civic Life in the Italian Renaissance*, trans. Peter Munz, New York.
———1970. *Dal Rinascimento all'Illuminismo*, Pisa.
———1983. *Astrology in the Renaissance: The Zodiac of Life*, trans. Carolyn Jackson and June Allen, London.

Garosi, Alcide. 1958. *Siena nella storia della medicina, 1240–1555*, Florence.

Garver, Eugene. *Machiavelli and the History of Prudence*, Madison.

Germino, Dante. 1966. 'Second Thoughts on Leo Strauss's Machiavelli', *Journal of Politics*, 28, pp. 794–817.

Gilbert, Allan H. 1938. *Machiavelli's Prince and Its Forerunners*, Durham, NC.
———1965. *Machiavelli: The Chief Works and Others*, 3 vols., Durham, NC.

Gilbert, Felix. 1951. 'On Machiavelli's Idea of *Virtù*', *Renaissance News*, IV, pp. 53–55.
———1953. 'The Composition and Structure of Machiavelli's *Discorsi*', *Journal of the History of Ideas*, 14, pp. 135–56.
———1957. 'Florentine Political Assumptions in the Period of Savonarola and Soderini', *Journal of the Warburg and Courtauld Institutes*, 20, pp. 187–214.
———1965. *Machiavelli and Guicciardini: Politics and History in Sixteenth-Century Florence*, Princeton, NJ.
———1972. 'Machiavelli's "Istorie Fiorentine": An Essay in Interpretation', in *Studies on Machiavelli*, ed. Myron P. Gilmore, Florence, pp. 75–99.
———1973. 'Machiavellism', in *Dictionary of the History of Ideas*, ed. Philip P. Wiener, New York, III, pp. 116–26.

Gill, Joseph, S. J. 1964. *Personalities of the Council of Florence*, Oxford.

Gilmore, Myron P. (ed.). 1972. *Studies on Machiavelli*, Florence.

Gombrich, E. H. 1970. *Aby Warburg*, London.

Gordon, Benjamin Lee. 1959. *Medieval and Renaissance Medicine*, New York.

Gramsci, Antonio. 1970. *The Modern Prince and Other Writings*, trans. Louis Marks, New York.

Grant, Edward. 1987. 'Medieval and Renaissance scholastic conceptions of the influence of the celestial region on the terrestrial', *Journal of the Renaissance Studies*, 17, pp. 1–23.

Graubard, Mark. 1958. 'Astrology's Demise and Its Bearing on the Decline and Death of Beliefs', *Osiris*, 13, pp. 210–62.

Guicciardini, Francesco. 1932. *Dialogo e Discorsi del Reggimento di Firenze*, ed. Roberto Palmarocchi. Bari.
———1972a. *The History of Italy*, trans. and ed. Sidney Alexander, New York.

————1972b. *Maxims and Reflections (Ricordi)*, trans. Mario Domandi, Philadelphia.

————1984. 'Considerazioni sopra i Discorsi di Machiavelli', in *Guicciardini: Anti-Machiavelli*, ed. Gian Francesco Berardi, Rome.

Hahm, David E. 1977. *The Origins of Stoic Cosmology*, Columbus, Ohio.

Hale, J. R. 1963. *Machiavelli and Renaissance Italy*, New York.

————1971. *Renaissance Europe: 1480–1520*, London.

————1977. *Florence and the Medici*, London.

Hariman, Robert. 1989. 'Composing Modernity in Machiavelli's *Prince*', *Journal of the History of Ideas*, L, pp. 3–29.

Headley, John M. 1988. 'On the Rearming of Heaven: The Machiavellism of Tommaso Campanella', *Journal of the History of Ideas*, XLIX, pp. 387–404.

Heller, Agnes, 1981. *Renaissance Man*, trans. Richard E. Allen, New York.

Hexter, J. H. 1956. 'Il principe and lo stato', *Studies in the Renaissance*, IV, pp. 113–38.

Hippocrates. 1950. *The Medical Works of Hippocrates*, trans. John Chadwick and W. N. Mann, Springfield, Ill.

Hulliung, Mark. 1983. *Citizen Machiavelli*, Princeton, NJ.

Jaeger, Werner. 1968. *Aristotle: Fundamentals of the History of His Development*, trans. Richard Robinson, Oxford.

Jones, Rosemary Devonshire. 1972. *Francesco Vettori: Florentine Citizen and Medici Servant*, London.

Kent, Dale. 1978. *The Rise of the Medici Faction in Florence: 1426–1434*, Oxford.

Kibre, Pearl. 1936. *The Library of Pico della Mirandola*, New York.

Klibansky, R., Panofsky, E., Saxl, F. 1964. *Saturn and Melancholy*, London.

Kristeller, Paul Oskar. 1961. *Renaissance Thought: The Classic, Scholastic, and Humanist Strains*, New York.

————1964a. *The philosophy of Marsilio Ficino*, trans. Virginia Conant, Gloucester, MA.

————1964b. *Eight Philosophers of the Italian Renaissance*, Stanford.

————1980. *Renaissance Thought and the Arts*, Princeton, NJ.

————1988. 'Humanism', in *The Cambridge History of Renaissance Philosophy*, eds. Charles B. Schmitt and Quentin Skinner, Cambridge, pp. 113–39.

Kuhn, Thomas. 1957. *The Copernican Revolution*, Cambridge, MA.

Lachterman, David R. 1991. 'Strauss Read from France', *The Review of Politics*, 53, pp. 224–45.

Lefort, Claude. 1972. *Le travail de l'oeuvre Machiavel*, Paris.

Le May, Richard. 1962. *Abu Ma'shar and Latin Aristotelianism in the Twelfth Century: The Recovery of Aristotle's Natural Philosophy Through Arabic Astrology*, Beirut.

————1987. 'The True Place of Astrology in Medieval Science and Philosophy', in *Astrology, Science and Society: Historical Essays*, ed. Patrick Curry, pp. 57–75.

Livy. 1976. *The Early History of Rome: Bks. I–V of The History of Rome From Its Foundation*, trans. Aubrey De Selincourt, Harmondsworth, Middlesex.

Locke, John. 1960. *Two Treatises of Government*, ed. Peter Laslett, Cambridge.

Macek, Josef. 1980. *Machiavelli e il Machiavellismo*, trans. Luciano Antonetti, Florence.

Machiavelli, Bernardo. 1954. *Libro di Ricordi*, ed. Cesare Olscki, Florence.

Machiavelli, Niccolò. 1950. *The Prince and the Discourses*, trans Luigi Ricci, E. R. P. Vincent, Christian Detmold, with an Introduction by Max Lerner, New York.

————1964. *Legazioni e commissarie*, 3 vols., ed. Sergio Bertelli, Milan.

————1965a. *Il Principe e Discorsi*, ed. Sergio Bertelli, Milan.

————1965b. *Machiavelli: The Chief Works and Others*, 3 vols., trans. Allan Gilbert, Durham, NC.

———1968. *Il Principe*, ed. L. Arthur Burd, Oxford.

———1970. *Il Principe*, ed. Giuseppe Lisio, Florence.

———1971. *Machiavelli: Tutte le opere*, ed. Mario Martelli, Florence.

———1975. *The Discourses of Niccolò Machiavelli*, 2 vols., trans. Leslie J. Walker, new Introduction and Appendices by Cecil H. Clough, London.

———1981a. *Il Principe*, ed. Federico Chabod, Turin.

———1981b. *Il Principe e altri scritti*, ed. Gennaro Sasso, Florence.

———1985. *The Prince*, trans. with an Introduction, Harvey C. Mansfield, Jr., Chicago.

———1986. *The Prince*, ed. with an Introduction, Peter Bondanella, and trans. Peter Bondanella and Mark Musa, Oxford.

———1988a. *The Prince*, eds. Quentin Skinner and Russell Price, Cambridge.

———1988b. *Florentine Histories*, A New Translation by Laura F. Banfield, and Harvey C. Mansfield, Jr., with an Introduction by Harvey C. Mansfield, Jr., Princeton, NJ.

Maimonides, Moses. 1986. 'Letter on Astrology', trans. Ralph Lerner, in *Medieval Political Philosophy*, eds. Ralph Lerner and Muhsin Mahdi, Ithaca.

Mansfield, Harvey C. Jr., 1979. *Machiavelli's New Modes and Orders: A Study of the Discourses on Livy*, Ithaca.

———1981. 'Machiavelli's Political Science', *The American Political Science Review*, 75, pp. 293–305.

———1985. *The Prince*, Chicago.

———1988. 'Translators' Introduction', *Florentine Histories*, trans. Laura F. Banfield and Harvey C. Mansfield, Jr., Princeton, NJ.

———1989. *Taming The Prince: The Ambivalence of Modern Executive Power*, New York.

Mainardi, Giovanni. 1521. *Epistolarum Medicinalium Libri XX*, Florence.

Marchand, Jean-Jacques. 1974. 'Una Protestatio de iustitia del Machiavelli: L'Allocuzione ad un magistrato', *Bibliofilia*, LXXVI, pp. 209–21.

———1975. *Niccolò Machiavelli: I Primi Scritti Politici 1499–1512*, Padua.

Maritain, Jacques. 1956. *The Social and Political Philosophy of Jacques Maritain: Selected Readings*, eds. Joseph W. Evans and Leo R. Ward, London.

Martelli, Mario, (ed.). 1971. *Niccolò Machiavelli: Tutte le Opere*, Florence.

Martin, Alfred von. 1963. *Sociology of the Renaissance*, New York.

Martines, Lauro. 1969. *Lawyers and Statecraft in Renaissance Florence*, Princeton, NJ.

McNair, Philip. 1976. 'Poliziano's Horoscope', in *Cultural Aspects of Italian Renaissance*, ed. C. Clough, Manchester, pp. 262–76.

Meinecke, Friedrich. 1957. *Machiavellism: The Doctrine of raison d'etat and Its Place in Modern History*, trans. Douglas Scot, New Haven.

Mossini, Lanfranco. 1962. *Necessità e Legge nell' opera del Machiavelli*, Milan.

North, J. D. 1980. 'Astrology and the Fortunes of Churches', *Centaurus*, 24, pp. 200–10.

———1986. 'Celestial influence – the major premise of astrology', in *'Astrologi hallucinati': Stars and the End of the World in Luther's Times*, ed. Paola Zambelli, Berlin and New York, pp. 45–60.

Oakeshott, Michael. 1975. *On Human Condition*, Oxford.

Oakley, Francis. 1964. *The Political Thought of Pierre d'Ailly*, New Haven.

Olschki, Leonardo. 1945. *Machiavelli the Scientist*, Berkeley.

Parel, Anthony (ed.). 1972. *Political Calculus: Essays on Machiavelli's Philosophy*, Toronto.

———1990a. 'Allocution Made to a Magistrate', *Political Theory*, 18, pp. 525–7.

———1990b. 'Machiavelli's Notions of Justice: Text and Analysis', *Political Theory*, 18, pp. 528–44.

———1991. 'The Question of Machiavelli's Modernity,' *The Review of Politics*, 53, pp. 320–40.

Paschetto, Eugenia. 1984. *Pietro d'Abano: Medico e Filosofo*, Florence.

Pattie, T. S. 1980. *Astrology*, London.

Pezzella, Salvatore. 1982. *Astronomia ed Astrologia nel medioevo da un manoscritto inedito (sec. XIII) della città di Firenze*, Florence.

Pedicino, Vincenzo. 1963. 'Medicina e astrologia nella concezione di Giovanni Manardo', *Atti del convegno internazionale per la celebrazione de V centenario della nascita di Giovanni Manardo, 1462–1536*, Ferrara, pp. 213–17.

Phillips, Mark. 1977. *Francesco Guicciardini: The Historian's Craft*, Toronto.

Pico della Mirandola, Gianfrancesco. 1930. *On Imagination*, trans. Harry Caplan, New Haven.

Pico della Mirandola, Giovanni. 1572. *Opera Omnia*, Turin.

Pincin, Carlo. 1966. 'Le Prefazioni e la Dedicatoria dei *Discorsi* di Machiavelli', *Giornale storico della letteratura italiana*, CXLIII, pp. 72–83.

Pitkin, Hanna Fenichel. 1984. *Fortune is a Woman: Gender and Politics in the Thought of Niccolò Machiavelli*, Berkeley.

Plamenatz, John. 1972. 'In Search of Machiavellian *Virtù*, in *The Political Calculus*, ed. Anthony Parel, Toronto, pp. 157–78.

Plato. 1968. *The Republic of Plato*, trans. Allan Bloom, New York.

Plethon, Geroge Gemisthos. 1966. *Traite des lois*, trans. A. Pellissier, ed. C. Alexandre, Amsterdam.

Plutarch. 1819. *Plutarch's Lives*, 6 vols., trans. John Langhorne and William Langhorne, London.
———1974. Plutarch's Lives, ed. Alan Wardman, London.

Pocock, John G. A. 1971. *Politics, Language and Time: Essays on Political Thought and History*, New York.
———1975. *The Machiavellian Moment: Florentine Political Thought and the Atlantic Republican Tradition*, Princeton, NJ.

———1978. 'Machiavelli and Guicciardini: Ancients and Moderns', *Canadian Journal of Political and Social Theory*, 2, pp. 93–110.
———1981a. '*The Machiavellian Moment* Revisited: A Study of History and Ideology', *Journal of Modern History*, 53, pp. 49–73.
———1981b. 'Virtues, Rights and Manners: A Model for a Historian of Political Thought', *Political Theory*, 9, pp. 353–69.

Polybius. 1972. *The Histories of Polybius*, trans. W. R. Paton, London.

Pontano, Giovanni. 1520. *De Prudentia, lib. 5; De Fortuna, lib. 3; De immanitate, lib. 1*. Florence.
———1530. *De Rebus Celestibus Libri XIV*, Basel.

Prescott, William. 1837. *History of the Reign of Ferdinand and Isabella*, vol. 2, Philadelphia.

Prezzolini, Giuseppe. 1967. *Machiavelli*, New York.

Price, Russell. 1973. 'The Senses of *Virtù* in Machiavelli', *European Studies Review*, 3, pp. 315–46.
———1977. 'The Theme of *Gloria* in Machiavelli', *Renaissance Quarterly*, XXX, pp. 588–632.
———1982. '*Ambizione* in Machiavelli's Thought', *History of Political Thought*, 3, pp. 383–445.

Price, Russell and Skinner, Quentin. 1988. *The Prince*, Cambridge.

Procacci, Giuliano. 1965. *Studi Sulla Fortuna del Machiavelli*, Rome.

Ptolemy, Claudius. 1980. *Tetrabiblos*, trans. F. E. Robbins, London.

Ricci, Luigi and Vincent, E. R. P. 1950. *The Prince*, in *The Prince and the Discourses*, Introduction by Max Lerner, New York.

Ridolfi, Roberto. 1959. *The Life of Girolamo Savonarola*, trans. Cecil Grayson, London.
———1963. *The Life of Niccolò Machiavelli*, trans. Cecil Grayson, London.
———1967. *The Life of Francesco Guicciardini*, trans. Cecil Grayson, London.

Rubinstein, Nicolai. 1942. 'The Beginnings of Political Thought in Florence', *Journal of the Warburg and Courtauld Institutes*, 5, pp. 198–227.

———1956. 'The Beginnings of Niccolò Machiavelli's Career in the Florentine Chancery', *Italian Studies*, XI, pp. 72–91.

———1966. *The Government of Florence Under the Medici 1434–1494*, Oxford.

———1968. 'Florentine Constitutionalism and Medici ascendence in the Fifteenth Century', in *Florentine Studies*, ed. Nicolai Rubinstein, London, pp. 442–62.

———1972. 'Machiavelli and the World of Florentine Politics', in *Studies in Machiavelli*, ed. Myron Gilmore, Florence, pp. 5–28.

———1987. 'Machiavelli Storico', *Annali della Scuola Normale Superiore di Pisa*, XVII, pp. 695–733.

Russo, Luigi. 1975. *Machiavelli*, 5th edn. Bari.

Sambursky, Samuel. 1959. *Physics of the Stoics*, London.

Santi, Victor. 1978. *La 'Gloria' nel pensiero di Machiavelli*, Ravenna.

Sasso, Gennaro. 1966. *Machiavelli e Cesare Borgia*, Rome.

———1967. *Studi su Machiavelli*, Naples.

———1980. *Niccolò Machiavelli: Storia del suo pensiero politico*, Bologna.

———1981. *Il Principe e altri scritti*, Florence.

———1987. *Machiavelli e gli antichi*, 2 vols., Milan.

Savonarola, Girolamo. 1513. *Opera Singulare del doctissimo padre F. Hieronymo Savonarola di Ferrara Contra Astrologiam Divinatricem*, Venice.

———1952. *Savonarola: Prediche e Scritti*, 2 vols., ed. Mario Ferrara, Florence.

———1973. *Trattato del Reggimento degli Stati*, Aalen, West Germany.

Schabert, Tilo. 1986. 'Modernity and History I: What is Modernity?', in *The Promise of History: Essays in Political Philosophy*, ed. Moulakis Athanasios, Berlin and New York.

Schmitt, Charles B. and Skinner, Quentin. (eds.). 1988. *The Cambridge History of Renaissance Philosophy*, Cambridge.

Skinner, Quentin. 1978. *The Foundations of Modern Political Thought*, 2 vols., Cambridge.

———1981. *Machiavelli*, Oxford.

———1984. 'The idea of negative liberty: philosophical and historical perspectives', in *Philosophy in History*, eds. Richard Rorty, J. B. Schneewind and Quentin Skinner, pp. 193–221.

Skinner, Quentin and Schmitt, Charles B. (eds.). 1988. *The Cambridge History of Renaissance Philosophy*, Cambridge.

Steneck, Nicholas. 1976. *Science and Creation in the Middle Ages: Henry Langenstein*, Notre Dame, IN.

Strauss, Leo. 1952. *The Political Philosophy of Hobbes: Its Basis and its Genesis*, trans. Elsa M. Sinclair, Chicago.

———1953. *Natural Rights and History*, Chicago.

———1959. *What is Political Philosophy? And Other Studies*, Glencoe, Ill.

———1969. *Thoughts on Machiavelli*, Seattle.

———1975. *On Tyranny*, revised and enlarged, Ithaca.

———1987. 'Niccolò Machiavelli', in *History of Political Philosophy*, eds. Leo Strauss and Joseph Cropsey, Chicago.

Tabanelli, Mario. 1978. *Un Astrologo Forlivese dal 1200: Guido Bonatti*, Brescia.

Tester, James S. 1987. *A History of Western Astrology*, Woodbridge, Suffolk.

Thomas, Aquinas, St. 1961. *Summa Contra Gentiles*, 3 vols., eds. Ceslai Pera, Petro Marc and Petro Caramello, Rome.

———1966. *Summa Theologiae*, vol. 28, ed. Thomas Gilby, London.

Thorndike, Lynn. 1936. 'The Debate for Precedence Between Medicine and Law: Further Examples From the Fourteenth to the Seventeenth Century', *The Romanic Review*, XXVII, pp. 185–90.

———1945. 'Albumasar of Sadan', *Isis*, 36, pp. 22–23.

———1955. 'The True Place of Astrology in the History of Science', *Isis*, 46, pp. 273–78.

———1958. 'De Complexionibus', *Isis*, 49, pp. 78–409.

———1959a–c. *A History of Magic and Experimental Science*, vols. II, IV and V, New York.

———1960. 'Three Latin Translations of the Pseudo-Hippocratic Tract on Astrological Medicine', *Janus*, XLIX, pp. 103–30.

Tommasini, Oreste. 1911. *La Vita e gli Scritti di Niccolò Machiavelli*, Rome.

Trinkaus, Charles. 1970. *In Our Image and Likeness: Humanity and Divinity in Italian Humanist Thought*, 2 vols., London.

———1985. 'The Astrological Cosmos and Rhetorical Culture of Giovanni Gioviano Pontano', *Renaissance Quarterly*.

———1987. '*Antiquitas* versus *Modernitas*: An Italian Humanist Polemic and its Resonance', *Journal of the History of Ideas*, XLVIII, pp. 11–21.

———1989. 'Coluccio Salutati's Critique of Astrology in the Context of His Natural Philosophy', *Speculum*, 64, pp. 46–68.

Vasoli, Cesare. 1979. *L'Astrologo Forlivese Guido Bonatti*, Ravenna.

Vescovini, Graziella Federici. 1971. 'Su uno scritto Astrologico di Biagio Pelacani da Parma', *Rinascimento*, XI, pp. 79–93.

———1979. *Astrologia e Scienza: La crisi dell'aristotelismo sul cadere del Trecento e Biagio Pelacani da Parma*, Florence.

———1987. 'Peter Abano and Astrology', in *Astrology, Science and Society*, ed. Patrick Curry, London.

Villari, Pasquale. 1969. *The Life and Times of Niccolò Machiavelli*, 2 vols., trans. Linda Villari, New York.

Walker, D. P. 1975. *Spiritual and Demonic Magic: From Ficino to Campanella*, Notre Dame, IN.

Walker, Leslie J. 1975. *The Discourses of Niccolò Machiavelli*, 2 vols., London.

Walsh, P. G. 1967. *Livy: His Historical Aims and Methods*, Cambridge.

Wardman, Alan (ed.). 1974. *Plutarch's Lives*, London.

Wedel, Theodore Otto. 1920. *The Medieval Attitude Towards Astrology*, New Haven.

Whitfield, J. H. 1965. *Machiavelli*, New York.

———1969. *Discourses on Machiavelli*, Cambridge.

Zambelli, Paola. 1965. 'Giovanni Mainardi e la polemica sull'astrologia' in *Giovanni Pico della Mirandola nella storia dell' umanesimo*, 2 vols., Florence, vol. 1, pp. 205–79.

———1986. (ed.) '*Astrologi hallucinati*': Stars and the End of the World in Luther's Time, Berlin and New York.

Zanier, Giancarlo. 1977. *La Medicina Astrologica e la sua teoria: Marsilio Ficino e i suoi critici contemporanei*, Rome.

INDEX